SUICIDAL

POSSESSED TO SKATE

Author and Editor: **Sean Cliver**
Layout and Design: **Eric Simpson**
Design Assistant: **Callie Simpson**
Copy Editor: **Sharon Harrison**

Copyright © 2004 Lobster Lips Productions, Inc.

The information contained in this book is based on material supplied to Lobster Lips Productions, Inc. and Concrete Wave Editions. While every effort has been made to ensure its accuracy, and to attribute and credit all work, Lobster Lips Productions, Inc. and Concrete Wave Editions do not under any circumstances accept responsibility for any errors or omissions. When and if at all possible corrections will be made in future editions.

All deck images were obtained solely by the Author through private collections, or supplied courtesy of private collectors. With respect to the privacy of these individuals, all contributors and sources are credited in the acknowledgments with no association to possessions unless expressly requested otherwise.

ISBN 0-9735286-2-1

Published by:
Concrete Wave Editions
1054 Center Street, Suite 293
Thornhill, Ontario L4J 8E5
Canada
concretewavemagazine.com

Distributed by:
Blitz Distribution
Huntington Beach, California
(714) 379-0020
For sales information, contact: Tory Boettcher
toryb@blitzdistribution.com

For those crippled with nostalgia: www.disposablethebook.com

This book was first printed on really crummy paper stock in October 2004. Luckily it sold out and was then reprinted in January 2005 with better quality wood pulp and 16 pages of additional material. A few people, like that Chris Solomon joker, crucified me for doing so, but screw them. It's my book and I can do whatever the hell I want! But I'm not entirely heartless. This third edition features nothing new or different at all, aside from that quaint little bar of descending numbers used to denote subsequent printings. Check it out, it's like all official and shit:

10 9 8 7 6 5 4

Printed and bound in China

Contributing Writers:
Steve Alba / Francesco Albertini / Brian Brannon / Todd Bratrud / Don Brown / Steve Caballero / Ron Cameron / Thomas Campbell / Dave Carnie
Garry S. Davis / Eric Dressen / Peter Ducommun / Daniel Dunphy / Ray Flores / Todd Francis / Tim Gavin / Alan Gelfand / John Gibson / Claus Grabke
John Grigley / Jef Hartsel / Tony Hawk / Mike Hill / Christian Hosoi / Andy Howell / Wes Humpston / Andy Jenkins / Jason Jessee / Natas Kaupas
Tim Kerr / Jeremy Klein / Jim Knight / Jason Lee / James Levesque / John Lucero / Barry McGee / Mike McGill / Marc McKee / Chris Miller
Lance Mountain / Rodney Mullen / Johnny "Mojo" Munnerlyn / Bruno Musso / Corey O'Brien / Gavin O'Brien / Jim Phillips / Pushead / Don Redondo
Steve Rocco / Rob Roskopp / Devin St. Clair / Craig Stecyk III / Tod Swank / Andy Takakjian / Ed Templeton / Jim Thiebaud / Bernie Tostenson
Mike Vallely / Per Welinder / Simon Woodstock

Contributing Photographers:
Jimmy Anderson / Joe Antonik / Marco Bianco / Eric Blais / Al Boglio / Grant Brittain / Steve Buddendeck / Tim Butler / Mike Carroll / Chris Chicarella
Christian Cooper / Garry S. Davis / Jacques Doetsch / Joshua Etherington / Mark Felt / Joel Fraser / Jesse Geboy / Jason Goodman / Jim Goodrich
John Guderian / Nick Halkias / Tony Hallam / Bill Heiden / Greg Hill / Mike Hill / Andy Howell / Chris Ilaria / Spike Jonze / Stephen Joy / Bryce Kanights
Alan Keller / Jim Knight / Rick Kosick / Kevin Marburg / Tim Medlin / Chris Miller / Damon Mills / Johnny "Mojo" Munnerlyn / Lee Murphy / Matt Newell
Pushead / Tony Roberts / Aaron Rose / Devin St. Clair / Michael Schmidt / Justin Sharp / Eric Simpson / Jeff Snavely / Tim Steenstra / Bernie Tostenson
Jeff Tremaine / Francisco José Burgos Villarrubia / Adam Wallacavage / Doug Winbury / Tobin Yelland

Cover:
Lance Mountain sacrifices prime face time for the benefit of full graphic coverage in Kelly Belmar's pool. Incidentally, the construction of this pool was financed entirely by the dollars generated from screening board graphics for Steve Rocco's companies from 1988–1992. Photo: Eric Simpson

Contents

Blind / Guy Mariano / by Marc McKee / 1992

was a fairly quiet kid in high school. Didn't stick out of the crowd, rarely voiced an opinion, and tried my best to avoid class participation. I mostly just drew in the margins of my notebook or on the brown paper bags I'd modified into schoolbook covers. But one day in a random history course that now escapes me, this girl was rattling off some fairly daft presumptions about the work of a famous artist. Unable to stand this nonsense any longer, I surprised everyone by verbally backhanding her with the stern suggestion she go to hell and not forget to pack all her arty theories for the infernal descent into Satan's back 40. Well, I wasn't exactly that harsh, but I did state in no uncertain terms that not all art has deep meaning, nor must it be tortured until screams of social relevance are extorted.

With that one simpleminded retort, all my hard-earned years of "art-class champ" credibility were chucked right out the window. No longer was I awarded the benefit of doubt around school as a deep and introverted soul obsessed with death and the human condition—now I was just some weirdo who drew skulls and zombies because he was a dork and nothing more.

Despite my status as a professional artist today, I still don't understand this strange obsession for stapling lofty explanations to the butt of every artistic act that comes down the pike. Nor do I see why it's considered so morally reprehensible to think an artist may have created something just for the hell of it, because they thought it might be funny or look cool. Who knows, perhaps I'm just a dumbass when it comes down to the cerebral affairs of art and theory, but I've always felt the critical deconstruction process does nothing more than pump up inflatable egos and strip the fun and spontaneity from everything—especially the art of skateboarding.

Over the past decade, many "hipper-than-thou" magazines have run extensive essays on the cultural impact of graphic design born out of skateboarding, but most if not all of these articles make me wince. Nothing is more irksome than a writer who clearly has no personal attachment to skateboarding yet still sees fit to perform academic autopsies on an artist's otherwise whimsical motivation to depict an accidental gun death in a suburban household setting.

Truth told, the primary impetus behind this broad selection of graphics and their historical origins is that I'm tired of seeing something I love bastardized by outsiders touting an art degree, a grab bag of "extreme" clichés, and a limited knowledge of the scope of work at best. They may have the best of intentions in filleting the art of skateboarding and serving it up in a semi-digestible manner for those not familiar with the attitudes and imagery—I certainly can't fault them for their appreciation—but I know for a fact they don't share the same visceral attachment as the kid who once walked into a skate shop and felt his nebulous existence go supernova in response to the graphics that would one day become his whole world.

So if there are any cultural parallels or dots to be connected from the subterranean basement of the skateboard sect to popular mainstream society, feel free to do so in the privacy of your own head. Me, I simply appreciate the graphics for what they are and the ridiculous journey they've taken me on for the last two decades. | Sean Cliver

DISPOSABLE

A HISTORY OF

SKATEBOARD ART

by Sean Cliver

Part One: Skate or Die

At the risk of sounding like one of those rabid zealots who posts up on a street corner spouting born-again testimonials with all the fervor of a soul formerly bent on barreling down a highway to hell, I wholeheartedly believe that skateboard graphics saved my damned life. Sure, it probably sounds like I'm just trying to wring some cheap justification for this book out of a few random turns of luck, but quite honestly, were it not for this unconventional commercial art form there would be no explanation as to how I averted the everyday tragedy of falling into a routine job and losing myself in the shuffle of a bland life in an equally bland land.

Case in point, and with no geographical pun intended, I grew up in Stevens Point, Wisconsin, one of a zillion faceless townships spackling the nooks and crannies of the Midwest. I was the typical American nightmare in the making: not a whit of cultural color to enhance my life and no real clue as to my lot within it. My only saving grace was that I'd managed to develop a modest amount of artistic talent, but even then I was mostly a half-assed byproduct of the Marvel Comics universe at best. Idle fantasies were entertained of one day becoming a professional comic-book artist, but all my attempts at developing a functional style were rather poor, the anatomy wooden, lifeless, and in no way conducive to cranking out those illustrated ballets with muscle-bound fruit-loops kicking the crap out of each other on a page-to-page, month-to-month basis.

There was, however, one legitimate skill I did have going in my favor: a knack for tedious, time-consuming detail work. Unfortunately, this anal attribute mostly pointed toward an arthritic future of technical illustration, a bleak occupation where I'd most likely slave over renderings of nuts and bolts until all that remained of my drawing hand was a gnarled, useless claw. Real cheery prospects for a kid about to get booted into the world with a high school diploma in one hand and a .00 Rapidograph inking pen gripped in the other.

So for all I knew and cared at the age of seventeen, the world ended ten feet beyond the city limits of Stevens Point—up until 1986, that is, when the punk/skateboard culture slammed into the region and breathed subversive life into the outcasts pooled at the bottom of our small town populace. I was neither here nor there in terms of a tidy social classification, but my best friend at the time, Brad Overacker, was engrossed in the hardcore music scene. He soon picked up a skateboard to accompany the rebellious lifestyle that went against everything our community held in high regard—most notably the pathological reverence placed upon the holy trinity of traditional sports: football, baseball, and basketball. Subsequently, Brad started to move within a different circle of friends, and I fast realized this was the proverbial moment in time for me to sink or swim if I hoped to have a social outlet in my waning teenage years.

Following Brad's lead, I picked up my first skateboard at a discount retailer on the outskirts of town for 30 dollars. The deck was a chunk of shit—not a Nash by brand, but the next worst imported thing—with a textbook illustration of a dinosaur for a graphic. Unbeknownst to me, this uninformed purchase was a grievous misstep into the world of skateboarding, but it was a decided step nonetheless, and one that was definitely in the direction of something I found to be more fun than anything else to come before it. Best of all, it didn't involve rampant team

The F-14 Fighter Jet was designed by me—or rather swiped by myself—from a Navy recruiter's folder. I had no intention of joining the Navy, but it went along with our military presence ignited by Stacy Peralta. VCJ put a bull's eye behind it and added the detail with my signature below.

For my next model, I always admired the classic Ray "Bones" Skull and Sword graphic, so I wanted a cool-looking skull graphic. I expressed that to George Powell and VCJ, and they came back with a really cool-looking skull except it had giant devil horns on it, which I hated. So VCJ asked me, "What elements surround you that you like?" I said I liked snakes, and VCJ figured why not add some lightning bolts to it as there are plenty of both in Florida were I grew up skating. | Mike McGill

spirit, communal locker room showers or anything else a hop, step, and a sip away from the crazed atmosphere of a Jim Jones high school pep rally. All that was required was a decent patch of cement and a high threshold for pain and good old-fashioned small town intolerance.

For whatever insecure reasons, I remained a fringe participant in the local skate scene for a few months and never once set foot within Silver Spoke, the hybrid BMX/skateboard shop that played ground zero to all the societal misfits in the area. When I finally did work up the nerve to brave the shop's intimidating atmosphere, my tenuous existence in life suddenly caromed onto a more concrete path as I took in the awesome spectacle of a hundred skateboard decks lining the walls like psyche-delic fixtures in an accomplished stoner's pad.

Captivating and arcane, the images screened upon the boards were wildly diverse in theme and ranged from new wave/punk graphic design to broad illustrative concepts. No matter what artistic avenue was taken, though, each and every graphic embodied the raw energy of a secret society rolling just beneath the radar of the mainstream, each one a specially crafted skeleton key to this fantastic underground that I now craved entrance to above all else.

I stood and stared at the walls for the better part of an hour thoroughly enthralled by the skateboards. Taking into account all the work

and effort that must have gone into their creation—from ethereal origin to final manufactured product—it was baffling to think the graphics were all knowingly bred for destruction. Even more curious to me was that not all the graphics were skilled works of art; in fact, the caliber of illustrations ran the gamut from crude and amateurish to highly professional in quality and technique—an overall spread of talent that held an alluring air of inspiration to a kid who just spent the last ten years being bludgeoned into submission before the daunting abilities of comic-book artists such as Neal Adams, Frank Miller, Berni Wrightson, and Steve Rude. Whereas my initial goal to work in the comic industry seemed quite unattainable, drawing images for skateboards just felt like something I had a slim chance at doing.

The one brand that stood out amongst all the other companies was Powell Peralta. Despite a host of graphics rudimentary in concept—dragons, skulls, swords, and snakes—the designs managed to transcend their inherent silliness to become clean and powerful icons. Several other companies, like Kryptonics, took an illustrated stab at similarly trite themes, which were fun in that whole "skulls, blood, gore" way but paled in comparison to the arresting images on the Powell products.

After long surveying their lineup of decks, I finally made the decision to upgrade from my current plywood embarrassment to a Powell Peralta

Blockhead / Street Style / by Dave Bergthold / 1986

Blockhead / Team / by Ron Cameron and Dave Bergthold / 1986

Blockhead / Sam Cunningham / by Dave Bergthold / 1985

Circle-A / Ricky Winsor / artist unknown / 1988

Circle-A / Bob Schmelzer / by Kevin Marburg / 1988

Fogtown / Van Gogh / artist unknown / 1985

Dogtown / Stonefish / by Michael Sieff / 1985

Dogtown / Red Dog / by Kevin Ancell / 1986

Dogtown / Street Cross / by Michael Sieff / 1986

Dogtown / Web / by Michael Sieff / 1986

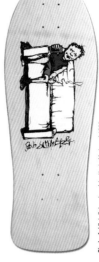

Dogtown / Eric Dressen / by Michael Sieff / 1987

Dogtown / Micke Alba / by Michael Sieff / 1987

G&S / Foil Tail / by Lynn Rutke / 1984

G&S / Billy Ruff / by Lynn Rutke / 1984

G&S / Neil Blender / by Neil Blender and Lynn Rutke / 1985

Madrid / Mike Smith / artist unknown / 1984

Madrid / Claus Grabke / by Claus Grabke / 1986

Madrid / Bryce Kanights / by Bryce Kanights / 1987

Plan 9 / Misfits / by Glenn Danzig / 1986

Kryptonics / Art and Steve Godoy / 1986

Kryptonics / Ripstik / artist unknown / 1984

Kryptonics / Team / artist unknown / 1985

Kryptonics / Team / artist unknown / 1986

Rip City / Black Flag / by Raymond Pettibon / 1986

Santa Cruz / Ramp/Street Concave / by Jim Phillips / 1984

Santa Cruz / Ramp/Street 10" / by Jim Phillips / 1984

Santa Cruz / Micke Alba / by Jim Phillips / 1984

Santa Cruz / Duane Peters / by Jim Phillips / 1983

Santa Cruz / Micke Alba / by Moto / 1985

Santa Cruz / Keith Meek / by Jim Phillips / 1986

Santa Cruz / Terrorist / by Jim Phillips / 1987

Hosoi / Monty Nolder / by Justin Forbes / 1988

Sims / Mike Folmer / artist unknown / 1983

Sims / Kamikaze / by Bernie Tostenson / 1984

Town & Country / Quad / artist unknown / 1984

Powell Peralta / General Issue / by V. Courtlandt Johnson / 1983

disposable|

Zorlac / Street Skate / by Jeff Newton / 1983

Zorlac / Devil Fish (First Version) / by Lady / 1986

Uncle Wiggley / Tony Magnusson / by Doug Ring / 1984

Uncle Wiggley / Argyle / by Doug Ring / 1985

Uncle Wiggley / Team / by Doug Ring / 1984

Uncle Wiggley / Fishstik / by Doug Ring / 1985

Santa Monica Airlines / Team / by Chris Buchinsky / 1987

Santa Monica Airlines / Street Heat / artist unknown / 1986

Schmitt Stix / Monty Nolder / by John McGueigan / 1984

Schmitt Stix / Joe Lopes / by Bryce Kanights / 1986

Schmitt Stix / ATV / by Paul Schmitt and Bruce Whiteside / 1984

Schmitt Stix / Rip Saw / by Chuck Hults / 1987

Vision / Leopard / by Tom West / 1983

Vision / Zebra / by Greg Evans / 1984

Vision / Reptile / by Tom West / 1983

Skull Skates / Christian Hosoi (Max) / by Ivan Hosoi and PD / 1985

Skull Skates / Johnny Ray / by Johnny Ray / 1986

Skull Skates / Mutant / by PD / 1986

Mike McGill pro model, a choice based solely on its striking graphic of a snake coiled around a skull. This concept, if offered up on the wall of a tattoo parlor as "Skull and Snake #32," would probably be more suited to the flabby ass of a biker chick, but on a skateboard—through the precision line work of an artist whose only telltale mark was the cryptic insignia of "VCJ"—it was the most incredible thing I'd ever laid eyes on.

With a price tag of $48.50 on the deck alone, I knew full well that relying on my weekly paper-route earnings would be like trying to chop down an oak tree with a bowie knife. Approaching my parents for a little financial aid was futile as well. My dad had drawn that line in the dirt when he learned of my first skateboard purchase and reminded me with a hint of displeasure that I was far too old to be wasting money on stupid wooden toys. Luckily, Brad's parents just opened a comic and sports-card store in town, so I cannibalized my age-old collections of baseball cards and comics and cashed out these two juvenile fascinations to pursue another of immediate and greater purpose.

Returning to Silver Spoke with a little over 150 dollars in hand, I spent it all on what could only be called an "overly complete" setup. In hopes of preserving the sanctity of the McGill Skull and Snake graphic, I purchased every godforsaken plastic accessory available to armor the deck with—nose guard, rails, tail rails, tail skid, copers, and a lapper. So what should have been a functional

skateboard now looked more like a U.S. military-issue vehicle. Any scratches or scuffs that did manage to penetrate this weighty, plastic defense system were dutifully touched up with paint markers and ink pens—a ludicrous process that upstaged my homework assignments on many a night.

In the coming months, I underwent a lifestyle transformation and happily slipped into the lower echelon of the high school caste system. A fairly bold move considering it now placed my meek frame within the crosshairs of every dimwitted redneck and jock who found the phrase, "Skate or die!" to be the highest form of public ridicule. I also ceased to draw comics the Marvel way and became hell bent on drawing evil skulls in a train-wreck of rendering styles gleaned from VCJ, Pushead, and the assorted art shown on albums by The Misfits.

My notebooks and folders bore the brunt of this newfound fascination and turned into sketch-intensive graveyards of skeletons and zombies in varying states of rot and decay, a subject matter that soon contaminated all my art-class projects as well. After putting up with a succession of gore-based themes, my art teacher finally intervened by telling me to stop wasting my talent. Conversely, I could have said the same for all the pointless hours spent drawing inane still-life arrangements of dead weeds and other obscure shit stuffed in vases, but I merely shrugged my shoulders and continued on my morbid way.

Suicidal Skates / Possessed to Skate / by Rick Clayton / 1985

Santa Cruz / Corey O'Brien / by Jim Phillips / 1988

I went into a tattoo shop looking for ideas and found a reaper that this tattoo artist drew. I bought a photocopy of it for 50 dollars. The reaper was holding a crystal ball in front of him and I wanted to put the Santa Cruz dot in there, but it was Jim Phillips's idea to do the fireball instead. The background came from a Virgil Finlay book, and I told Jim to draw the dots as small as he could; he thought they might not be able to screen the little dots, but he did it anyway. For the font on my name, I brought in my Hell Comes To Your House compilation record and had him put those crosses on there just like on the back of the record. Jim came up with the skull on the tail, and I still think it's his best work next to all the Indy logos. One of the old screeners told me they were making ten- to fifteen-thousand of them a month. I was getting a dollar per board and received seven-thousand dollars a month for a year. I got into a lot of trouble with the IRS for not giving them their cut. It was still selling thousands when I changed graphics, but I got so sick of looking at it that it had to go. | Corey O'Brien

CRAIG JOHNSON

zorlac™
©1986

Steve Caballero

Powell Peralta / Steve Caballero (First Version) / by V. Courtlandt Johnson / 1980

Original concept sketch / 1980 / by Steve Caballero

When it was time for my first graphic in 1980, it took me a while to think of something cool. Then Stacy Peralta gave me six Caballero decks printed with a Propeller graphic. He said this was a prototype because we had to shoot an ad as soon as possible, but he asked what I thought of it. I wasn't too stoked on the graphic since I had been riding a Ray "Bones" Rodriguez deck for over two years prior and couldn't believe this is what the artist came up with for my pro model. I shot the ad, but I was bummed. I wanted something that represented me, so I picked a dragon because I liked the way they looked and I was born in 1964, the Year of the Dragon.

I drew the first rough sketch of what I wanted, and then Court came up with the next few until he created something we both agreed on. He was great to work with because he was fast and an amazing artist. The first deck that came out didn't have my personal signature on it, and I really wanted it to be on there since Ray "Bones" had one on his. So the next batch of boards had my signature on them. I don't know why the bearing was dropped from the graphic later on. Powell still liked it because it was a good seller, we just changed the shape a couple times and dropped the bearing. What's cool about that Dragon graphic is that it first came out in 1980, and my next one didn't come out until 1986.

For my next graphic, an artist at my dad's work came up with a Chinese dragon that I really liked. I wanted to keep the same feel, and I thought this dragon would work well but it only lasted a year, maybe because it was drawn by someone other than Court. I never questioned why the graphic was changed so quickly. I was too stoked that I was even getting model after model. Plus, my board sales kept on rising every year so there were no complaints on my end. In 1980, I went from making about 500- to one-thousand dollars a month—getting a dollar royalty per board sold—to making eleven- to sixteen-thousand dollars a month in board sales alone in 1987, so I trusted Powell's every judgment on graphic change and design.

In 1987 we went for a Japanese-style dragon. The first run only had the dragon image, but then full-length graphics were coming into style, so Powell wanted to add something to the background. They chose this image of bats that connected together to look like bones as well. The whole reason they chose that background—as well as my name being shaped in a bat logo—was because I was always wearing Batman shirts at the time. I got a lot of flack from Powell for not representing any Powell T-shirts in any of the photos I was getting in the mags, which I felt was pretty lame considering I was making thousands of dollars for the company, but at the same time they capitalized on it by making the graphic have a Batman feel. **Steve Caballero**

Powell Peralta / Steve Caballero (Second Version) / by V. Courtlandt Johnson / 1981

Powell Peralta / Steve Caballero / by V. Courtlandt Johnson / 1981

Powell Peralta / Steve Caballero / artist unknown / 1986

Powell Peralta / Steve Caballero / by V. Courtlandt Johnson / 1988

Caballero concept sketch / 1980 / by V. Courtlandt Johnson

Caballero concept sketch / 1980 / by V. Courtlandt Johnson

The "Mutt" name came from my surfer friend Keith. Surfers were pretty much the whole skate crowd in the mid '70s Florida scene, and the bad asses were all "surf dogs." My shaggy hair and young dork, awkward nature didn't entitle me to any kind of full breed status—Mutt stuck. The Robotic Dog was my first graphic on Powell Peralta and it was a direct consequence of the whole Mutt thing. The day I got my first one, I proudly walked up to show my father. His genuine reaction was, "Looks like a damn rat," or something really close to that. The artist [V. Courtlandt Johnson] was always really cool to me. The Chessboard graphic came from the whole nerd/tech aspect of freestyle. The crown on the finger was his interpretation of the way he said I carried the "title," back when I used to win a lot of contests. **Rodney Mullen**

Powell Peralta / Rodney Mullen / by V. Courtlandt Johnson / 1981

Powell Peralta / Rodney Mullen / by V. Courtlandt Johnson / 1985

Contrary to this teacher's brash assumption, I now had several people involved with local punk/garage bands approaching me for artwork to use on T-shirts and concert flyers, as well as a few custom works on blank boards. The meager proceeds from these jobs went directly toward my all-consuming obsession for skateboards—a preoccupation that almost came to a brutal head in the spring of '87 when I brought home a Suicidal Tendencies Possessed to Skate deck.

By coincidence, I bought this new board on the very same day a "low slip" arrived in the mail from school (these warnings were sent to parents mid-quarter to alert them if their kid was not maintaining a passing grade in a specific class). Aside from being my first low slip ever, this was a particularly grave matter because the class I was floundering in was German—a subject taught by my dad at the junior high level. The untimely combination of this family disgrace with the blatantly satanic pentagram on the bottom of my new deck would certainly have made for a fucked-up evening in the household, but as my "skate fate" would have it, my mom was laid up sick in bed for the day and unable to check the mail. Discreetly shredding the inflammatory notice, I spent the rest of the evening working on a custom griptape job for the Suicidal deck with no one the wiser.

Following my graduation from high school in 1987, I relocated to Madison, Wisconsin, a far more progressive city fifteen times the size of my hometown, where I enrolled in a low-rent commercial-art program at Madison Area Technical College. Semesters were 500 dollars a pop and basically consisted of five to six art-oriented classes geared toward finding a job, as opposed to most college fine-art programs, where a premium is paid to find oneself. Despite the dime-store tuition, my skills increased exponentially, as I was now scribbling to some degree virtually every day of the week. I did, however, find a few professors no more open-minded than my high school art teacher, and once again I was told that such juvenile pursuits as skulls and gore would lead me nowhere near a prosperous path in graphic design. Inspiration often stems from strange sources, and mine was swiftly taking seed in bucking the overbearing tide of my instructors, a rebellious state of mind already well ingrained through skateboarding.

Aside from my total immersion in art, the foremost bonus to living in Madison was a strong skateboard scene that supported two decent shops, Flying Fish and California Connection. Within months of frequenting California Connection on an almost daily basis, I finagled a job on the weekends assisting customers and setting up complete skate-

My first pro model actually came out in 1979, when I rode for Eurocana in Sweden, and the graphic was illustrated by Jan Richter, a fast slalom skater and a cool artist. I was always into how Jan drew the character with such perspective. When Stacy called and said Powell Peralta wanted to make a pro model for me, I started thinking of concepts that would be a reflection of my homeland Sweden. A lot of things came to mind, anything from topless girls on the beaches of Sweden to hardcore, bloodthirsty Vikings with horns and stuff.

Through discussing it with VCJ, the Viking concept developed further to where we added the fangs to make it more fantasy crazy-like. To top it off, we wrote my name in Runic letters, the alphabet used by the Vikings around the eighth century. The Runic stone reads, "Search and strive, push beyond with strength, yours not theirs, that is the key." Back in 1984 I came up with it just sitting around thinking about progress and what it meant to me. The ultimate validation that the graphic was strong came when I received a Polaroid shot of this guy Barry Smith in Toledo, Ohio, who had a tattoo artist do the Viking skull on his whole damn back. |Per Welinder

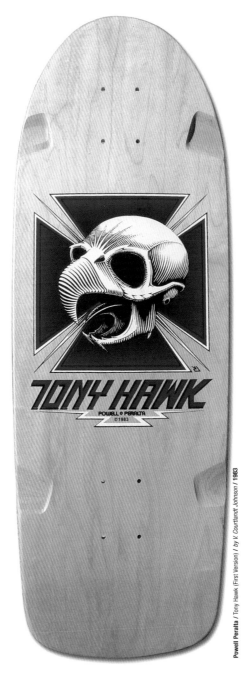

Powell Peralta decided to give me a signature model, so it was only natural that I would have a hawk as a graphic. A friend of mine, who is now a comic-book illustrator but was only thirteen at the time, drew a few ideas that were basically sketches of different types of hawks. I handed them to Powell thinking they would come up with a unique version or creature for the final graphic, but I guess George and Stacy thought it was exactly what I wanted, and Court basically copied one of his drawings, but added a lightning bolt to the talons and made it into a swooping pose. It looked a little meaner and had more detail, but it didn't have the Powell "edge." It was more like an illustration in a textbook, but I was way too happy with having my own model to complain about it. Needless to say, it had poor sales, so George and Stacy decided to take a different approach. They let Court come up with something truly unique—what I refer to as the "Screaming Chicken Skull"—and I loved it. I had that graphic for nearly ten years, and we ended up rereleasing it as a Birdhouse deck. Many of my graphics since then have been loosely based on the original. | Tony Hawk

boards. In exchange for my hours of service, I recycled my under-the-table earnings for discounted store product, thus enabling me to sustain the fix for a new deck every few weeks or so. One of the biggest perks to my half-ass employment was constant exposure to all the new boards and graphics. VCJ remained my preferred artist of choice, but not an idle afternoon passed when I didn't attempt to dissect Pushead's painstakingly detailed work for Zorlac, or the colorful intricacies achieved by Jim Phillips with his creative mixture of line work and separations on the various Santa Cruz models.

In March 1988, while flipping through an issue of *Thrasher* magazine, I ran across a Powell Peralta ad with the headline "Artist Wanted" amid a collage of sketches. In classified ad format, the small print invited people to send in four samples of their work for a chance at gainful employment with the company. This was somewhat hard to take seriously, considering Powell already had who I believed to be one of the best artists in the industry, but the hell if I was going to pass an open window of opportunity—especially one that pertained not only to the ultimate dream job but a chance at vindication before the skeptical eyes of my art professors.

After rummaging through some drawings from the past few months, I chose what I thought to be four distinct samples of my capabilities—I use the word "distinct" rather lightly because three of the four drawings consisted of skull-based imagery—and sent them in on a whim and a prayer to the Powell headquarters based in Santa Barbara, California.

A couple months later, I'd all but forgotten about the art contest when a package arrived in the mail from Powell Peralta. Included inside was a half-expired Bones Brigade calendar and a form letter stating I had officially made the "first cut." I viewed this as an accomplishment all its own but didn't hike my hopes up much beyond that. Besides, it was now summertime in Wisconsin, a season not to be taken lightly as a diehard skateboarder in the Midwest, and I was skating to the exclusion of all other thoughts and pursuits.

Near the tail end of August, I received a phone call from the company informing me that I was now considered to be one of the final four prospects to fill the artist position. They requested to see more samples of my work, so I assembled a slide sheet of what few semi-respectable class projects I could from the previous semester, showcasing anything from a color-marker comp of a kitchen blender to a technical line drawing of an old Camaro. Hence, my true surprise when three weeks into my third semester at MATC I received another call from Powell, this time asking if I was available to fly out to Santa Barbara for a job interview. Never one for conversational or profes-

My first pro model was on Titus Skateboards in Germany. I'd always been loyal to Titus, even when Santa Cruz asked me for the first time to join their team. I said no—stupid, really—but at some point Powell Peralta offered me to join the team, and I said yes. It was very hard for me to work with Stacy because he always wanted to be your "father figure," giving all sorts of advice I didn't think I needed. As a teenager, all I wanted was to get away from my father—I didn't need a new one.

Anyway, there was talk about a model, and we worked on a shape and I thought up the graphics. The original idea is from an art magazine. There was this fire face, and I changed it around to my needs. I worked part-time in an advertising agency, so I had all the tools for color separations and sent the whole thing to Powell. The board came out much too long and wide. On top of that, Stacy wanted to bring out the board for Germany only, possibly for England. I didn't understand the idea behind that at all, but he said no one would buy a board from someone who is not from the U.S. I realized that I hadn't found a sponsor in Powell that really believed in me, so I quit and went to Madrid Skateboards. The only batch Powell ever made was less than 50 boards. | **Claus Grabke**

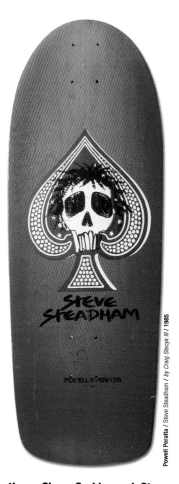

Powell Peralta / Claus Grabke / by Claus Grabke / 1985

Powell Peralta / Steve Steadham / by Craig Stecyk III / 1985

I was at Powell once and saw these Claus Grabke and Steve Steadham boards with very square edges. I thought they were seconds or bootlegs that they [Powell Peralta] was trying to stop from being made, but then I was later told by Stacy that Powell was trying to make boards overseas through a distributor—I think it was Shiner—so they wouldn't have to ship them overseas and the prices would be better. But I guess George didn't like how the boards looked and shut it down.

|**Lance Mountain**

Powell Peralta / Ray "Bones" Rodriguez (First Version) / by V. Courtlandt Johnson / 1978 (courtesy of Jimmy Anderson)

Powell Peralta / Ray "Bones" Rodriguez (Second Version) / by V. Courtlandt Johnson / 1980

Powell Peralta / Skull and Sword (First Version) / by V. Courtlandt Johnson / 1983

Powell Peralta / Skull and Sword (Second Version) / by V. Courtlandt Johnson / 1988

I always thought the old Ray Rodriguez Skull and Sword graphic from Powell was really incredible. It just kind of stunned me way back then. It's like those old heavy metal songs ... back then Iron Maiden and Black Sabbath just seemed so heavy-duty and intimidating, you're this kid and it just blows you away. I guess you try to keep that in mind with working on skate graphics, that even if you think it's dopey or something, there'll be some kid out there who could connect with it if you do it just right.

|Todd Francis

sional etiquette, I stammered something to the equivalent of, "Fuck, yeah!" as I'd never been to California before—or anywhere west of Minnesota, for that matter.

In the coming days I threw together a makeshift portfolio, all the while letting my imagination sprint off into a geographical fantasyland—mostly due to a simpleton's grasp of an approximately 160,000-square-mile state—as I envisioned all the pro skaters and legendary spots I would finally witness firsthand. However, a glimpse of my flight itinerary evaporated my dreams into thin air: Powell booked me in and out of Santa Barbara in exactly 24 hours. Granted, I was in no position to complain, but one fucking day in California was the torturous equivalent to letting a lifetime penitentiary inmate just set foot in a Nevada whorehouse before ruthlessly yanking him back into confinement without even seeing the naked goods.

Beyond all belief, I found myself seated in George Powell's office within an hour of touchdown in Santa Barbara on October 4, 1988, my portfolio splayed out before him and Nick Dinapoli, the department manager of the Design Group, as the art staff was formally referred to within the company. George was somewhat intimidating, not unlike any other company president, I suppose, and I attempted to field his questions the best I could. There were, however, gaping holes in my knowledge of art history and most every reference he made sailed right through them like darts tossed at a chain link fence. Worse yet, when George asked who some of my favorite artists were, I spat out VCJ without even a second thought to how silly it sounded. By far, the most difficult part was maintaining my concentration on the interview instead of daydreaming about stuff like the whereabouts of Stacy Peralta and the Bones Brigade team riders, and if I'd get the chance to go skating with them later on.

Toward the end of the interview, which I presumed to be going rather poorly, a tall man in what looked to be his early forties wearing all white clothing rolled into George's office on a pair of skates and introduced himself as Court. This was in fact Vernon Courtlandt Johnson, the artist behind the enigmatic initials that I'd so long admired. He flipped through my portfolio, politely commenting here and there as I mumbled in embarrassment over my vastly inferior work, and then asked if I wanted to go and grab some dinner with him.

Before doing so, we stopped off at the Design Group office to check out his personal studio. For a nineteen-year-old art student and skateboarder who worshipped Powell Peralta's graphic lineage, this was nothing short of nirvana, and my jaw dropped in reverential awe as I gazed upon a massive assortment of sketches and original art—most memorably the new Mike Vallely Elephant graphic—that littered Court's enclosed workspace.

The majority of his latest drawings concerned two Tony Hawk concepts, both of which were a radical departure from his longstanding Skull and Cross graphic, and a rash of insect studies. When we finally left the office, my mind was reeling in response to this unbelievably privileged glimpse I'd just had at the inner workings of Powell's art department, and I'm surprised I didn't crash the rental car as Court navigated us toward the restaurant in downtown Santa Barbara.

Over the course of dinner, the soft-spoken artist politely put up with all my inane questions regarding the Bones Brigade and assorted Powell Peralta trivia (I swear, I even grilled him on the decision Powell made in 1987 to produce "Boneite" decks, an ill-fated construction of maple veneers pressed with a tarpaper-like material that only added extra weight and water absorbency to the skateboard—in effect making it a big wooden tampon), but every so often the conversation did steer toward matters of art.

Powell Peralta / Alan Gelfand / by V. Courtlandt Johnson / 1981

Powell Peralta / Jay Smith / by V. Courtlandt Johnson / 1981

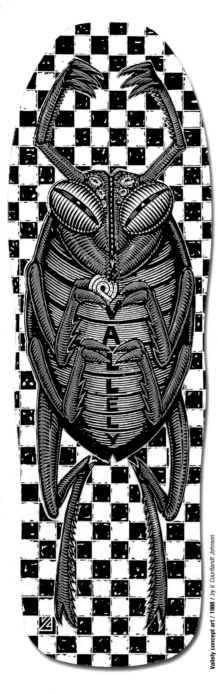

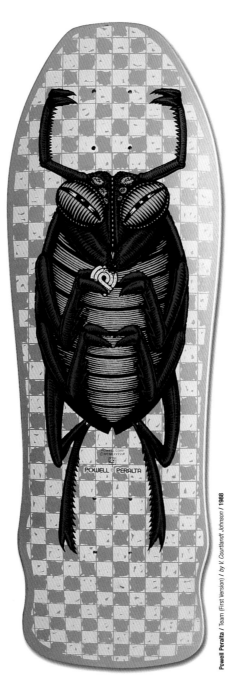

I learned that most of Court's illustrations were done on white scratchboard, and his style was influenced by the black and white renderings of M.C. Escher, a Dutch artist whom I was unfamiliar with at the time. We also talked about his origins at the company—he was a former brother-in-law to George—and how he started out in production before really taking up the graphic torch with Ray "Bones" Rodriguez's landmark Skull and Sword design.

Despite his being one of the most legendary skateboard artists of all time, Court spoke most earnestly of a therapeutic/spiritual practice called "balancing," where someone would stand before him as he scrutinized and lightly tapped specific points on their body to correct any perceived physical or mental imbalances. For lack of a more thorough understanding I'd simply chuck this into the "New Age" bin, but apparently it was something he was heavily into—so much so that he admitted to a current disenchantment in working at Powell and openly mused about taking a sabbatical in the coming months. Little did I know it would be a permanent departure.

The next morning I left without a clue to my fate other than a sinking gut feeling that I'd blown the interview in whole. Several weeks went by with no word from Powell, and my last strains of hope died along with everything else in the Midwest as fall descended with the cold, steel precision of a seasonal guillotine.

When I finally heard from the company, I'd mentally prepared myself for a consolation prize—a free T-shirt at best. Instead, I was dumbfounded by an offer of full-time employment, the pertinent details of which involved an opening salary of $18,000 a year and a one-way ticket back to Santa Barbara. I briefly discussed this once-in-a-lifetime opportunity with my parents—both of whom remained somewhat skeptical to an actual profession being built around skateboards—and they eventually gave me their stern but fair blessing to drop out of school and accept the position.

With only two months left to go in my third semester, I stuck it out at Powell's behest. I put this time to good use by getting in my last delinquent kicks, skipping classes and slacking off, smugly content in the knowledge I had a full-time job tucked safely in my back pocket come January of 1989.

In 1987, Stacy Peralta called me up at my parents' home in New Jersey, informed me I was going pro, and told me to think about what I wanted for a board graphic. I distinctly remember the moment, sitting in my bedroom on the phone with Stacy, as it was the continuation of this unbelievable dream coming true. I also remember watching TV several nights later and seeing a National Geographic program about elephants. This program really hit home with me as it focused on the plight of the African elephant, that it was endangered and how it was being slaughtered for its tusks. I was blown away. How could this majestic and beautiful animal, the largest land mammal on the planet, be endangered at the hands of man?

The program stuck with me, and I wanted an African elephant for a board graphic as a symbol and reminder of how beautiful and tragic life can be at the same time. But I was afraid to tell Stacy or anyone at Powell Peralta that I had chosen an elephant; it just didn't sound cool and I felt awkward about trying to articulate why I wanted an elephant. I did, however, mention it to Mark Gonzales, who was visiting the East Coast and staying with me at my parents' home for a few days, and he replied that elephants were cool and that he liked to draw them all the time. That was all the inspiration I needed. If Gonz says that elephants are cool, well to me that was the same or better than God saying it. So I called up Stacy and told him I'd decided upon an African elephant.

Not long afterward I attended my first pro street-style contest in Oregon. One night in the hotel, Stacy and Craig Stecyk presented a board graphic for me to look at. It was of a cockroach—a bug. I didn't understand why they were showing me this, and they asked me what I thought of it. I said I thought it looked cool, but I couldn't really think about it any further as it didn't speak to me. They said they were glad I was okay with it because it was going to be my graphic. I immediately protested, but they went on to explain that VCJ and George Powell really liked this graphic and wanted it to be the next pro model and how it would be best for me to accept it. But I fought back and swore I would never have a bug on the bottom of my board. They couldn't believe how strongly I felt about it. They really thought I'd just accept whatever they threw at me.

This incident probably marked the true beginning of the end for my relationship with Stacy and Powell Peralta. From then on, he always saw me as a thorn in his side, and I think he also realized that my protesting their prearranging this marriage between me and my board graphic was enough to make me quit if it were pressed any further. So they eventually backed off and told VCJ it was going to have to be an elephant.

I'm not sure what happened internally at Powell, I think there were a lot of bad feelings from George and VCJ that I did not accept the graphic, and part of me believes that maybe VCJ refused to do my graphic at that point because all I started hearing about was how Powell was looking for a new artist with a new style to do this particular graphic for me. That summer, while demo-ing with the team in my hometown, Stacy presented me with a graphic that an artist who was a friend of Kevin Harris' had done from Vancouver, Canada. He'd already shown it to Tommy Guerrero and Jim Thiebaud, and they both thought it was cool and a much-needed departure for Powell's graphics at the time. It was a graffiti-style elephant in a city setting with machine gun tusks firing upon a bunch of rats and my name was done in graffiti on a wall behind the elephant. I did like it for what it was, but felt

Valley concept art / 1988 / by V. Courtlandt Johnson

pressured to accept it. I knew I didn't really want it to be my graphic, but it was an elephant and I felt like I'd caused enough problems, so I decided to just let it be. Luckily, George and VCJ weren't down with it at all. I think the idea of this graphic being a part of the line and sitting next to VCJ's work inspired him to get back on the case. Before I knew it, I was meeting with him in Santa Barbara and looking at many different elephant sketches of his. He'd apparently thrown himself into the work, researched the African elephant and created his own relationship, which wasn't very far off from mine. Talking to him and seeing how he worked, I really gained an appreciation for him—his art and sensibilities. I knew then that the final graphic would be right.

I went back to New Jersey, and over the next few weeks he sent me many different designs. One that he sent—and that I believe we strongly considered—did not have the tribal pattern and shield design in the background of the elephant but instead had a repeating pattern of an image of a hunter. It wasn't long before we settled on the graphic that would eventually become the board. I remember him sending me a photocopied version of it with a note that read, "This is it." Although I agreed, I don't think I could have argued it. VCJ felt strongly about it, and by that time I trusted his instinct.

I am definitely happy with the design, and I reckon it's still the best board graphic I've ever had, if not the best graphic of all time. Then again, I prefer the VCJ Bones Brigade era stuff over everything that has come since. To me, those were and are what skateboards are supposed to look like, and to be so lucky as to have had a board in that series by that artist is something I'm thankful for. Through the years I believe the graphic has taken on a deeper meaning and significance for my audience; I know it has for me, and so I've continued to utilize the elephant to express and represent myself in skateboarding. —Mike Vallely

Lance Mountain

Powell Peralta / Lance Mountain (First Version) / by V. Courtlandt Johnson / 1985

When Variflex first told me I was gonna get a board in '81 or '82, I tried to come up with ideas for a graphic. I thought a bull's eye would be cool and I was pretty much set on that. At the time, I had a job watching a condo construction site so people wouldn't steal wood—funny, right?—and I was sitting in the car one night, when I thought of having a lancer or

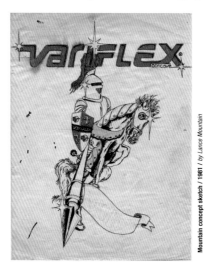

Mountain concept sketch / 1981 / by Lance Mountain

a knight, because my dad was in a horse guard regimen called the 17th 21st Lancers. So I did a sketch of a knight, but my drawing wasn't very good. Variflex took the idea from there and cleaned it up, but it still wasn't as good as I wanted. When I got on Powell Peralta I wanted the same thing—VCJ could have done it amazing—but for whatever reason they didn't want to do it. Instead, they wanted my head on the board, maybe even blowing up with all sorts of ideas coming out. But I'd rather not have a board than that for a graphic.

Craig Stecyk was going to do something—I would've used the graphic he drew on the board I rode in the first Bones Brigade video—but I was shown some caveman drawings by VCJ and I liked those. The first version of the Future Primitive graphic had a big, blob, frog guy doing a layback air, but I didn't really like the main character. I told him to make it look more like a real skate trick. The sec-

Mountain concept sketch / 1988 / by Lance Mountain

ond version had Tony Hawk doing a finger-flip on it, but I asked if he could change it again. The third version was the invert, and there were three or four more changes to that same graphic over the years. Right around the time my son and I had an ad for minis, Powell was thinking about making mini boards and a handful of samples—maybe five or ten, if that—were made with a single Future Primitive character on them.

Later on I still wanted a knight for my street model, but they wouldn't do it. So I tried drawing it over and over by copying VCJ's style. Just to draw it was a real stretch for me, and to do it like VCJ was impossible, but I kept working on it in hopes they would see that it could look good, and then VCJ would do the graphic. But every time I'd show it to them, instead of wanting to do it better they would just tell me what was drawn wrong and how to do the style and shading better. It took forever and I had to draw it about eight times, but it got better every time, and I learned a lot about graphics that I was able to use later on. But it was never as good as VCJ could have drawn.

|Lance Mountain

Variflex / Hand painted by Lance Mountain / **1981**

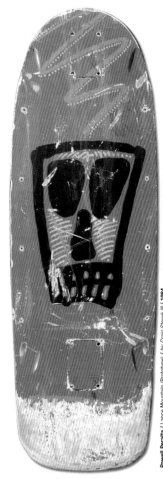

Variflex / Lance Mountain (Second Version) / artist unknown / **1982**

Powell Peralta / Lance Mountain (Prototype) / by Craig Stecyk III / **1984**

Powell Peralta / Lance Mountain (Second Version) / by V. Courtlandt Johnson / **1985**

Powell Peralta / Lance Mountain (Third Version) / by V. Courtlandt Johnson / **1986**

Powell Peralta / Lance Mountain (Prototype Mimi) / by V. Courtlandt Johnson / **1987**

Powell Peralta / Lance Mountain (Boneite Experimental) / **1987**

Powell Peralta / Lance Mountain / by Lance Mountain / **1988**

Part Two: The Promised Land

One of the foremost questions I'm asked is how to go about becoming an artist in the skateboard industry. Unfortunately, my response to all is muddled at best. I don't have a single clue as to how anyone would go about finding a job as such, because I lucked into the position through a completely unorthodox manner— an art contest of all things—with no real effort on my part. I was simply whisked out of the Midwest by a tornado of fortuitous events and delivered unto the promised land of the skateboard industry in California. Were someone to have told me then that I would become a firsthand witness to the simultaneous fall of one great skateboard empire and the rise of another, I surely would've laughed. After all, I was just some random skater from Wisconsin with no prior industry contact whatsoever.

On January 5, 1989, I reported for work at Powell Peralta, then located on Gutierrez Street in the lower east side of Santa Barbara. The company was spread out over a number of buildings around the immediate area, and I was surprised to find the art department looking radically different than during my job interview three months prior. For one, VCJ's private office was entirely gone; the walls were torn down and a generic cubicle slapped together in its place. Secondly, he was gone too. Court's planned sabbatical became a resignation after thirteen years or so with the company, and with a creeping dread it dawned on me that I was meant to be his successor. Considering I had about as much faith in my artistic abilities as the Pope does in that Hindu chick with eight flailing arms, this was a very unsettling prospect. Not only did I have a monumental set of shoes to fill, if I did not manage to sufficiently do so I would forever be known as the person responsible for the pivotal downfall of Powell's venerated graphic heritage—awesome.

The majority of my first morning on the job was spent gathering art supplies from around the office—one of the great scores being an isosceles triangle on which the name "V. Courtlandt Johnson" was written. After lunch, Nick Dinapoli called me over to his desk. Apparently, George Powell was still on holiday vacation, so without any precise instructions to pass on from him Nick suggested I call Steve Caballero to discuss new graphic ideas. Thanks to my natural born blank expression, the fact I'd all but shit my pants was adequately disguised because: a) you don't just call up Steve Caballero; and b) you don't just replace a Steve Caballero graphic. But sure enough, Nick went ahead and gave me his home number anyway.

I left a bumbling message explaining my newly acquired position and why I was calling, but I figured I must have made a real ass of myself because he never returned the call. Weeks later, a rumor broke in the office that Cab was seriously weighing an offer to ride for Santa Cruz Skateboards. It would also come to light in the coming month that both Mike Vallely and Rodney Mullen were in the process of defecting to a much-maligned foster company of Santa Monica Airlines named "SMA Rocco Division" (soon to be known as the more notorious World Industries), owned by Steve Rocco, a former professional for Sims Skateboards who'd gotten the boot for insubordinate behavior. This was all pretty disheartening, because now not only were the Powell graphics going to suck, but the preeminent Bones Brigade team appeared to be coming apart at the seams.

I did this graphic myself—as if that was hard to figure out—while I was still riding for Sims. The reason no one saw it is because only a few were produced before Brad Dorfman kicked me off the team. After Skip Engblom convinced me to cash out my credit card to buy boards and start a company, I realized I had no graphics to put on them. So I went down to Vision while everyone in the art department was at lunch and "repossessed" them. It is a collage of my favorite things: friends, family, Winnie the Pooh, etcetera. At the time, skaters rarely did their own graphics, unless they had real talent like John Lucero.

Once I realized that even someone with negligible skills such as myself could produce graphics and ads, I felt a sense of empowerment like I never had before. Of course, that feeling only lasted a few months. By then my skills on the Xerox machine had peaked and I resorted to using Rodney Mullen's college buddies and Jesse Martinez's friend who worked at a tattoo parlor. Thank god Marc McKee came along and rescued us. |Steve Rocco

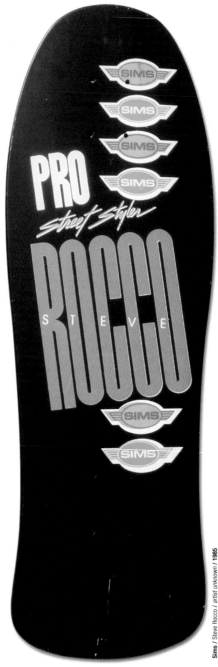

Upon George's return, I fast learned that as president he controlled each and every aspect of the business. Nick may have been the Design Group's on-site manager, but George was undoubtedly the formal art director who insured not a single item went into production without his approval. So, once a week, an afternoon was designated as "design review," a nerve-wracking block of time set aside in George's busy schedule when he would go around the office to assess everyone's progress. The staff was fairly minimal, with Jim Knight and I as the primary designers. Jim was the only other actual skateboarder in the art department, and he handled the photography and layout chores on the product posters and Bones Brigade Intelligence Reports, along with the design of various T-shirt, sticker, and wheel graphics. George spent most of his time with us critiquing, musing, and meting out art direction.

These often proved to be frustrating engagements, as George was a perfectionist to a fault—a fault that was not only aggravating to an artist but damn near everyone else in the company, because it significantly delayed the introduction of new products to market. Still, no matter how maddening it was—and it really was at times—I came to respect this quality in George and learned far more on the job at Powell than if I had stayed in school just to earn a silly piece of paper.

While I was being groomed to become a deck artist, my initial work assignments were no more grandiose than designing a border for a Winged Ripper banner and creating a new freestyle wheel graphic. I believe George viewed me as a lump of creative clay that he could mold and shape to his liking, and in a semi-fatherly way took me under his wing to broaden my artistic horizons. He encouraged me to check out books from the library regarding the art of primitive cultures, the German Expressionists, graphic design from the Third Reich, and, for obvious reasons, M.C. Escher. Mostly I just spent a great deal of time rummaging through the Powell art archives—these huge envelopes bulging with a treasure trove of old sketches, color comps, abandoned concepts, and finished illustrations—trying to decipher exactly how VCJ went from point

SMA Rocco / Steve Rocco / by Steve Rocco and Jules Kaupas / 1988

SMA Rocco / Jesse Martinez / by Doug Smith / 1988

SMA Rocco / Think Crime / by Steve Rocco / 1988

A to point B on the classic graphics that ultimately labeled an era of skateboarding.

Where was the other half of the company's namesake throughout all this? Well, Stacy Peralta's appearances at the factory were actually quite rare, as he lived down south and worked out of the fabled Powell L.A. office, where all the really fun stuff went down, like the advertising and video shoots he produced with his longtime creative collaborator and mentor, Craig Stecyk. Once or twice a month however, Stacy and Craig would come up to Santa Barbara and pop into the art department to monitor the situation and bolster morale when needed.

During these visits, Stacy often appeared to be distant and steeped in serious thought, but he was generally good-humored and spoke with a genuine sincerity and insight. Stecyk was always a more than welcome intrusion in the art room with his fuck-all attitude and antics, especially during the design-review sessions where George's domineering tone always seemed a bit tempered in Craig's presence for whatever reason—possibly

Unreleased T-shirt design / 1989 / by Marc McKee

Hand painted surfboard *by Craig Stecyk III / circa 1970*

Powell Peralta / Vato Rat / *by Craig Stecyk III / 1984*

Powell Peralta / Steve Steadham / *by Craig Stecyk III / 1985*

Truth be told, I never think about these sorts of things. Nor do I archive or portfolio shit. It was a long time ago, and all sense of authorship and intent were purposely shed at the moment things were done. Along the trail I suffered a blunt-force head trauma that affects my ability to recall things. The good news is that because of this documented medical condition I no longer have a clue.

Philosophically I never was much moved toward such vainglorious posturing anyway. Whatever anybody else says is fine with me. Dogtown, Zephyr, POP. I was around all that and painted hundreds of different boards, glyphs, crosses, logos et al. Skipper Boy claims he and I were sipping Silver Satin and Kool-Aid on the Blue Bus bench when I uttered something about it being "a dog's life in a dog town." Everybody makes mistakes, and maybe that's one of mine. As to who later went and copyrighted, sold, or traded anything I once did, I really don't remember. There were a few things I had already done on my own that they used. But always it was modified by others and reviewed by committee and fundamentally transformed into whatever it was an engineer thought he wanted. All of which I guess was the point.

There never was anything done up there that escaped the brutal mechanism. Ray Rodriguez once showed me this great skull drawing that he'd done. I idly mentioned that it should be on his first board. Now decades later someone in that camp is still trying to redraw another mutated version of the Sword and Skull. No subsequent renditions they ever did were as good, simple, honest or correct as Ray's. Anything or anyone innovative or independent anywhere near that scene was driven out or beaten into submission. It did not matter if you were Mofo or the Czar's brother-in-law. Monotony and blind replication would eventually destroy you. Some played to win and others played to lose. As for me, I did not play at all and it worked out well. | **CR Stecyk III**

because the two of them were dia-metrically opposed in most every respect.

In the wake of VCJ's abrupt departure, two Tony Hawk graphics were left in varying states of com-pletion, so I managed to use them as training wheels to find my artistic legs at the company. The first design, the bizarre and alien-like Claw, was finished for the most part, aside from the front logo of the accompanying T-shirt design. So I did some ghost work by creating what was supposed to be a Powell logo in the center of the claw but actually looked more like a weird butthole.

The other graphic, an odd con-glomeration of wings sprouting off the head of a hawk in opposing directions, was meant for a new street model of Tony's but lan-guished in disarray as no one knew what to do with the art in Court's absence. Stacy actually felt very strongly about this particular deck, viewing it as a prime opportunity to break stride from what he perceived as the "tired-and-true" approach to graphics Powell was long famous for. The obvious advantage to taking such a risk was that even if the graphic flopped, the deck would still sell an outsized amount just by its association to Tony, since the popu-larity of his name alone could sell a duck turd taped to a 2 x 4.

The first decisive and mutually agreed-upon idea was to solely pro-duce the Street Hawk as a black deck instead of the usual full palette of six-to-eight basecoat colors. While this may sound like a simple process, it was anything but. Only after viewing no less than twelve decks sprayed in varying states of blackness—matte, glossy, semi-gloss, satin, pearl, and all the combi-nations thereof—was the specific black finish selected after several design-review meetings. Meanwhile, the remains of the graphic were tossed in my lap to fumble with as a debate ensued between George and Stacy on how it should be applied to the board. Whereas Court's original illustration was that of an organic creature meant to occupy the tradition-al space between the front and back truck holes, George suggested I re-render it in a cold, metallic manner, a style that would complement the custom black finish on the deck. Finally, and after much deliberation, a minimalist approach was taken at Stacy's request, and the graphic rele-gated to the size of a small sticker.

Powell Peralta / Tony Hawk / by V. Courtlandt Johnson / 1989

Powell Peralta / Tony Hawk / by V. Courtlandt Johnson and Sean Cliver / 1989

In a way I guess this was my first deck design, but there was no amount of pride taken on my part as I felt like a fraud for batting ninth inning cleanup work on the vision of another artist. Regardless, my partic-ipation in the arduous process of developing the final Street Hawk graph-ic did serve to school me in the degree of thought and effort taken to achieve an end product at the company. At least I now understood why the Powell decks stood out leagues beyond the competitors from a pure-ly aesthetic point of view.

Whereas George was keen to the fact I could satisfactorily mimic Court's style—he actually commended my abilities by calling me a "sponge" one day—I'm inclined to believe Stacy was a bit disappointed.

Powell Peralta / Butterfly (Prototype) / by Chris Buchinsky / 1987

Powell Peralta / Butterfly (Prototype) / by Chris Buchinsky and Jim Knight / 1987

Lucero (Prime Time Dist.) / John Lucero / by John Lucero / 1988

Foundation / Tod Swank / by Tod Swank / 1990

When I first started working at Powell Peralta in June of 1987, VCJ was still working there, but I didn't see him much at first. He would stop by only to see if the company had built the walls of his new office space yet, and I got the feeling it was a stipulation of his return.

There was another artist working there by the name of Chris Buchinsky. He had done the Ripper animation for the beginning of the videos and was working on some deck art. He was originally working on concepts for a Jesse Martinez pro model, but Jesse was let go from the team—rumor was the reason for his departure had to do with getting into fights and running from police while wearing the company colors. I'm not sure if the Butterfly deck was a concept originally intended for Martinez, but Buchinsky re-worked the design at least a dozen times before he was eventually let go, too.

In order to salvage the graphic and all the hours spent to produce it, I was given the job of "cleaning it up." I was excited to be a part of making an actual deck graphic, but at the same time I thought the Butterfly graphic was cursed in some way. Under George's direction I changed the graphic quite a bit, giving it a new body, different antennae, the shadow barbed wire, and other modifications. The "CB" artist tag was also dropped.

After many revisions—and a few prototypes actually printed—George decided not to produce it. Court's walls were finished, he came back to work, and they made his Bug deck instead.

Jim Knight

The whole idea in the first place with the art contest was to find an artist with roots grounded in skateboarding, but I don't think Stacy counted on my being so heavily influenced by the very artist I was meant to replace. It also didn't help matters much that I'd come into the company at an odd point in time when the first significant shifts of power were afoot in the industry.

By 1989, a major revolution took root as the popular face of skateboarding began to change from vertical to street, and a whole new generation of skaters was on the verge of usurping every last bit of thunder from their "rock star" elders. Another faction of pro skaters, led by Rocco, Tod Swank, Mike Smith, and John Lucero (albeit rather briefly), made a break from their sponsors to form small "skater-run" companies. Across the corporate divide from them stood Powell Peralta, Vision, and Santa Cruz: the big three that had dominated the marketplace and grown fat on the excess of the sport's popularity in the '80s, only they now found themselves skirting the double-edged sword of success in a subculture that thrived on rebelling against that very thing.

This was a considerable change in sentiment that Powell was not swift to acknowledge, or at least not at the breakneck pace in which skateboarding was reinventing itself from the ground up. Then again, the company was still comfortably breaking sales records month after month and preparing

Powell Peralta / Steve Caballero (Prototype) / by Craig Stecyk III / 1989

Powell Peralta / Mike McGill (Prototype) / by Craig Stecyk III / 1989

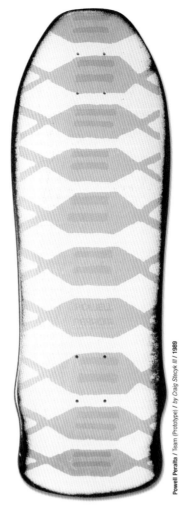

Powell Peralta / Team (Prototype) / by Craig Stecyk III / 1989

Powell Peralta / Steve Caballero (Prototype) / by Van Arno / 1989

to move into a gargantuan new warehouse—a former lemon-packing plant, if that wasn't an omen in itself—so no one was exactly screaming to crank the steering wheel in any other direction. All except Stacy, that is.

With regard to the graphics—a few of which dated back to the early '80s and were still being produced on outmoded deck shapes and constructions—Stacy felt the company had rested far too long on its skull and bones laurels. So, under Stacy's sole direction, Stecyk brought up three new deck designs that were covertly worked on under the omniscient blip of George's radar. The graphics were all of a primitive style, consisting of tribal masks and motifs, and Stacy's goal was to have a set of finished prototypes created to present his case to George for a definitive change in art direction.

And so it came to pass that George walked headlong into the graphic ambush during a regularly scheduled design review, with both Stacy and Craig laying in wait. For the duration of the meeting George kept a good face, but I could tell he was genuinely hurt by the direct challenge to his artistic sensibilities—not to mention the fact the entire operation was carried out in a clandestine manner. In the end, George left the fate of the graphics up to the individual pros, Caballero and McGill, but they too rejected the designs (as would several others down the food chain, like Ray Underhill; the Medallion became a red-headed stepchild kicked from rider to rider until Hawk finally took it). During this same meeting, two other graphics were proposed for a street graffiti-oriented Tommy Guerrero design and a Native American-themed Caballero, both com-

missioned by Stacy from an artist by the name of Van Arno, but George nixed these concepts as well. All told, this failed coup d'état left an indelible mark on Stacy, and his frequency of visits to the Santa Barbara facility slowly tapered off to a trickle over the coming year.

To Stacy's credit, yes, Powell Peralta did need a graphic makeover (in addition to many other things); however, the idea of designs tailored to a 30-year-old's level of art appreciation may not have been the right call, especially when the target market consists of twelve- to eighteen-year-old kids. This sophisticated sense of direction was shooting way over their heads, whereas Steve Rocco, with the aide of newfound artist Marc McKee, managed to aim directly into the heart of this consumer mentality with the graphics for World Industries.

Though initially scoffed at by industry veterans, the Rocco III and Mike Vallely Barnyard models proved to be a flashpoint in the history of skateboard graphics as fluorescent, cartoon-based concepts imbued with a witty approach to corporate icons and characters upstaged the popular graphic design/punk-oriented themes of the '80s. Thus, World situated itself as an underdog threat to the entire industry as Rocco successfully focused his ludicrous yet shrewd marketing abilities on creating a silly and subversive image that was readily digestible to any kid with a flair for rebellion.

Marc McKee

The first skateboard graphic I ever did was the Mike Vallely Barnyard for World Industries back in 1989. The way I met Steve Rocco was through this guy R.L. Osborn, who had this BMX bike company I'd been doing graphics for. He was a pro BMX freestyler from the '80s who had this big house in Hermosa Beach, and both Steve and Rodney Mullen were renting rooms from him at the time. Anyway, Steve had seen the stuff I had been doing for R.L., and even though it consisted mainly of drawings of pit bulls and skulls and roses intertwined with barbed wire, he said he wanted me to do a graphic for him. Actually, some of the stuff I'd done for R.L. included some T-shirt designs that had caricatures of people that looked like they were out of Mad magazine, so maybe it was more that stuff that Steve was into.

Up till then, the World graphics all looked like the Venice/Dogtown-looking stuff that Jesse Martinez and Jef Hartsel had on their boards, or the Powell-style wood-cut drawings—only not as good—that were on Rodney's and Mike Vallely's first World boards. And then there were the cut-and-paste jobs Steve did himself with the aid of the copy machine. Talking to Steve it was obvious that he had definite ideas of what he wanted, and that they weren't necessarily best conveyed in the form of Xeroxed collages or 16th century woodblock prints.

The Martinez and Hartsel graphics were good, but I guess the guy who did them, Doug Smith, wasn't all that "dependable." When Rocco got him to do the graphics for Jesse's first board, he gave him some money to go to the art store to get all the proper supplies. I think he may have been living on the street at the time, and he could draw but just didn't have any pens and paper. So Steve gave him some money to get the right stuff and then, about a week later, he brought in the finished piece drawn on the back of a pizza box. I guess he spent the money on weed—and pizza. He was a good artist, though. He drew everything with a Sharpie pen with a tip that he'd cut down with a razor blade to make the finer lines.

The main idea for the Barnyard was definitely Mike's, down to the "please don't eat my friends" line on the top graphic, but there were also a few other things inserted into the graphic that Steve wanted, like the polluting factory with the SMA World logo and the ghetto duck. Steve

SMA Rocco / Jesse Martinez / by Doug Smith / 1989

World Industries / Mike Vallely / by W.T. Lageose / 1989

would always want to throw a million different things into the background or wherever, and sometimes it was like what he was describing was less like a graphic and more like a short animated feature. I think the Animal Farm theme of having the farmer getting killed by the animals was my idea and maybe the beginning of my preoccupation with drawing violent cartoon characters.

The second graphic I did for World was pretty much the prime example of the one thing that World graphics would really become known for: blatant disregard of copyright law. The Rocco III was one of the first in a long line of rip-off graphics and the one that would eventually come back to cause the most trouble. On his previous graphic, Steve had photocopied a page from a Winnie the Pooh book, where Pooh was walking around with a honey jar stuck on his head.

For his next board, the idea was to have the honey jar in pieces on the ground, with Pooh's head in full view, only with now with devil horns, pitchfork and goatee, and, for some reason, new-wave wraparound shades. In the next few years the evil Pooh went unnoticed by Disney, and during that time we came out with numerous other rip-off graphics. The only thing negative that ever happened was that we would get these cease-and-desist letters from their lawyers which, because of the limited production runs of our boards at the time, basically amounted to a legal slap on the wrist. By the time we got the letter we had usually long stopped producing whatever it was they were after.

Occasionally we had to send back actual inventory so they would be sure that we had stopped. This happened once for sure when we made the Mario board for Jeremy Klein, and I think even then we only sent them a few boxes of boards since they really had no way of knowing how much stock we still had.

It wasn't until years later, when we rereleased the Rocco III as a snowboard graphic, that we finally got into some shit with Disney. I think we settled out of court for 60K. The thing that really sucked was that we could've gotten off by arguing that it wasn't really Winnie the Pooh since the Disney character never had horns or a pitchfork, but unfortunately we had to present some of our sales records that showed the board referred to as the "Pooh Devil." **Marc McKee**

SMA Rocco / Steve Rocco / 1989

World Industries / Mike Vallely / by Marc McKee / 1989

World Industries / Steve Rocco / by Marc McKee / 1989

The Barnyard was my coming out as a vegetarian, in a sense, so the bottom graphic was going to be this funky folk-art piece of animals grazing and the top graphic was going to be a quote in simple bold, black Helvetica, "Please don't eat my friends." I left this idea with Rocco, but while I was on tour he got together with Marc McKee and tweaked things. When I returned they had the entire graphic completed. I hated it. To me it was stupid and childish. Rocco, however, felt strongly about it. He talked about George Orwell's book Animal Farm and how this graphic was a play on that with the animals rebelling and fighting back.

He made a good case, and I began to warm up to the design. It definitely looked different than anything I'd ever seen before, and I slowly came around, but I had two demands. One was that the top graphic be a continuation of the bottom scene with the quote worked into it, and the second was to remove what I determined to be a vulgar and pointless image of a horse mounting another horse—the horse that was getting mounted is still on the board, you can see her smiling face peeking out from behind the barn. I wouldn't approve the graphic otherwise. This was easily the best-selling model I've had. Back then I was pulling consistent ten- to thirteen-thousand-dollar checks each month for almost a year, thanks to that board. To this day I have people come up to me and credit the Barnyard for introducing them to the ideologies behind vegetarianism. |Mike Vallely

World Industries / Ron Chatman / by Marc McKee / 1990

World Industries / Stik-o-rama / by Marc McKee / 1990

World Industries / Jesse Martinez / by Marc McKee / 1989

World Industries / Jesse Martinez / by Marc McKee / 1990

World Industries / Mike Vallely / by Marc McKee / 1989

World Industries / Mike Vallely / by Marc McKee / 1990

World Industries / Mike Vallely / by Marc McKee / 1991

Unfinished Jason Lee design / 1991 / by Marc McKee

> Marc McKee is probably the single most important artist of skateboards. I don't think people even really realize his impact and his retardedly unbelievable skills. For a certain period in the early '90s, the World Industries stuff and his composition defined what a skateboard graphic was and subsequently is. Words are hard to use to describe his mastery—Marc rocks.
>
> **Thomas Campbell**

With the decision to bump two of Powell Peralta's street-based amateurs into the professional ranks, I was finally thrust into uncharted waters with Ray Barbee and Steve Saiz as my proving grounds. To my favor both had no prior graphic history with the company, which enabled me to work from a clean slate free of milestones erected by VCJ. Although I started working on both simultaneously, Barbee's proved to be the easiest and stemmed from his initial concept of a rag doll. Taking loose elements from his style, along with his trademark baseball cap and beads, I managed to pull an image out of my ass that was wholly unlike anything produced by Powell to date: a simple cartoon drawing. I wasn't exactly sure if this would be construed as a good or bad thing in the marketplace, but I took solace in the fact Ray's easygoing and popular personality would be the linchpin to its success if anything.

The Saiz graphic, on the other hand, was a much more difficult process if only because Steve had his heart set on this "goop monster" he had drawn. I tried a few renditions of this Hulk-like creature bursting out of a puddle with "Saiz" spelled out in the mess held above its head, but the whole thing reeked of Santa Cruz for some reason. Moreover, George wasn't remotely interested in pursuing it, either. I also toyed around with a skeletal lizard in a flaming tree—a concept Stacy visibly cringed at on first sight—but then sidetracked into a Native American theme, based on Steve's predominantly Spanish heritage. Any ground that I may have gained in Stacy's eyes with the Barbee design was quickly lost as I adapted a style reminiscent of Court's to accomplish the final Saiz art, all the way down to using white scratchboard as the medium. If that alone didn't cause Stacy to despair, then my next design for Caballero surely did, because it was nothing more than a continuation of his dragon theme with yet another heavy nod to Court. So much for the great change in graphic direction at Powell Peralta!

At the Action Sports Retailer trade show in September 1989, I was walking through the aisles of the slum section (an area where all the negligible companies are commonly sequestered in small conference rooms far removed from the main arena), and stumbled upon the World Industries booth. In striking contrast to the all-out 800-square-foot effort of Powell Peralta—a company that took immense pride in its inventive booth concepts—World had nothing more than a folding table with some chairs strewn about it. While surveying the new World products, I noticed a short man of pinkish pallor checking out my ID badge. With hand outstretched and a gleam in his eye, he approached me saying, "Hey, you're Sean Cliver! You did the Ray Barbee graphic!"

This was in fact Steve Rocco, the very man painted out to be everything going wrong in the skateboard industry, and here he was now shaking my hand and telling me how much he admired the first original graphic I'd drawn and how it saved Powell from becoming a laughingstock in the industry. Looking back on that moment now, like a critical freeze-frame in a Martin Scorsese film, this was probably the beginning of my end at Powell.

Mountain concept art / 1989 / by V. Courtlandt Johnson

Following the Future Primitive theme we were struggling to get an idea for a new graphic. I had a knee problem during this time, and since the skull theme was Powell's thing VCJ came up with this "knee bone voodoo skull" idea-I think it would be funny to do now, but at the time it wasn't something I wanted on my board.

Then, in 1989, Lance Jr. drew a lot of these little stick guys on a stack of computer paper I had. I think every parent gets stoked on what their kid draws, they hang the art up on their wall or refrigerator or whatever, so I just figured I would hang it up as my board graphic. I don't know why I really used the drawings beyond that, but once I did that one I just started taking all the drawings he did and began making paintings from them. I'd take his line work, draw around it, and put colors in it. It's basically become my known style, and I still do it all the time. I did two other Powell boards like that, too.

That time with graphics was weird ... it was just about being real simple and having nothing on your board. People were trying to do anything different because everything had been done and things were coming out real quick. People wouldn't wear their own shirt anymore; they'd only wear other people's graphics. It was starting to be a really strange time in skateboarding, I think, and the Dough Boy came from that same time of just real minimal graphics.

I had these cartooning books that showed animation of these guys running, and I thought it would be rad to have a straight little strip of them under the wheels on one side of the truck from nose to tail. I thought it would be cool to have the guy running, tripping, then he falls and is kinda bummed when he gets up. I drew it out so that he was jumping over my name and then tripping and falling over Powell Peralta. I turned it in-I don't even know why I was turning graphics in, they didn't really want us to turn graphics in-but George didn't like it.

The way it was drawn, I guess he thought people would read into it, like I was the guy was tripping over the Powell name and falling and being bummed on it. So he wanted it changed to where the character bounces off the name and flips off the board really happy. It changed the direction of the whole thing, so ultimately it wasn't even the same idea I wanted. It turned out fine, but it was just weird. I didn't really think of people reading into stuff, but I guess they do. To me it was just this little dude who was more embarrassed then bummed when he fell, and all I really wanted was just a straight line on the board. Years later, I ran it on a Firm board the way I originally wanted to.

|Lance Mountain

Powell Peralta / Lance Mountain / by Lance Mountain Jr. and Lance Mountain / 1989

Powell Peralta / Lance Mountain / by Lance Mountain Jr. and Lance Mountain / 1990

Powell Peralta / Lance Mountain / by Lance Mountain / 1990

Powell Peralta / Lance Mountain / by Lance Mountain / 1991

Lance Mountain / Huntington Beach, CA / 1989 / photo by Rick Kosick

Mountain concept sketch / 1990 / by Lance Mountain

Powell Peralta / Mike McGill / by John Keester / 1990

Powell Peralta / Steve Caballero / by Sean Cliver / 1990

Powell Peralta / Team / by John Keester / 1991

Powell Peralta / Ray Barbee / by Sean Cliver / 1990

No more than a year into my tenure as the head artist, Powell Peralta ran a similar "star search" advertisement to the one I'd been reeled in with. It's not that I was doing a bad job. On the contrary, George seemed happy with how I was developing, and I had yet to commit any outright graphic atrocities, but the times were changing at a rapid clip. A design that previously held its own for a year or more in the skate shops with consistent sales now only struggled to the six-month mark on marginal, waning numbers. This was mostly due to a change in marketplace sentiment, where the more nimble companies were capable of introducing new models with a greater frequency, thereby satiating the younger generation's increasing lust for fresh graphic stimuli and functional board shapes for modern street tricks. For the larger companies this posed a serious problem—it wreaked havoc in scheduling production runs of decks where massive quantities were the norm to keep shipping departments stocked at all times.

So to keep up with the increasing graphic turnover rate and maintain sales projections, another artist was an absolute necessity at Powell. The winner this time around was John Keester, a 33-year-old artist from Sonoma, California. Technically speaking, John was a far better artist than I was, and it threw a healthy degree of competition into the mix. There was, however, one distinct difference between the two of us: my proximity to the hardcore skateboarders who were responsible for shaping the next phase of skateboarding.

When not entrenched in my strict nine-to-five routine, I was frequent-

ly out skating the schoolyards and other Santa Barbara spots with the locals and amateurs on the Bones Brigade roster, or traveling to various demos and contests in California. Consequently, between my fascination with Rocco's absurd industry antics and a constant exposure to the latest rumblings on the street, I was well aware of the fading perception of the Powell brand name. Skateboarders were no longer responding to its skull-based images, aside from the garden-variety twelve year olds picking up their first deck on their parents' dime. These kids may have been Powell's bread and butter throughout the latter stages of the '80s, but in 1990 the cyclical popularity of skateboarding was already on the downswing and prepubescent lemming hordes were no longer buying decks. They were onto the new trend on the block: Rollerblading. Accordingly, this exodus left a dwindling market of cynical teens that had long outgrown Powell's legacy.

Overall, my burden of awareness manifested itself as a crap attitude at the office. I openly clashed with George in design-review meetings to the point that he simply dismissed my opinions as jaded. Keester, on the other hand, didn't rub against the company grain so much and was content to generate further graphics in the Powell vein. However, this isn't to say I was doing anything better myself. I was still eking out variations on past proven themes, like Caballero's dragons and the wrought-iron stylization of a dagger for Tommy Guerrero's last pro model on Powell before he, too, up and left the flagging Bones Brigade to start Real Skateboards with Jim Thiebaud under Fausto Vitello's San Francisco-based empire, Deluxe.

Powell Peralta / Tommy Guerrero / by Kevin Ancell / 1986

Powell Peralta / Tommy Guerrero / by V. Courtlandt Johnson / 1986

Powell Peralta / Tommy Guerrero / by Sean Oliver / 1989

Real / Tommy Guerrero / by Jeff Klindt / 1990

Guerrero concept art / 1985 / by Mofo

The original idea was based on a "street machine," and Mofo had a photo of an old hot rod from around the '40s with the V-8 symbol on the front it. We also added a Mexican flag-looking eagle with a snake to the background, and then submitted the idea to George. Of course he didn't like it. Then [Kevin] Ancell took it on and totally diminished the original idea from the car and just took the front of the grill—that's how the dagger came about, because it's actually the centerpiece from the grill with the V-8.

So Ancell did the first graphic, and that was sort of going for a cholo lowrider feel with the lightning bolt decorations around the side with the roses. I dug it, and they screen-printed it. I guess George was out of town when this happened, though, because when he came back he didn't like it and wanted to change it. So then it became Court's job, and he came up with the flames and dagger with only the "V" remaining—it was the total derivative of what Mofo had started with a grill of a car. I liked Ancell's best, personally.

|Tommy Guerrero

Tommy Guerrero / 1986 / photo by Grant Brittain

Real / Jim Thiebaud / by Natas Kaupas and Kevin Ancell / 1990

Real / Jim Thiebaud / by Jef Whitehead / 1991

Real / Jim Thiebaud / by Kevin Ancell / 1993

After my experiences with Powell and NHS, I wanted my first board on Real to mean something and have a lasting impact. Skateboarding was at a point where graphics that didn't really mean shit were just being churned out, and I saw it as an opportunity to do more than just cut-and-paste images that looked cool. I was also at a point in my skating where I wasn't really sure how much more time I had to be out there, and I figured it was time to change it up and try to say something with the vehicle of board graphics.

I thought the image of a hanging Klansman was about as powerful as you could get. There was no side-stepping the message. Natas had left SMA to start 101, but he helped me out by drawing the idea up. When the board came out it was great. Some shops were afraid to carry the board. Some sent it back. The hate mail I received was so funny. Then there were the skaters who got behind the message and sent Polaroids of the graphic tattooed on their arms and legs. Soon after the board was released, I organized a tour of the Deep South—three weeks on the road skating with the locals and sessioning all their spots. Some skinheads showed up at one of the demos and hung out watching while we all skated and got ready for whatever they were going to bring. Turned out they were SHARPS [Skinheads Against Racial Prejudice] and had made shirts of the graphic and wanted to give me one. At the end of the day, none of the people who sent hate mail and death threats had the balls to step to a group of skaters who knew deep down that they were unstoppable.

Jim Thiebaud

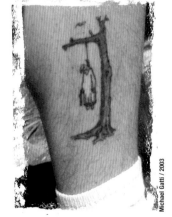

Michael Gatti / 2003

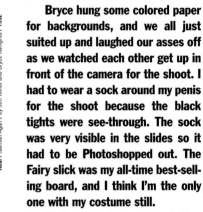

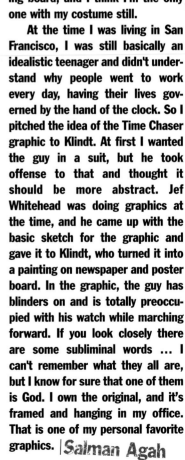

I remember going to a shop with Jeff Klindt to purchase some costumes. I didn't really care what my costume was going to be—I was more stoked to be a part of Real Skateboards, an emerging fresh company in skateboarding, and hang out with Jim Thiebaud and Tommy Guerrero. It was raining very hard that night, and I was brought to the Studio 43 warehouse, where Bryce Kanights, Tommy, Jim, and Jeff were with lots of beer. We all hung out and sipped on some Miller Genuine Draft—I think Tommy and Jim were partial to that brand at the time.

Bryce hung some colored paper for backgrounds, and we all just suited up and laughed our asses off as we watched each other get up in front of the camera for the shoot. I had to wear a sock around my penis for the shoot because the black tights were see-through. The sock was very visible in the slides so it had to be Photoshopped out. The Fairy slick was my all-time best-selling board, and I think I'm the only one with my costume still.

At the time I was living in San Francisco, I was still basically an idealistic teenager and didn't understand why people went to work every day, having their lives governed by the hand of the clock. So I pitched the idea of the Time Chaser graphic to Klindt. At first I wanted the guy in a suit, but he took offense to that and thought it should be more abstract. Jef Whitehead was doing graphics at the time, and he came up with the basic sketch for the graphic and gave it to Klindt, who turned it into a painting on newspaper and poster board. In the graphic, the guy has blinders on and is totally preoccupied with his watch while marching forward. If you look closely there are some subliminal words ... I can't remember what they all are, but I know for sure that one of them is God. I own the original, and it's framed and hanging in my office. That is one of my personal favorite graphics. | Salman Agah

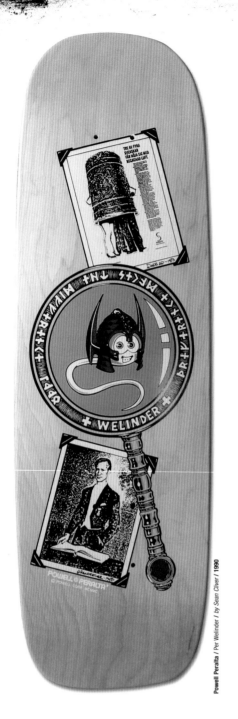

Powell Peralta / Per Welinder / by Sean Cliver / 1990

While other companies scrambled to reinvent themselves with fresh, young teams and a more street-oriented direction (one of the most successful being Schmitt Stix, as they miraculously escaped the shadow of Vision's death pall by folding and reemerging as New Deal, a company fronted by Andy Howell's distinctly urban and graffiti-inspired graphics), Powell Peralta remained steadfast in sticking to its guns but floundered in exactly how to go about bridging the old and new generations—especially when it came to graphics. The most absurd incident that comes to mind was the internal stink that arose over Per Welinder's last deck, a hybrid double-tail shape that was stranded somewhere between the size of freestyle deck and a full-size model. If anything, this unorthodox size should have been the point of contention, but instead it stemmed from a silly genealogical graphic Per and I worked on to portray three current generations of Welinders and his intent to keep the Swedish family name going. This proposed fourth generation was depicted by a manic train of spermatozoa winding down from the nose of the deck to the tail—a magnifying glass bringing one helmeted warrior to the fore—in pursuit of a cartoon female egg with eyelashes and lipstick.

The design was 90 percent of the way through the approval process, with T-shirt samples printed and separations being cut for the deck art, when Stacy paid a rare visit one afternoon. When I spied him silently staring at the Welinder shirt samples spread out on the floor for design review, I knew the day was not going to end well. Sure enough, Stacy later expressed his distaste to George, stating that he was disappointed we were now stooping to such base levels to compete with the likes of Rocco. His was not the only voice of condemnation in the company. The entire female accounting department was up in arms over what they deemed to be a "sexist and crude" image. The next day, George came in, and the sperm and egg were wiped clean from the background, castrating the graphic of all its original humor value—not to mention a good majority of its design sense, too.

Meanwhile, World Industries delivered a Randy Colvin pro model to shops that was sealed in a black plastic bag with a yellow sticker reading, "Censorship is Weak as Fuck." The graphic on the deck inside featured an explicitly fluorescent portrayal of a naked woman sprawled on her back masturbating. Obviously, many mom 'n' pop shops throughout the nation had more than a few problems with this graphic, but Rocco pinned their morals to the mat with a threat to "blackball" them if they refused to carry the deck. This meant they were forbidden from ever ordering anything distributed by World Industries again, or at the very least denied certain high-demand products bearing the names of Mike Vallely, Mark Gonzales, or Jason Lee. Since the survival of many of these shops depended on Rocco's products, many capitulated to his Napoleonic demands, even if it meant disposing of the Colvin deck upon receipt.

WARNING:
Censorship
is
Weak as Fuck

Board cannot be returned once factory Plasto-Pak™ seal is broken.

world industries

Needless to say, it was getting more and more frustrating for me at Powell, especially when the graphics being generated by World Industries and Blind were the ones I now wanted to skate and wear. Instead, I let myself get pushed into pursuing inane tribal/primitive directions for riders like Mike McGill, Nicky Guerrero and Steve Saiz. I only did so in a desperate attempt to try and appease Stacy, but this is, of course, the cardinal sin for any artist. I wasn't being true to myself, the resulting graphics were abysmal, and I still feel bad that scores of maple trees were sacrificed on my no-good artistic account.

Unreleased T-shirt design / 1990 / by Saen Cliver (courtesy of Per

Ever since I was a 12-year-old Italian kid staring at skateboard magazines, I dreamed about doing graphics. On my first trip to the U.S. in '87, I did a little work for Schmitt Stix but then met Tony Magnusson at Lance Mountain's ramp. We were both passionate about the design aspect of skateboarding, and he was thinking of switching Magnusson Designs into a new company called H-Street. It sounded rad to me. It had a true urban feeling—an ideal area that could exist in any town around the world. A week later I did the first H-Street logo with hand-drawn graffiti lettering set over a conventional font. Tony was stoked on it, because the company was still just an idea then. I guess my logo provided a further kick to make it happen. For the time, Scott Obradovich and I did a few graphics for Magnusson Designs. It's so amazing to draw a graphic and then see it for real on a skateboard—it is unmatchable. Then I had to go back to Italy. My visa was over. Months later, Tony called and said H-Street was now a true company.

When I came back in '88, H-Street was being run from T. Mag and Mike Ternasky's place. Art and Steve Godoy were doing many of the graphics while I concentrated on other details of the company, like designing ads, T-shirts, decals, and wheels. I then drew the Arrow logo that made the brand recognizable worldwide. I thought of it as a sort of street sign—a crossroad to whatever direction you wanted to go. Soon after Mike Ternasky produced the Shackle Me Not video, he showed Scott and I this raw, hip-hop-style sketch. He believed it might be the future of art in skateboarding—all twisted and zoomed, yet clean and simple. From there, we launched a new H-Street style with Matt Hensley's first deck. H-Street was a tremendous experience, although none of my graphics are my favorite, except perhaps for the Hensley King-Size Eagle. I also feel a bit lame I didn't bust out a significant graphic for Danny Way.

Francesco Albertini

51

Randy Colvin

Was it because he pushed mongo? Probably not, but for some reason Randy Colvin always got the most fucked-up graphics of all of our riders. Actually I think it was mainly due to geography since he lived in Arizona and didn't make it into the office that often to see what kind of stuff we were slapping his name on, such as:

Censorship: This graphic was conceived as a statement against censorship, but I think it's safe to say that it was really just an excuse for putting the first full frontal nudity on a skateboard—now it would probably be described as great marketing. We got custom black bags to package the decks in and heat-sealed them with a warning sticker that said if the bag was opened the decks would not be able to be returned. Rocco's idea was that people would have to buy the deck without being able to see how gnarly the graphics were since I don't think many shops displayed it on their board walls. The way I drew the girl still bugs me—I don't think I had done enough research up to that point.

Velvet Safari: When I started working on this graphic that was supposed to be like one of those cheesy '70s velvet blacklight posters, I had no clue it would be possible to actually apply that black velvet stuff to a board. By some strange coincidence though, when Chicken and Kelly Belmar—the guys at the place where our boards were screened—saw this graphic they said they could do it and they knew exactly where to get the stuff. Right next door to them was a toy place where one of the things they did was apply the fuzzy shit for the hair on G.I. Joes. It was just a matter of being able to silkscreen the glue on a deck, and then all they would have to do is sprinkle on the powder and wait for it to dry. I heard a few people say the fuzz was nice for grabs.

New Kids on the Block: This is evidence that we were doing things entirely without Randy's approval. But that's not to say we didn't have his interests in mind. On the original version of this deck there was a big swastika above Jordan's head that we decided it would be best to remove.

Colvinetics: In the original sketch it was Jasonetics for Jason Lee, basically a joke on the whole Hollywood/Scientology connection. Needless to say, he was not into it, so we gave it to Randy. At least we didn't sic the Scientologists on him when they sent us a cease-and-desist letter.

Rasta Rebel: Another graphic that Randy had nothing to do with and I wish I could say the same for myself. I have no idea what I was thinking with this one, but I was probably stoned at the time.

|Marc McKee

World Industries / Randy Colvin / by Marc McKee / 1990

World Industries / Randy Colvin / by Marc McKee / 1990

Dear George,

After seeing all the ads lately (especially yours) making fun of new or small companies I realized how stupid I was for having one. Dude, you were right small companies are cut ! Anyway, I've talked to Jason and Rudy, and we all agree we should try to be big-time just like you guys. Here's a picture of our new graphics and logo. I hope they're OK. And if there's anything else that we're doing wrong, just make another ad and we'll change it.

Sincerely,

Mark Gonzales

P.S. Do you think I should kill myself ?

BLIND

not a small company anymore

In 1991, Powell Peralta ran an advertisement mocking the trend of small, skater-owned companies in Thrasher magazine, featuring Lance Mountain, Ray Barbee, and Tony Hawk dressed in goofy clothing upon which the fictitious company names "Me Me Me," "Scum Bucket," and "Bad Person" were printed. Perhaps ill-advised, the ad was an obvious stone thrown at the World Industries camp that provided Rocco the golden opportunity to play "David" to Powell's "Goliath." Now if there is one thing I understood about Rocco, it's that he loves being challenged by anyone with an air of superiority, and he will devote all his time, energy, and resources to ripping apart an opponent with the tenacity of a cornered wolverine. So, with an open chink revealed in the armor of Powell, Rocco smartly played his cards as the innocent victim to the corporate bully and devised an entirely new battleground where graphics would be the weapons of choice.

In a memorable ad titled, "Dear George," Blind debuted three new graphics for Rudy Johnson, Jason Lee, and Mark Gonzales. The designs parodied classic Powell designs and proved to be immensely popular with skaters. Rather than stand idly by while the company lost further ground, I thought a humorous rebuttal was in order and drew up an idea for a Blind Ripper graphic. My initial idea was to screen the decks with the exact same top graphic as the Blind decks, thinking at the very least a few dimwits would unknowingly put some sales in Powell's corner, but George thought Rocco might sue for doing so—a notion I found rather funny since George was already in the process of investigating a legal recourse to the decks produced by Blind. (Apparently, the difference in top logo didn't even matter; more than a decade later I discovered some still believed the deck to be produced by Blind and not Powell.) Arguably, the Blind series heralded the end of Powell Peralta's dynasty and successfully knocked the industry giant flat on its lumbering ass for the next decade to come—all due to a silly little marketing war played out for the enjoyment and participation of the consumer.

The whole war with Powell Peralta started when Rocco got their two best ams, Rudy Johnson and Guy Mariano, to ride for Blind. Rodney Mullen and Mike Vallely had left Powell a year earlier to help start World Industries, so this was really salt in the wound. Soon after, Powell ran this ad with Lance Mountain, Tony Hawk, and Ray Barbee wearing T-shirts with dollar signs on them and pondering the idea of leaving Powell to start their own companies—pretty funny since it was intended as a joke but turned out to be true.

It would have been nearly impossible for Steve to let the ad go unanswered, so the next Blind ad that came out had this big headline on it, "Dear George," with a note from the Gonz—but in reality written by Steve—that said we were wrong and he was right and that we would try to be more like a big company with a new line of graphics we were sure he would like. First it was stolen riders—stolen graphics seemed like the next logical step.

Before we released this series there was a big question mark as to what George Powell's reaction would be. My original idea for tweaking the Welinder Screaming Skull was to give it braces with that crazy headgear they used to make kids wear with all the springs and pulleys. Because we had already received a few cease-and-desist letters from some other companies we had stolen logos from, Steve wanted to make sure these graphics were different enough from the originals so we could actually sell them and not have to stop as soon as we got one of those letters that arrives by certified mail.

I don't know where this number came from, or if it has any legal basis, but somehow we had the idea that a graphic has to be at least "ten percent" altered from the original in order for it to be free from being any kind of copyright infringement. I don't know how you can quantify to what degree one image is different from another on a percentage basis, but we thought if we met the criteria we'd be okay. Anyway, when I finished the skull with braces, Steve thought it was still less than ten percent different from the original. So I ended up drawing a new version with the football helmet.

The Jason Lee Dodo Skull was originally drawn for Danny Way, who was still on Blind at the time. The reason we changed it to be Jason's pro model was that the rivalry between Danny and Tony Hawk was kind of intense at the time, so Steve and Rodney Mullen thought the graphic would be seen as too much of a direct dis on Tony, instead of just one board in a series of boards that were more aimed at making fun of Powell. After the graphic came out with Jason's name on it, a lot of people thought the choice of the dodo skull, with its huge beak, was supposed to be some kind of caricature of Tony, but I seriously didn't put that much thought into it.

|Marc McKee

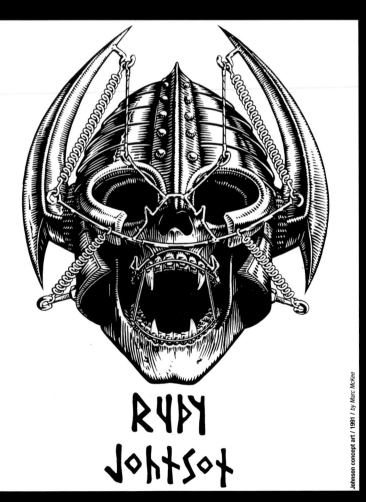

Johnson concept art / 1991 / by Marc McKee

BLIND ⊚ SKATEBOARDS
©1983

Way concept art / 1991 / by Marc McKee

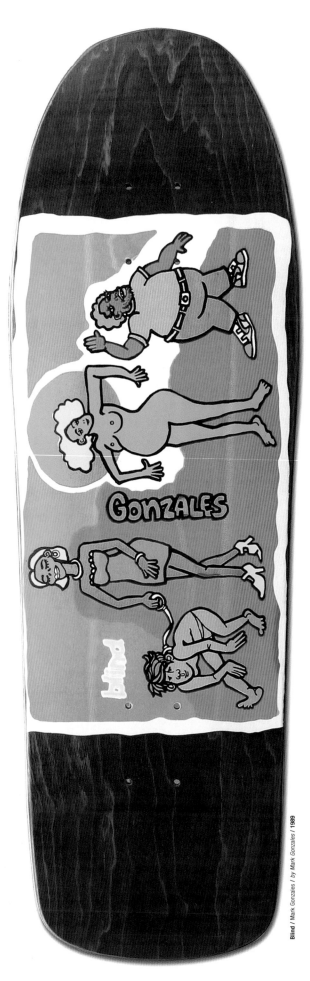

Blind / Mark Gonzales / by Mark Gonzales / 1989

I was pretty honored to have my first board done by Mark [Gonzales], because I always liked his crazy-ass self-drawn graphics on Vision. For the graphic, we just came upon this book that had all these cartoon body parts and he thought it would be rad to draw something like that. At the time I had my first car, a little Toyota. I guess Mark loved that car because he used to have one, so he randomly threw the word "Toyota" on the graphic. People were really confused by that, and I heard that in San Francisco some people were like, "Who's Toyota Johnson?"

The Aborted model, that one Mark and [Steve] Rocco were so excited about producing that it was out of my hands. I knew it was gonna cause some sort of controversy, and I guess it was banned from a lot of shops. **Rudy Johnson**

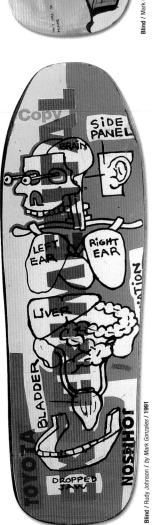

Blind / Mark Gonzales / *Hand painted by Mark Gonzales* / **1991**

Blind / Mark Gonzales / *Hand painted by Mark Gonzales* / **1991**

Blind / Mark Gonzales / *Hand painted by Mark Gonzales* / **1991**

Blind / Mark Gonzales / *Hand painted by Mark Gonzales* / **1991**

Blind / Rudy Johnson / *by Mark Gonzales* / **1991**

Blind / Rudy Johnson / *by Mark Gonzales* / **1991**

Blind / Mark Gonzales / *by Mark Gonzales* / **1991**

Blind / Mark Gonzales / *by Mark Gonzales* / **1990**

I remember Mike Vallely getting pissed off at me because of the ad we used to promote the Burger graphic. It was only coincidental, as I later explained to him out of fear, but I was standing in front of a Burger King with a shaved head, like Mike's, holding a Whopper with a big fat smile on my mug. I can see why he could have thought I was making fun of him. Anyway, I like that graphic. That board generated my biggest royalty check. **Jason Lee**

Blind / Jason Lee / by Marc McKee / 1990

Blind / Jason Lee / by Christian Jacobs / 1990

Blind / Jason Lee / by Marc McKee / 1991

Blind / Jason Lee / by Marc McKee / 1991

The Burger graphic came out after I had quit World Industries. Rocco may have tried to persuade me to use this graphic before I quit—I do vaguely remember that being discussed—but I flat-out denied him. I really could have cared less about it except for the ad that Rocco ran advertising the board. It featured Jason Lee with his head shaved, wearing a buttoned-up flannel—as I did at the time—holding a burger. Being the hardcore vegetarian I was, I definitely took this personal. So when I saw Jason next I confronted him about it. He played ignorant, and in some ways perhaps he was, but I still gave him a tongue-lashing for being a pawn in Rocco's petty attacks. Jason apologized, and I let him off the hook. I didn't really have nor did I want to have a problem with Jason, but I was definitely hurt by the fact he participated in this obvious attack. |Mike Vallely

Blind advertisement / 1991

After two years' worth of graphics under my belt, I seriously began to fear my well of inspiration would dry up, but somehow things almost always managed to work out in the clutch. Generally the riders would come up with a basic concept—like Ray Underhill and his dime-store cross necklace that some girl had given him on tour—and take out half the battle. Other pros were no help whatsoever and provided little to no input other than "just something cool." I think this may have been the case with Bucky Lasek's first pro model, where I used the "association" formula by starting with his hometown of Baltimore, which lead to a baseball theme derived from the Orioles, but then subtracted the world's most boring sport to leave a stadium scene peopled by a number of recognizable faces and characters. Mike Frazier was another such pro with no real concern for his graphic, but inspiration finally expressed itself on paper after a bout of extreme frustration in trying to see-to-eye with George on a concept. There remained, however, one rider I had supreme trouble with, and that was Tony Hawk.

For whatever shortsighted reason I was completely unable to see past a creative morass of wings, beaks, feathers, talons and other avian-like imagery whenever a new Hawk model dropped into the production pipeline. When Tony adopted the bastard Medallion graphic of Stecyk's I thought for sure this would finally break this restrictive chain of thought, but then he hit me from out of left field with a concept for his next deck spelling out "Toe Knee Hawk" in a pictograph manner. I was skeptical about this idea (I believe my lack of enthusiasm was awfully apparent), but didn't have anything better to offer him, either. I was hoping to redeem myself on his next deck, but Tony had a specific idea in mind for this one too: the simulated appearance of a used deck. This wasn't necessarily a bad idea, but it did have this weird Spencer's novelty-shirt feel, kind of like that anatomically correct rib cage sported by Nigel Tufnel in Spinal Tap. The Used Deck graphic actually made it all the way to the prototype stage, but George wasn't satisfied with the screened appearance and vetoed its production in favor of a minimalist, one-color blot design. Keester would eventually manage to sum up all my frustrations with Tony's visual last name by drawing a mouse caught in the shadow of an oncoming hawk. The top graphic of which revealed the mouse holding a shotgun with a smattering of feathers floating about him—a curious twist considering this would indeed be Tony's last pro model on Powell before he quit to found Birdhouse Projects with Per Welinder in 1992.

Powell Peralta / Tony Hawk / by Sean Cliver / 1990

Powell Peralta / Tony Hawk (Prototype) / by Sean Cliver / 1991

Powell Peralta / Tony Hawk / by Sean Cliver and Jim Knight / 1991

Powell Peralta / Tony Hawk / by John Keester / 1991

Tony Hawk / Carlsbad, CA / 1990 / photo by Grant Brittain

There wasn't much democracy in terms of graphics at Powell Peralta, but they had a great track record for what worked, so I wasn't one to argue very often. When skating started changing during the street era, it was necessary to churn out new graphics every few months to stay fresh. Making a scratched-up board was my idea, but the process of getting it made was much too slow. The idea was spent before it even got screened. Powell was still trying to create graphical icons with longevity, but it no longer mattered to the street generation.

|Tony Hawk

Amid rising concerns throughout the company in mid '91, Stacy saw fit to take one last run at liberating the art department. Prominent department heads from production, marketing, promotions, and sales were all gathered together in a meeting where it was sternly put forth to George that he relinquish control of the Design Group. As opposed to the first not-so-diplomatic intervention in '89, this time around the reasons were all stated in a very sound and business-like manner, the likes of which George understood: first and foremost being an urgent need to speed up the approval process on deck, T-shirt, and wheel designs. As it stood now, between George's desire to produce a high-end clothing line, his ongoing fantasy with creating the ultimate skateboard truck, and recent explorations into developing a Chinese market for skateboards, a.k.a. Powell Golden Dragon, he was simply stretched far too thin and, as a result, significantly delaying the introduction of new products to boost lagging sales. In the end, George begrudgingly bowed to the pressure and stepped aside to allow the art department greater creative control—but not without a certain amount of misgivings.

Freedom was ours at last, and under the self-proclaimed banner of the "Triad," Jim, John, and I began cranking out designs in a timelier manner. All good things must come to an end, though, and so did our freewheeling times in the art department soon after George returned from an extended trip to China. By coincidence, a design review fell into his schedule on his first day back in the office and he appeared in the art department with a very strange energy about him. Not thinking too much about it, I proceeded to express a less than enthusiastic opinion while group-critiquing a bone-oriented McGill concept of Keester's, and effectively lit the fuse for everything that would transpire next.

Immediately after finishing up with John, George strode into my office where he pointed to a recent design I'd done for Frankie Hill—a representation of Clint Eastwood—and vehemently demanded an explanation as to why I would expose the company to a potential lawsuit, like I suddenly turned out to be a "sleeper cell" terrorist operative or something. I suspect he'd paid a visit to our offices the prior evening to pre-inspect our work, because he was obviously cocked and ready to fire off a few heated rounds in my direction from the moment he'd walked in. Normally cool and composed, George was now fuming like I'd never seen before.

Aghast at his opening salvo, I stammered that I had no such intentions. Besides, even if legal representatives of Eastwood contacted Powell, I assumed a cease-and-desist letter would likely be the legal extent of the matter—or at least so I'd learned from Rocco's hit-and-run tactics on a slew of copyrighted material such as the Miller Brewing Co., Dr. Seuss, Sanrio, the Church of Scientology, Nintendo, Burger King, David Bowie, and the Goodwill Corp., but the hell if I was going to use his damnable name to defend my case at this point in time. (In hindsight, what's most funny about all this is that no more than a year later Powell was responsible for ripping off graphics from every corner of the trademarked universe, including *Star Wars*, Slayer, *Love and Rockets*, Marvel Comics, and even World Industries.) George eventually regained his composure, but I knew a line had been crossed in our relationship and the damage done was irreparable.

I should note, however, that George was intrigued by the idea of doing subversive stuff. In fact, we wasted many a Design Review mulling over concepts we all knew could never be produced under the squeaky-clean banner of Powell Peralta. One memorable instance of these brainstorming

Powell Peralta / Mike McGill / by John Keester / 1991

Powell Peralta / Frankie Hill / by Sean Cliver / 1991

Powell Peralta / Team / by Sean Cliver / 1991

Ray Barbee concept sketch / 1991 / by Sean Cliver

Powell / Chris Senn / artist unknown / 1992

Powell / Lance Conklin / by John Keester / 1992

Powell / Wade Speyer / by John Keester / 1992

Powell / Steve Caballero / by John Keester / 1993

Powell / Mike Vallely / by Jerry Mahoney / 1994

follies occurred when George finally committed to producing slick-bottoms (a sublimation printing process that enabled photos and paintings to be reproduced on a plastic "skin" adhered to the bottom of a deck), and we spent a couple sessions belaboring the idea of having two photos of a penis and vagina blown up to the full proportions of a deck. The intent was to then screen over the images with a "scratch off" material, similar to that found on a lottery ticket, so whoever purchased the deck would have no clue as to what the graphic was until the distinctive genitalia were revealed after use. I swear we honestly stood there staring at these mockups Jim Knight created from extreme close-up shots in porn magazines, while George stroked his chin and pondered the ramifications of pursuing such a direction.

Then there were other ideas merely drawn up as jokes, like an off-color Ray Barbee comp with the rag doll in a Satanic Black Mass scenario. George found this image to be rather striking design-wise, but we both agreed it would present far too many problems for the sales force, not to mention a little conflict of interest with Ray's personal beliefs. Another Barbee comp of mine portrayed a black Uncle Sam, but Ray wasn't at all comfortable attaching his name to anything controversial. The design was then dumped onto a generic team model that just about confused the shit out of everyone, especially with the authentic Civil War-era handbill reproduced on top that advertised "Negroes For Sale." So there were good times to be had in the art department, just not enough to keep my runamok mouth out of trouble.

From the moment I started working for Powell in 1989, I walked into the office most every day expecting to be fired. There was no specific reason for me to feel like a dead man walking, but for nearly three years I existed in this tenuous state of mind until November 1991 when my fears were finally laid to rest. Thanks to a worldwide recession, evaporating market share, and a building that had "Titanic" stenciled all over it, everyone in the company knew full well that something had to give in response to the dismal financial outlook. Before long, rumors began circulating amongst employees about "Black Tuesday," the anticipated day of reckoning when mass lay-offs would be leveled across the board just before Thanksgiving. I punched in at 9:00 a.m. sharp that day dressed all in black to commemorate the somber mood.

Oddly enough, I didn't anticipate being one of the heads to go rolling out the door. After all, I was the artist with seniority. I was the artist who fancied himself the "real" skateboarder. I was the artist who spent a few indiscreet weekends on Rocco's boat The Guppy, and returned to work sporting the latest World Industries clothing. I was the artist that certain people within the company were now referring to as a "loose cannon." I was the artist who just may have grown too fucking big for his britches, and that was quite an outsized opinion to have back then, as pants were already taking on ludicrous proportions.

Returning from my lunch break amid an exodus of former employees, I'd no more then sat down at my desk to resume work on a new graphic for Adam McNatt, a stylized drawing of Claudia Schiffer from a Guess advertisement (why this wasn't deemed to be any worse than the Hill Eastwood graphic, I have no clue), when George walked into my office and closed the door. Then and there I knew my days as an artist at Powell Peralta were over. He said the decision had not been easy, and to soften the blow he tossed me a bone, saying that if I ever had any ideas for graphics in the future that I was more than welcome to make an appointment with him to come pitch them.

Up until he finished the termination spiel, I hadn't said much of anything at all, just nodded my head in numb acknowledgment. George looked at me expectantly, waiting for what, I don't know, but I merely

Adam McNatt concept sketch / **1991** / by Sean Cliver

Powell Peralta / Steve Caballero / by Sean Cliver / **1991**

Powell Peralta / Steve Caballero / by Sean Cliver / **1991**

Powell Peralta / Chris Senn / by Sean Cliver / **1991**

101 / Natas Kaupas / by Andy Jenkins / **1991**

The Firm / Lance Mountain / by Lance Mountain / **1992**

The Firm / Ray Barbee / by Lance Mountain and Ray Barbee / **1992**

The Firm / Lance Mountain / by Lance Mountain / **1992**

shrugged my shoulders, made a motion to the envelope in his hand and said, "Cool, are those my door-prize checks?" I'm pretty sure this wasn't what he expected, nor wanted to hear, and with an icy chill he handed over a few weeks' severance pay and told me to leave the building immediately. Apparently, George needed to corral the surviving employees and shore up what little morale remained for the long hard nuclear winter that lay ahead of the company—and this was before he even knew of Stacy's impending resignation in the coming months.

Walking out of the building, I figured a quick act of defiance was in order to save face. So I hopped in my car, drove straight to a local skate shop and, for the first time in three years, paid for a brand-new deck. This was actually a thrilling moment for me, as I was finally able to venture outside the confines of Powell-produced boards. I scanned the racks and eventually selected a Natas Kaupas Patriot model on his new company 101— yet another popular brand instigated and distributed by Rocco. For whatever reason, this graphic spoke to me, and I stripped my current Powell deck of all its parts, threw it in the trashcan, and set up the Natas to skate over to the Unemployment Agency—one moment a semi-renowned skateboard artist, the next a lowly statistic.

The next morning I was allowed to return to Powell and clean out my office of all personal belongings. I believe someone was supposed to oversee my doing so, but Jim and John both felt too awkward and left me to my peace. All bitterness aside, I honestly had no intention of taking anything that wasn't mine, but, like any self-respecting 22-year-old artist with no legal conceptions to speak of, I took one look at the half-finished art for the McNatt Schiffer graphic and couldn't bear the thought of anyone else polishing it off. That was mine. Besides, if George no longer wanted me around then surely he had no use for any of my dumb ideas, either. So I rolled up the pertinent materials, threw them in a box, and went on my not so merry way.

I may have kept a stiff upper lip on the outside, but I was actually demoralized. Working at Powell Peralta had become my sole identity, and now, severed clean from the company, I was at a total loss. The only illogical thought I mustered during a brief period of hysteria was to gather up all the stray decks and clothing I'd amassed at home over the years—most one-of-a-kind production samples and other rarities—and cart them down to the Santa Barbara swap meet. In no more than a few hours, I converted the abundance of goods into 500 dollars*, an amount I hoped would buy at least one more month's time to allow my mind to stop spinning its wheels and seriously figure out how in the hell I was going to salvage my existence in the skate industry, let alone California.

Befittingly, one of the last graphics of mine to be produced by Powell Peralta was for Ray Barbee's fourth and final model (both Lance Mountain and Ray would soon quit the team to independently start The Firm). Released on a black satin-finish deck, the one-color graphic depicted the rag doll ascending into the heavens in angelic garb with a scroll reading, "It is finished," in half-ass Latin. Most prophetic, however, was the top logo that consisted of a tombstone engraved with "Powell Peralta 1989-1991." An eerie and inadvertent epitaph for my career there as well.

* By current collector valuations, this stash of rare Powell product would most likely be valued at more than $3000. While foresight isn't one of my strong points, I've found that short-term idiocy has always come quite naturally.

Powell Peralta / Ray Barbee / by Sean Cliver / 1991

John Keester

Powell Peralta / Longboard / by John Keester / 1990

It still makes me laugh that I got my job at Powell Peralta by responding to an ad they ran in Thrasher magazine. Well, contest really. "Hey, want to be a skateboard artist? Send us some shit." Next thing you know I'm working at the newly refurbished, former lemon-packing-plant-turned-skateboard-company in Goleta, California. I'm not sure what I expected going into it. I was just so pumped up to be doing art for skateboards that I didn't really consider what the actual working environment would be like. I'd just hoped to be continuing the VCJ tradition and do badass skull and dragon designs, to evolve the style and give it my spin.

Instead, Powell wanted to break that image and do something new, I guess. The first graphic that made it to production for me was the Bones Brigade World Tour 1990 T-shirt with the Ripper as a bomber pilot. George liked it and gave it the green light. I was happy because I finally had something to focus on, but once I started to work on it I could tell about half the company was clearly not behind that direction. So the naive, new guy discovers there may be some political undercurrents to watch out for—and there were.

It ended up feeling very corporate in nature. That was reflected in the design reviews that occurred early on, they seemed very serious and official. It was an effort to get a drawing okayed and into production. George had standards. There was a lot of scrutiny that generated many iterations of refinement, and you could count on several different versions and color combinations and color tunings before anything went to press. I always had respect for George's desire to produce the highest quality product; in fact I appreciate that now more than ever. But I also recall that many of those design review sessions were very tense with unnaturally long silent periods where a certain amount of eye rolling occurred.

George sometimes had a way of over-thinking and over-working things. He had a highly discriminating eye, but he was an engineer, not an artist. Art and engineering have two distinctly different ways of looking at the world. That's what's hard about being a commercial artist, you don't always get to express it your way; sometimes you're just the hands. It was clear that it was George's company, so George had a big say in the style and taste of the graphics. I'm not so sure his style and taste reflected the skate demographic of the day, but that's where our day-to-day direction came from.

My first designs were generic graphics, like the Rose and Bone longboard. Then I got rider graphics, and the McGill Stinger was my first pro design. I really liked doing work for screenprinting, the limitations make you get creative with ways to get the effect you want. You've got to be tricky to squeeze the most out of a little. I really put Dave Schad, who did most of the separation work and screen preparation, through the paces with the McGill Aquarium, trying to use partially transparent inks overlaid with each other in ways that would produce additional colors.

But one of the best parts of working at Powell was the variety of work we got to participate in. Not just deck, T-shirt, and sticker art, we got to help design and create the trade-show stuff and video artwork. Then a clothing line was launched, which was dubious from the start considering the reputation of the company at that point. Another set of cool graphic challenges, but as it turns out, probably not the best thing for Powell to do at that place and time. It caused a lot of internal concern, and it seemed to split the energy of the company.

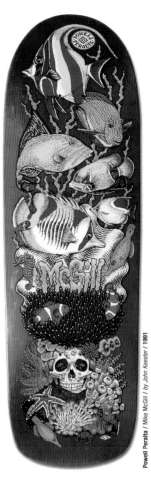

Powell Peralta / Mike McGill / by John Keester / 1991

Things went from bad to worse. Powell was feeling the pinch. Finally the inevitable happened and there was a pay reduction and a layoff that included Sean [Cliver]. That was a big turning point for the company and me. Powell had to find ways to be competitive, and that's when things can escalate and get ugly. That's when you end up with things like the case of "Schiffer vs. Schiffer"—heh, something I'm proud to be a part of.

It was then that I realized the process had gradually changed. Powell was going to try and be fast to the marketplace and do what appeared to be working for other companies. Rip-offs were definitely one of those things: it was like a game of who could collect the most cease-and-desist orders for the graphics they put out. So that's when I started doing stuff like Slayer, *Love and Rockets*, Street Fighter, Tank Girl, and *Star Wars* graphics, which again for me is great practice, but not so fulfilling artistically.

George always stayed involved with the art to some degree, but there were more pressing issues for him in those days. Where at first it took a lot of revisions to get a graphic to final, I was now churning out crap by the bucket load. We had moved into the full-color sublimated graphic phase as well. That meant I was starting to do full-on paintings, which I really loved, but I was a novice and not so fast. So that, in conjunction with the increased volume of work, meant that the quality got stepped on all the way around. The graphic content had become far less appealing, and the work environment had become very strange and depressing.

Mike McGill / Encinitas, CA / 1990 / photo by Grant Brittain

In the end, it seems like my visit at Powell was a witness to the fall of a once-great civilization. Time and circumstance had conspired to end an empire. It was obviously sad for me because my perfect job went sour, but it's also hard for me to be involved and watch a place that holds such a prominent place in the history of skateboarding go down like that. I finally got my portfolio together and started shopping around. I had been going back to school to learn computer software like Illustrator and Photoshop, so when a job at a video-game developer cropped up I gave it a shot. They ended up hiring me, so that is what I am still doing now over a decade later. I spend more time skating virtually than in reality these days.

When I look back at the Powell Peralta years I usually view them as the best of times and the worst of times for various reasons. But I still like that job the best of any I've had. I think there's something about skateboarding that's just in your soul, it's part of your being, and there's just no escaping that pull. I hope to get another chance to do some board art. A graphic on a skateboard goes the full cycle from creation to destruction. In fact it's created specifically for someone to go grind it back into the elements it was made from. And I think that's the beauty of it, because the art is simply symbolic of the spirit and soul of the movement it represents.

|John Keester

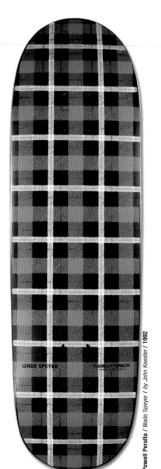

Powell Peralta / Wade Speyer • by John Keester / 1992

Powell / Steve Caballero • by John Keester / 1992

Powell / Wade Speyer • by John Keester / 1993

Powell / Wade Speyer • by John Keester / 1993

Powell / Chris Senn • by John Keester / 1993

World Industries / *Rodney Mullen* / by Marc McKee / 1991

Blind / *Rudy Johnson* / by Spike Jonze / 1991

101 / *Natas Kaupas* / by Andy Jenkins / 1991

disposable|

Part Three: The Evil Empire

Ask any crystal-stroking hippie on the streets of Berkeley, and they'll swear up and down on Mother Earth's great green name that nothing good can ever come from negative energy. I'm inclined to believe otherwise, because if harnessed properly it can be a most beneficial kick in the ass for an artist. And what better place to demonstrate this principle than at the epicenter of everything considered to be negative in the skateboard universe during the early '90s: World Industries.

It's commonly known that one should never underestimate the wrath of a woman scorned, but I'd say an artist comes in a scathing second in terms of exacting revenge. Typically I'm not the cold, calculating sort, but my being axed from Powell Peralta certainly did instill me with the burning desire to make George regret his decision. In actuality, he had both our best interests at heart by cutting me loose at the first convenient opportunity (although it wouldn't be for several years until I finally acknowledged this "mercy killing" of his), but my appropriation of the McNatt Schiffer graphic certainly compounded matters in a way that could only be classified as the "chaos theory" at wild work.

I completed the art at home in the days following my termination, thinking I could possibly use it as a springboard into a new job—although where exactly I had no idea. However, I soon received a call from Craig Stecyk, who gave me a friendly heads up that if the McNatt graphic wasn't "found somewhere in the art department" I may be faced with a legal complication courtesy of the Powell Corporation. Apparently, as it was then explained to me, an artist gives up all ownership rights as a salaried employee. Therefore the graphic and concept were deemed the property of the company as it was first devised under their roof. To my immature mind this smacked of creative prison rape, but I surrendered the artwork over to Jim Knight so it could be "found somewhere in the art department" the next day. I did so, however, with an exponentially larger chip on my shoulder against Powell.

As per usual, it's always darkest before the dawn, and my salvation came in the form of a random phone call the next morning from Steve Rocco, who asked if I wanted to work for World Industries—halle-fucking-lujia. I immediately drove down to their offices to negotiate the terms, and when I asked how much the position offered, Rocco replied, "I'll pay whatever it takes to have the best skateboard graphics in the industry." With that we agreed upon a magic rate of twenty dollars an hour in freelance time—a proposition that scared the absolute shit out of me after three comfortable years of salaried employment with full health benefits. A true master in the art of persuasion, Rocco explained how this really was a much better deal by saying if I worked 60 hours a week, then that translated into the hefty sum of twelve-hundred dollars, a great deal more money than I was making at Powell. I couldn't argue with that, especially since I wasn't too concerned about a social life outside of skateboarding in the first place.

101 / Gabriel Rodriguez / *by Marc McKee* / **1991**

101 / Kris Markovich / *by Marc McKee* / **1991**

Blind / Rudy Johnson / *by Marc McKee* / **1991**

Blind / Jason Lee / *by Marc McKee* / **1991**

World Industries / Chris "Dune" Pastras / *by Marc McKee* / **1991**

Blind / Jordan Richter / *by Marc McKee* / **1991**

World Industries / Chris Branagh / *by Marc McKee* / **1991**

101 / Gabriel Rodriguez / *by Marc McKee* / **1991**

Naturally, Rocco was very curious about George, if not downright bewildered by some of his business decisions of late. I rattled off a few satisfying tidbits of what went on behind the scenes at Powell—he found the concept of design review hysterical—along with the recent tale of the McNatt Schiffer debacle, at which point his ears perked up. "Redraw the graphic and we'll do it first!" he said with devilish, high-pitched glee, knowing full well that Powell was hampered by production and marketing schedules that would prohibit them from releasing the McNatt board until January 1992. I was somewhat hesitant at first—not wishing to evoke the legal fury of George—but Rocco assured me that nothing at all would happen. I couldn't help but trust his judgment, seeing how he'd just blatantly ripped off a cavalcade of Warner Brothers' characters without a single legal anvil being dropped from the corporate behemoth.

Rocco decided to release the graphic universally on all five Blind pro models, along with a special commemorative top logo consisting of a direct quote spoken from George to Rodney Mullen when he left the Bones Brigade to join World Industries in 1989. I recreated the art that night and in just over a week's time the Blind Schiffer decks were in stock and ready to be shipped. This was my first true taste of Rocco's wicked business ethics, and I loved it. Not only that, but vengeance was mine and far more quickly than I could have ever imagined.

To be honest, the idea of living in Los Angeles really freaked me out, so I thought I'd try staying in Santa Barbara and work out of my home, commuting two to three times during the week. Late in December, Natas Kaupas sent up some reference material for a new 101 graphic with Bod Boyle, who was going to the Powell Peralta Skate Zone, a massive indoor park that occupied a whole bay in the factory. Natas asked if this was going to be a problem, but against my better judgment I told him it shouldn't be—even though I knew full well I was flirting with disaster.

My initial plan was to slip in and out of the building via the side park entrance, but then I got cocky and stupidly decided to exit out the company store adjoining the Skate Zone. There I ran into Jim Fitzpatrick, the head of promotions at Powell. Jim was one of the people whose company I'd genuinely enjoyed during my employment, and he always managed to make things fun no matter how dismal it seemed at times. We were only speaking for a few minutes when, sure enough, George entered the room by fateful coincidence. He locked eyes with me in a flash, and as he swiftly strode over in our direction, I felt a chill of guilt ripple through my spine, like a thirteen-year-old kid who'd been caught going through the underwear drawer of his best friend's mother.

In a rising crescendo, George called me a "total asshole" and demanded I leave the building immediately. I guess he was pretty upset about the whole Schiffer fiasco—the Blind series forced their hand into entirely redesigning the McNatt graphic—but perhaps more so by the fact the fledgling artist he'd nurtured turned out to be a petty Frankenstein's Monster. Luckily the door was right behind me, so I slipped out with a quick, "Sure, no problem." This was the last exchange of words I'd ever have with George.

Blind / Jason Lee / by Sean Cliver / 1991

Powell Peralta / Adam McNatt / by John Keester / 1992

" We're still friends, but business is business and war has been declared"
George Powell- 1989

This board is dedicated to all the Powell employees who lost their jobs in the war.

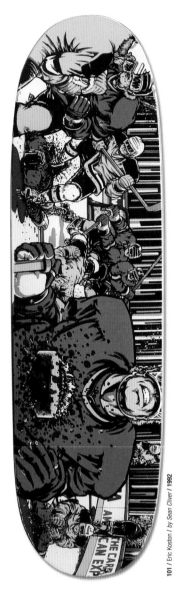

101 / Gabriel Rodriguez / by Sean Cliver / 1992

101 / Eric Koston / by Sean Cliver / 1992

101 / Eric Koston / by Sean Cliver / 1992

101 / Gabriel Rodriguez / by Sean Cliver / 1992

Clearly Santa Barbara no longer held any love for me, and the repeated four-hour commutes to and from Los Angeles were beginning to wear on my nerves and bite into my work schedule. So I threw in the towel on my big-city fears, put everything in storage, and moved down to Hermosa Beach, where Rocco graciously let me stay at the upscale modern house he shared with Rodney Mullen until I found a place to live. The 101 Gabriel Rodriguez Penalizer graphic was drawn and painted in his living room while I watched his state of the art big-screen Sony television, drank tons of bottled Cokes from his vintage coin-operated machine, and circled rental listings in *The L.A. Times*.

Working alongside Marc McKee in the art department at World was an incredible experience, if not downright intimidating. I knew the graphic bar was set pretty damn high at the company, so I stepped it up the best I could and finally managed to break

World Industries art office / 1992 / photo by Doug Winbury

free of playing an inferior doppelganger to VCJ and develop a style all my own. Natas was especially helpful in enabling this artistic transition of mine with concepts that were more scene-based, as opposed to relying on a single icon or image, and we developed a whole ultra-violent theme that carried through several 101 graphics.

Three years at Powell Peralta did leave me with a few scrupulous scars, though, the presence of which were embarrassingly made known when McKee came up with the idea to spoof the Garbage Pail Kids trading cards. While he debuted the initial rough sketches for the Fucked-Up Blind Kids to Rocco, specifically the one for Rear-End Rudy, I wondered aloud, "You can't really put that on a deck, can you?" Rocco immediately piped up at the inkling of a challenge by saying, "Who says you can't!"

It took me a few seconds to realize I'd actually spoken out loud, but he was absolutely right. Nothing was unimaginable, unattainable, or incapable of being produced in his delightfully twisted Wonka-land, and like him or not, you had to admire Rocco for not bowing down to anyone or anything during this time period. In 2002 Blind would release another Fucked-Up Blind Kids series, but apparently McKee wasn't allowed to put "Fucked-Up" on the boards, or at least not legibly so, because the words were always creatively censored in some fashion before being removed from the bottom altogether after demands from the sales department. As the saying goes, "Punk was cool. Too bad you missed it."

Despite the intense pressure to create the best graphics in the industry, at no point did it ever feel like a real job at World Industries, whereas the rigidity of the nine-to-five clock-punching schedule at Powell Peralta often broke my creative will to work beyond the office. On any given day, McKee and I walked into the office around noon and didn't leave for home until midnight or later, oftentimes maintaining this schedule six to seven days a week (to the casual observer it may have appeared we were extremely passionate about our work, but in truth we just had nothing better going on in our lives). This isn't to say we worked our fingers to the bone, because diversions were commonplace throughout the day, like when Rocco invited us to goof off on his armada of jet skis or go on a spur of the moment jaunt to Catalina Island.

The biggest distraction of all, though, came in the form of the team riders, who ruled the office environment like accomplished little tyrants. Most of them were in their mid-teens with little to no respect for anything or anyone—thanks largely to the actions of Rocco, I suppose—and they were constantly running in and out of the art room, tagging the walls, desks and even our original art. (In contrast, the Powell team riders were not allowed anywhere near the art department without formal business with the artists, because George was paranoid of creative leaks.) One night, McKee and I were working late as usual when Tim Gavin and Guy Mariano stopped by World out of boredom. Gavin started making photocopies of his penis on the Xerox machine, while a friend of theirs literally took a crap right in the middle of the art room floor flat on his back, ankles pulled up to his ears. On a few other occasions, hired strippers came to the building to entertain a large assortment of team riders and employees—including the UPS man—in the center of Mullen's former twelve-by-twelve office space. World Industries was pure anarchy in reckless motion, yet somehow it still managed to work beyond all belief—but not always without a cost.

Blind / Rudy Johnson / by Marc McKee / 1992

Blind / Guy Mariano / by Marc McKee / 1992

Blind / Henry Sanchez / by Marc McKee / 1992

Blind / Jordan Richter / by Marc McKee / 1992

Plan B / Sean Sheffey / by Carl Hyndman / 1991

Plan B / Danny Way / by Carl Hyndman / 1991

Plan B / Rick Howard / by Carl Hyndman / 1992

Plan B / Mike Carroll / by Carl Hyndman / 1992

Plan B / Sean Sheffey / by Sean Cliver / 1992

Plan B / Rick Howard / by Sean Coons / 1992

Plan B / Mike Carroll / by Carl Hyndman / 1992

Plan B / Matt Hensley / by Niko Achtipes / 1992

Plan B / Mike Carroll / by Niko Achtipes / 1992

Plan B / Pat Duffy / by Sean Coons / 1993

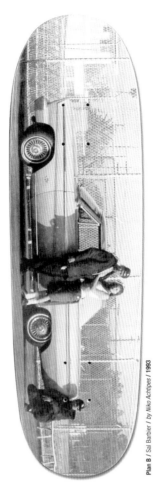

Plan B / Rick Howard / by Sean Coons / 1993

Plan B / Danny Way / by Sean Coons / 1993

Plan B / Sal Barbier / by Niko Achtipes / 1993

101 / Kris Markovich / artist unknown / 1993

Blind / Ron Bertino / by Sean Cliver / 1992

From the day it came into being the World Industries empire was perpetually in flux. Most of the pros who contributed to Rocco's success from '89–91 had left in volatile and argumentative circumstances: Mike Vallely quit to join New Deal; Mark Gonzales left Blind, the very company he founded; and Jason Lee, Jeremy Klein, Ron Chatman, Chris "Dune" Pastras, and Randy Colvin all left soon after I started working there. A few of these riders cited resentment over the latest company to join the World Industries lineup in late 1991, Plan B.

Mike Ternasky, a former H-Street partner and team manager, methodically handpicked all the riders for the successful launch of Plan B, but when it came down to a graphic direction someone seriously dropped the ball. The first several Plan B graphics were so bad, in fact, that they became the butt of every joke in the office, and Rocco kept telling Ternasky to concentrate on getting better artists. Since I'd come onboard recently, Mike approached me to do some work. Unaware of any political undercurrents at the time, I did one graphic for Sean Sheffey and was on the verge of starting one for Danny Way when Natas told me that if I continued to do work for Plan B he wouldn't be able to use my services for 101. The reason was understandable: he didn't want any similarity between the two companies. I much preferred the unique and quirky art direction of 101, so I dropped what I was doing for Plan B. This decision did not sit well with Ternasky and consequently led to an odd friction between the two of us, a situation made all the worse by the incessant sar-

Unfinished Ron Bertino design / 1992 / by Sean Cliver

castic remarks made by me and McKee regarding Plan B's graphics.

Eventually this elitist attitude got the better of me and I began working on a Ron Bertino graphic for Blind that mocked the hip-hop elements of Sal Barbier's decks and the horror elements of Danny Way's. The concept was a "fresh Freddy Krueger," dressed in an oversize baseball jersey and cocked cap, flashing a gang-sign with his gloved hand of blades. I was no more than a quarter through the pencil drawing when Rodney came into the art department and warned me to expect trouble in response to the graphic, which was now mistakenly being interpreted as a personal dig at Ternasky.

According to Rodney, Mike and Danny were at Rocco's house the night before and vocalized their anger over the graphic. Rocco said that Mckee and I were "out of control" and left it at that. Well, two hours after Rodney's warning, Danny aggressively confronted me in the hallway and told me that it would be in my best interest to quit making fun of Plan B. I've heard about fanatics who swear they'll die by their art, but I sure as hell ain't one of them, especially when it's just over a damn joke (incidentally, no actual blows were thrown, contrary to the largely exaggerated version portrayed in *Thrasher's* gos-

sip column). So instead of Fresh Freddy, Bertino received a graphic of Rocco's sole direction that was a swipe of the *Doonesbury* smoking advocate Mr. Butts, and each deck came shrink-wrapped with a "smoker starter kit," consisting of a single cigarette and wooden match.

When another round of World Industries pros fell by the wayside in mid '92, McKee and I developed the Rocco Tribute series to introduce the new crop of pros, namely Daewon Song, Shiloh Greathouse, and Chico Brenes. We'd long joked about creating graphics paying an over-the-top homage to Rocco for some time, but he remained leery of the general idea, maybe because he thought we were actually mocking him in a backhanded fashion. However, once we presented him with the concepts Rocco finally got behind the series.

There were four graphics in all, so we split the chores evenly. McKee rendered an ominous Orwellian take on Rocco's control over the skateboard marketplace á la *1984*, and a Romanesque fantasy featuring a harem of ladies pampering Rocco as he lay in repose on a chaise lounge chair with his trademark Motorola cell phone to his ear (back in 1992, these unwieldy bricks were still considered a luxury item). I was responsible for the deification of Rocco as one of those Roman Catholic dudes with a funny pope hat, and the modification of a famous Russian statue to depict Rocco standing

World Industries / Jovontae Turner / by Sean Cliver / 1992

Blind / Henry Sanchez (Limited) / by Sean Cliver / 1992

Blind / Henry Sanchez / by Sean Cliver / 1992

World Industries / Daewon Song / by Sean Cliver / 1993

victoriously atop a crushed Powell Peralta logo—a therapeutic favorite of mine. I can only imagine how offensive this series must have appeared to everyone else in the industry. They probably assumed Rocco had a lot of gall to produce something so obscenely self-aggrandizing, but that was merely the joke in itself.

Now when Rocco said he'd pay whatever it took to have the best graphics, I don't think he had in mind the invoices I'd be submitting down the road whenever a slick-bottom derailed my work schedule. A diehard pen-and-inker by trade, I lived in mortal terror of being assigned a slick-bottom, mostly because I'd dropped out of the MATC Commercial Art program prior to delving into the colorful arena of brush and pigment. I tried to weasel my way out of one such slick-bottom project, the Henry Sanchez Terminator graphic, by telling Rocco I had serious doubts that I could pull it off. I argued that I'd never attempted a total airbrush illustration before, but he wouldn't hear it. McKee had never messed around with oil paint before, but that didn't stop him from setting the gold standard for slick

designs with the Jeremy Klein Black Eye Kid and Jovontae Turner Napping Negro.

I nervously resigned myself to the Sanchez graphic, and hunkered down in my tiny studio apartment in Playa del Rey with an airbrush, a tank of compressed air, and a VHS tape of *Terminator 2*. (Incidentally, the whole "big idea" with the Terminator graphic was to screenprint Arnold Schwarzenegger's face over the robot, but this was only done with the first production run because the slicks varied in position from deck to deck and the robot's head was always sticking out to one awkward side or the other.) All told, no less than three weeks of insomnia and stress went into its creation and the invoice amounted to approximately 3,000 dollars. A few months later, I'd boldly bill this very same amount again after wrestling with an airbrush and gouache for nearly a month on Daewon's *Land Before Time* graphic. Luckily World's shady accountant cut the checks without question, as he was far more concerned with his pimped out '88 Toyota Celica ST than the amounts of money I was invoicing the company.

World Industries
Napping Negro
Jovontae Turner Model

World Industries / Jovontae Turner / by Marc McKee / 1992

World Industries and its subsidiaries had crossed every imaginable line in terms of taboo graphic material by 1992. Religion, sex, drugs, alcohol, wanton trademark infringement, American pride and bad Mexican prison art were all satirized with irreverent glee, leaving but one sacred frontier where few dared to openly tread: the racial stereotype. So, quite unsurprisingly, many were outraged when World unveiled the Jovontae Turner Napping Negro in its usual unflinching manner.

Although the timing of this graphic coincided with the rampant wave of political correctness washing through the United States in the early '90s, its roots were far more incidental in nature. Ultimately, it stemmed from a 101 graphic for Gabriel Rodriguez that featured a lesser-known Warner Brothers character, the Gremlin. This deck was inspired from a book on the animation of Warner Brothers that Marc McKee used as reference material in the art department. For better or worse, riders from the other teams began thumbing through the book as well, and the theme soon spread like syphilis in the ranks as it significantly blurred the lines of distinction between World, Blind, and 101.

Soon after this errant series ran its course, Jovontae discovered the dog-eared book and requested a graphic featuring "Coal Black and the Sebben Dwarves," a controversial cartoon produced by Warner Brothers in 1943. Since Jovontae's first model on World depicted a runaway slave in the Stretch series, McKee modified the character by employing the very same principle used on Natas' Devil Worship board: If you're gonna half-ass something then it's not worth doing at all. | Sean Cliver

World Industries advertisement / 1992

Daewon Song finished art / 1994 / by Marc McKee

Unreleased Chris Branagh design (Top Graphic) / 1992 / by Marc McKee

A lot of the early graphics I made were purely created for shock value. This one, for me, is still the most outrageous. It was intended as satire, but I'm not sure that this point got across, even with the accompanying full-page ad in Thrasher that Rocco wrote. It was pure sarcasm and worded like those ads for the Civil War chess set, which, I don't know, seem to be counting on the fact there are people still out there with an abiding fantasy of a victorious Rebel Army. Anyway, at the time it didn't seem to matter since all of our skaters, including Jovontae—whose deck it was and who was black—seemed to think the graphic was hilarious.

And the Napping Negro wasn't the end of it. Next came the Jovontae At Night graphic, which was just this all black board with two big white eyes and smiling teeth. To be fair, after these two decks came out we made every effort to make fun of as many other ethnic groups as were represented by our "ethnically diverse" skate team. There was the Chico Brenes Orange Vendor, the Daewon Song Hot Dog on a Stick, and finally the Chris Branagh Cabbage Patch, which showed a drunk Irishman asleep in a field of cabbage and potatoes, holding an empty bottle of whiskey and dreaming of a full one. Chris's parents kept this one from ever being made, which just goes to show that it's always the white guys who can't take a joke. **Marc McKee**

World Industries / Jovontae Turner / by Marc McKee / 1992

World Industries / Jovontae Turner / by Marc McKee / 1992

World Industries / Chico Brenes / by Marc McKee / 1992

Jovontae Turner concept sketch / 1993 / by Marc McKee

World Industries / Kareem Campbell / by Marc McKee / 1993

World Industries / Jovontae Turner / by Marc McKee / **1992**

Girl / Rick Howard / by Andy Jenkins / **1993**

Girl / Mike Carroll / by Andy Jenkins / **1993**

Bitch / Team / by Sal Rocco Jr. and John Thomas / **1993**

After a year or so at World, I began to take note of a significant change in Rocco. Great concepts were no longer the spirited drive behind each and every board graphic, as World began to seesaw between maintaining its image and the quest for cash. Filler decks with simple rip-off graphics and short production runs began to slip through the creative cracks at the company more and more often. McKee and I dubbed these boards as the "quick cash" models, an inside joke stemming from Jovontae Turner, who never once entered the art room without requesting a quick board graphic to pay for much needed upgrades on a vintage VW Bug he'd acquired. But this isn't to say all these graphics were dogs; the Jovontae at Night and Banana Board both had inherent humor value.

The upside to these sub-par graphics was that they were a cheap and effective solution to subsidize the more elaborate and time-consuming designs like the Rudy Johnson Sparkplug and the Eric Koston Buddha. Sadly, many other riders were keen on the idea of generating fast royalty checks and began to demand even more inane logo rip-offs. In response, Marc and I jokingly created the "magic graphic finder," a piece of paper with the shape of a skateboard cut out of its middle that could be placed over virtually any photo or piece of artwork to—voila!—reveal an instant graphic. I eventually lost my sense of humor, though, when Rodney told

me Chico wanted the Travelodge sleepwalking bear logo for his next graphic. I damn near threw my pen out the second-story window of the art department in response, because I knew it signaled the bland face of things to come. Consciously or not, I wound up doing such a horrible job in ripping off the Travelodge logo that Rocco yelled at me for doing so, and I had to redo the stupid thing for a second production run.

In the summer of 1993, Plan B team rider Rick Howard noticed a discrepancy in some wheel invoices—apparently, the numbers being ordered did not equate to the royalties being paid out—and orchestrated a mass defection of riders from Plan B, Blind, 101, and World. With an additional investment from Spike Jonze, Rick and Mike Carroll founded Girl Skateboards in September with the logo being an icon of a female similar to those found on women's restrooms. Rocco took this all pretty hard (he actually became very withdrawn and no longer maintained the personal contact he once did with the riders), but instead of lashing out in his typical manner he let his little brother Sal Rocco, Jr., who ran the shipping department, handle the public venting chores with the vengeful creation of Bitch Skateboards.

The Bitch logo was a violent parody of Girl's with the addition of a male icon holding a gun to the female's head. The shirts, hats, stickers and

Bitch / Megan & Rick / by Sal Rocco Jr. and John Thomas / 1993

Bitch / Mike Carroll / by Sal Rocco Jr. and John Thomas / 1993

Bitch / Tim Gavin / by Sal Rocco Jr. and John Thomas / 1993

Bitch / Eric Koston / by Sal Rocco Jr. and John Thomas / 1993

decks emblazoned with this volatile image quickly became the focal point of controversy in the El Segundo community, as parents banded together in a righteous attempt to oust the "misogynistic" business from the area. Local news stations picked up on the outrageous story and blew it even further out of proportion.

In addition to its main logo board, Bitch released four other decks with graphics that mocked Rick, Mike, Eric Koston and Tim Gavin by portraying them as penises of varying sizes and emotional states. After a modest success as a novelty act, Bitch then tried to pass itself off as a real company and started sponsoring riders and filming for a video (the fantastically horrifying footage of which remains missing to this day). Before long, however, the company self-destructed, and in the convoluted aftermath the Bitch name was licensed out the backdoor to a Japanese firm. The logo was then screened, stitched, and stamped onto anything from shoes to tie-dyed bikinis and boogie boards, all produced and sold overseas. Over ten years later the Bitch products can still be seen in Japan—oftentimes on the unlikeliest of people.

Rick Kosick / Tokyo / 2002 / photo by Jeff Tremaine

I did get the short end of the stick, literally, but I didn't mind at all. I think Eric Koston was the most bummed. I knew I had a small cock, and Mike Carroll knew he was a baby, but Eric did not know he was a puppet. I was just bummed to hear how much money Bitch made for being a novelty company.

Tim Gavin

When Rocco first started producing *Big Brother* in 1992, a skateboard magazine with little to no serious emphasis on skateboarding, McKee and I started assisting on it as a diversion from our day-to-day art duties. However, by 1994 we were devoting more than half our time to managing its editorial direction (Marc actually invested in *Big Brother* and assumed the formal role of editor). We were occasionally given grief for neglecting the graphics aspect of our jobs, but Rocco hired several other artists to pick up the slack.

When Mike Smith showed up out of the blue to revive Liberty Skateboards for the second or third time* with a spot of cash, a trampoline and a series of board graphics, Rocco let the company run its course before swiping the artist, Daniel Dunphy, to work for World. In the caustic fallout from Bitch, Judson Bryan was the only semi-competent person left holding a pen in his hand, so he was recruited to fill in any graphic voids for all the brands currently being distributed by World, including Blind, 101, Plan B, Prime, and Menace. John Thomas, the former Alva professional, was hired as a fulltime production artist, handling anything from laying out ads to running film for slick-bottoms, but he designed a few graphics from time to time as well. Even renowned Blockhead artist Ron Cameron did a few graphics after Rocco filched him from Acme out of spite for owner Jim Gray, but he soon drifted away to pursue the development of his own company. While this abundance of new artists did afford McKee and I the time to play hooky, the individual qualities of the assorted companies began to homogenize creatively.

---

* When Rocco first started World Industries, Liberty was one of the earliest brands to be distributed by the company but it never managed to catch on in popularity. Every so often though, Mike Smith would manage to scrape together some cash and finagle Rocco into letting Liberty eke out a few more decks—one even being a Sal Rocco, Jr. model prior to the creation of Bitch—to keep the dream alive.

Mike Smith / Torrance, CA / 1990 / photo by Rick Kosick

Liberty / Team (Prototype) / by Daniel Dunphy / 1992

Liberty / Mike Smith / by Daniel Dunphy / 1992

Black Label / John Cardiel / by Daniel Dunphy / 1993

Daniel Dunphy

I was first introduced to Mike Smith through a friend of mine who skated for Liberty. I don't know the details, but Mike was asked by Steve Rocco to find another artist to do his graphics—something about him using up too much of Marc McKee's time. Mike was a last-minute kind of guy, and he always came to me a day after the graphics needed to be done. So four weeks of work would be crammed into three nights, tops. I was rarely happy with the results—especially since I was limited to two to four colors per graphic—and I even had to cut the black key line with ruby because Mike didn't want to pay for film to be shot. At that time I was living in my parents' garage, drawing, cutting, and pasting all night long on the cold, cement floor with a thin rug between it and me. Bottom line, it was a foot in the door.

Somewhere between the third and fifth round of decks I did for Liberty some other people were taking notice of my work. One particular graphic parodied a deck series out of World Industries that depicted Rocco in various positions of power. I opted to dress him up in the World Pooh Bear costume and placed him in the midst of the mad tea party. Rocco hated it. Apparently, he'd seen the test prints at the printer and demanded that his face be removed from the graphic. Only one of these decks survived that I know of.

Around that same time, Mike hooked me up with John Lucero. John and I actually had a connection that neither of us were aware of: we both had the same high school art teacher. In fact, John's art was my first introduction to skateboards, because our mutual teacher exhibited his Madrid Jester deck on our classroom wall—I guess he helped John prepare the screens for it. I considered it to be an honor working for John, although I think I spent more time trying to convince him that he should be the one doing his graphics, not me.

The last series of graphics I did for Liberty was my favorite, and it included a Sal Rocco, Jr. pro model. I was able to put more time into those graphics—and more color—and convinced Mike that the decks should be printed at World. He was reluctant—probably because of the cost—but he finally came through. I think that was when he either sold or traded his boat to Rocco for the printing. Nevertheless, the decks turned out great.

Somewhere during the completion of those graphics, Lucero contacted me. He heard that Rocco wanted to hire me as an artist at World and hoped that he could beat him to the punch. He offered me 200 dollars a week, plus a beat-up Honda Civic, as I had no transportation. I took John up on his offer for maybe a week before I received a call from Rocco and within a couple of weeks I started at World. John was cool about it—or at least he never expressed any angst toward me—but Mike accused Steve of stealing me from him and somehow managed to get free ad space in a couple issues of Big Brother magazine. I was just glad to know I would soon be out of my parents' garage.

|Daniel Dunphy

Plan B / Rodney Mullen / by Daniel Dunphy / 1994

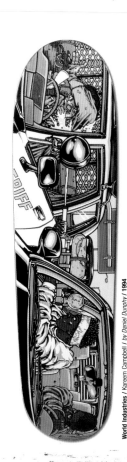

World Industries / Kareem Campbell / by Daniel Dunphy / 1994

World Industries / Kareem Campbell / by Daniel Dunphy / 1994

World Industries / Shiloh Greathouse / by Daniel Dunphy / 1995

Liberty Sal Rocco, Jr. design / 1993 / by Daniel Dunphy

Toy Machine / Ed Templeton / by Sean Cliver / 1994

101 / Clyde Singleton / by Sean Cliver / 1996

23 / Clyde Singleton / artist unknown / 1997

The idea for the 101 Clyde 'n' Hobbes graphic came from a Big Brother trip in '96 where not only did I verbally insult a group of schoolchildren, but I became a Mormon, an alcoholic, and a really bad spokesperson for marijuana all within a week's time. Plus, I didn't wanna tell nobody at the time, but peeing in toilets was so 19th century then. I was on some new shit, where I preferred to mark my—or anyone else's—territory with the nice scent of warm piss after a long night of debauchery. Hands down, that was the best graphic I've had due to the fact it showed the real assholery of me at the time.

I had at least ten of the Steve Steadham Powells, mainly due to the fact he was the only black professional skater at the time. I didn't have anything I could relate to with a Tony Hawk or Steve Caballero deck back then. Having long bangs and wearing Skate Rags wasn't going on in my 'hood, so whenever I saw Steadham in a mag, that's what I could relate to. Shit, I even started riding pools back then because he was doing it, but I couldn't fuck with that Zinka. From what I understand, Steadham called 23 one day regarding his graphic being used and wanted to put some stoppage to it. Yeah right. It would've probably helped if he actually drew it or owned Powell, neither one of which was an issue, of course. Then, some time later, he calls back and asks about riding for the team. Wow. Steadham getting on 23 would've been the equivalent to Kool Moe Dee joining Black Moon.

|Clyde Singleton

On one memorable day in '94, Rocco stopped by my desk while I was working on a graphic of a nude woman devoid of an epidermal layer. He stated that McKee and I had to "stop doing shit like this" because the shops were refusing to order anything controversial. (I subsequently offered the skinless lady graphic to Ed Templeton, who was badgering me to do some work for Toy Machine.) Evidently Rocco no longer wielded the power of intimidation he once held over the shops. The storeowners were the ones now calling the shots on what they would or would not carry, with the risk of being blackballed an impotent threat of the past.

More importantly, Rocco went on to tell us to stop wasting so much time and effort on individual graphics. He still greatly appreciated our work, but apparently, as he was now telling it, graphics no longer mattered in the marketplace. To provide evidence of this, he held up a top-selling Birdhouse T-shirt printed with a poorly drawn Jeremy Klein graphic. My knee-jerk reaction to this argument was, "Fuck that!" but even I had to admit the state of affairs had become quite ludicrous of late—especially at World, where most designs were produced only once, in small lots of 300-500 decks total, making the turnover rate so rapid on these disposable art pieces that Rocco might as well have been producing limited edition designer tampons.

While many companies benefited sales-wise from this spin cycle of new graphics in the mid '90s, the once rich "visual mythology" of the subculture was fast becoming a churning mud puddle. Despite the abundance of marginal ripped-off-logo-cut-and-paste-whatever-is-cool graphics flooding the shops, there still remained a few truly creative eddies, courtesy of artists like Thomas Campbell, Mike Hill, Ed Templeton, Chris Johanson, Ron Cameron, Andy Howell, Mark Gonzales, Barry McGee, Neil Blender, and Andy Jenkins, all of whom were now propelling the

medium into the ghettos of the fine-art community. Consequently, gallery shows sprung up around the world, as "skate art" began to be recognized as such and appreciated outside the traditional confines of the subculture.

Not long after this telling episode with Rocco, a general manager was hired to streamline the chaos of World Industries into a lean, mean corporate entity. It was a necessary evil, I suppose, and his imported man of choice was Frank Messman, a former freestyle skater who had just graduated from the "George Powell School of Business" after running the defunct Powell Peralta European distribution center in Amsterdam. This was a very shrewd business move on Rocco's part, as it enabled him to wash his hands of all the ugly things that needed to be done at the company to ensure its future success. Cool and methodical, Frank set about trimming the fiscal fat at the company. Locked security gates were erected in shipping, more sales and accounting personnel were hired, and, most painful of all, the artists were taken off hourly wages and reduced to piecemeal labor with a set amount of 350 to 500 dollars per deck graphic.

Rocco personally broke this news to McKee and I, citing that times were bad economically, but that one day he hoped to improve our rates. However, in the face of the company's "new world order," I'd learned that once money is taken away from you, you're not likely to get it back. As a consequence of this change in attitude at World, my graphic spirit soon broke. Where I once dreaded the "quick cash" designs the riders so favored, I now welcomed them as an easy opportunity to pay my own bills. This isn't to say I didn't take pride in a few boards here and there—the 101 Clyde Singleton Clyde 'n' Hobbes remains one of my favorites from this era—but to the many others I shelved my ego on I do hang my head in abject shame.

Blind / Rudy Johnson / by Marc McKee / 1992

101 / Adam McNatt / by Sean Cliver / 1992

World Industries / Chico Brenes / by Marc McKee / 1993

101 / Adam McNatt / by Sean Cliver / 1992

World Industries / Jovontae Turner / by Marc McKee / 1993

101 / Kris Markovich / by Sean Cliver / 1992

Blind / Henry Sanchez / by Marc McKee / 1994

101 / Adam McNatt / by Sean Cliver / 1994

101 / Eric Koston / by Marc McKee / 1993

World Industries / Chico Brenes / by Sean Cliver / 1994

Devil Man sketch / 1996 / by Marc McKee

World Industries / Team / by Marc McKee / 1996

World Industries / Team / by Marc McKee / 1996

How had the once insurmountable World Industries brand name fallen into such disrepair? Well, to summarize Rocco in brief, he could best be described as a little kid with a new toy: every fresh project is tackled with an extreme intensity, but then he gradually loses interest until it is tossed aside for the next exciting thing to come around. A prime example of this behavior was his ambition to start a skateboard magazine. No more than six issues into *Big Brother*, Rocco lost practically all interest in the volatile rag and ceased to have anything more to do with it (he finally rid himself of this perpetual thorn in the side of World's budget by selling it off to Larry Flynt Publications in 1997). Swiveling his attentions away from *Big Brother*, Rocco then focused on the creation of a shoe company known as DuFFS, but once it was off the ground and successfully running he emerged to find World Industries bereft of an image and lost in the sea of mediocrity.

Thus, Rocco rediscovered his first marketing love with World Industries and seized upon an offhand creation of McKee's, a red smiley-face with horns and a goatee—the earliest incarnation of the Devil Man—and gave him the green light to brand the character to the company. This was the first decisive direction for World Industries in a long time, and most importantly, a concept not contingent upon a distinguished team of pros (there's nothing quite so maddening as betting the farm on the irrational whims of teenage kids). These were also the first graphics that endured multiple production runs as sales spiked in response to the image makeover. McKee proceeded to pump out a number of Devil Man graphics and before long added two battling sidekicks, Flame Boy and Wet Willy, who would one day upstage the goateed lollipop himself. He also resuscitated Blind from its graphic purgatory with the creation of a morbid cartoon character known as the Reaper. This was an exceptionally noteworthy act, because ever since Mark Gonzales' departure in 1991, Blind had slowly achieved a shambling, zombie-like status, and with one fell swoop the Reaper exorcised the ghost of Gonz from his former company once and for all.

Unreleased Prime design / 1996 / by Sean Cliver

With the graphic revival of both World Industries and Blind in full profitable swing, Rocco's inner circle applied pressure to the other companies distributed under the flagship, namely 101 and Prime, to likewise improve their sales. Natas eventually let 101 die gracefully to pursue other interests in the field of graphic design, but the owner of Prime, Mark Oblow, devised a plan to mock the Devil Man with a series of Angel Man decks. He approached me to fulfill the concept, since I'd been doing more graphics for them of late. I completed the art and separations on the first deck, only to discover days later that Rocco had stomped his presidential foot down and vetoed the graphic's production along with any others attempting to poach the Devil Man's fame.

Apparently, Rocco didn't want anything to derail this new direction, and he took an even harder stance when Woodstock Skateboards, a small company run by Simon Woodstock and Rich Metiver, threw a few silly jabs at Rocco and the Devil Man. The price of Simon's folly, which consisted of a notorious ad run in issue 26 of *Big Brother* and a few innocuous deck graphics, was an out of court settlement that effectively slit the throat of Woodstock Skateboards when all was said and done. In the coming years, Rocco brought a similar hammer down on Jim Gray, when Acme made some derisive ads concerning the trademarked World characters. Considering his renowned impudence in the late '80s and early '90s, I thought this to be a largely hypocritical reaction on Rocco's part, but he simply dismissed this notion by claiming he had done nothing whatsoever to provoke these attacks on World Industries, whereas in the past he was merely defending himself from the larger bullies of the industry.

After a solid year of watching World Industries release a slew of decks featuring the Devil Man and Co., I brashly predicted that kids would fast tire of the characters' escapades and search out fresher graphic pastures. Well, I couldn't have been more wrong. World not only successfully upset the industry through its perversion of the hardcore marketplace in the early '90s, but then proceeded to steal the entire twelve-year-old kiddie market just as skateboarding was revving up for another cycle of "extreme" popularity that would carry all the way into the new millennium. Perched atop this latest and greatest wave, World attained a level of success few skate companies had ever seen before—and all mostly due to McKee's art direction.

Woodstock / Simon Woodstock / *by Jimbo Phillips* / **1997**

I get really bummed when I think about those boards and the defaming ad that correlated with them. It was a time in my life where I was on a lot of booze and drugs—I have been sober for five years now, praise God!—and I also felt like my days were numbered in skateboarding anyway, so I wanted to go out in a blaze of glory. I figured I would just do some graphics that slammed on Rocco and everything would be fine.

Rocco is a pretty tough character, but I could tell he was pretty bummed at me personally. I know that Frank Messman was really bummed about the whole deal too. I wish I could take it all back ... things were already getting really bad in my life. I had partied to the point I was beginning to experience some physical illness, and I knew I had to change something in my life in order to survive.

It was weird, I think the same day I woke up with what I swore would be my last hangover—the day I swore to stop partying—the phone rang. I picked it up and Rocco's lawyer was on the other end. He informed me I was being sued by World Industries and that I had to meet with him and Rocco to settle the matter. I told the lawyer that I would rather just die, but he was actually really cool about everything. The thing most people don't know is that Rocco and his lawyers enabled me to get off the hook pretty easy; they went hard after the guy who was doing my boards at the time instead, Richard Metiver. I get really depressed when I think about that part of it. I instigated the whole thing against Rocco, and Metiver got stuck with the bill. If I could, I would cut Metiver a check for the full amount of the lawsuit today, but I am flat broke these days. | Simon Woodstock

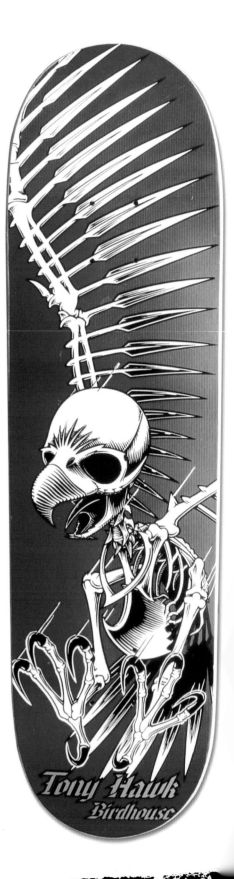

Part Four: John Henry

When I first informed an art instructor of mine in 1988 that I was dropping out of school to accept the position at Powell Peralta, he predicted my involvement in the field would span five years at most. He assumed I'd move onto bigger and better things with time, I suppose, but this profession was literally the top of the dream heap to me. I mean, how much better could life get than escaping Wisconsin, moving to California, and getting paid to draw pictures for skateboards? Despite fulfilling my dream to be an artist for a skateboard company, I somehow always managed to get tangled up in other less creative aspects of the business at both Powell and World Industries. The problem was, somewhere along the line in my arrested development I never developed the coolly efficient mindset for business or politics. So, like many others who naively entered the skateboard industry bright-eyed and bushy-tailed, I emerged in disillusionment as World no longer resembled the blissfully dysfunctional company I'd once so envied from afar.

After five years of working for Steve Rocco's conglomeration of companies, I received a call from Per Welinder, the co-owner of Birdhouse Skateboards, in November 1996. They were in a graphic pinch and he asked if I would be able to help them out with a design for Bucky Lasek. Apparently, Per had already received the nod from Rocco to approach me for work, so I figured I had no choice but to help out. Per and Rocco were longtime friends, but I still felt weird about the situation, like I'd been whored out in some fashion and Rocco no longer valued my skills enough to keep them under exclusive lock and key. If nothing else, I guess it just underscored the fact I was a freelance gun-for-hire and nothing more.

Jeremy Klein handled the art direction at Birdhouse, and although he was famous for his gross negativity and distaste for practically everyone and everything—aside from candy, video games, Asian girls, and Macs—we hit it off fairly well in terms of a working relationship. Better yet, Klein was very exact in stating what he wanted done for the graphic, eliminating all the time-consuming guesswork on my end. This was a novel change of pace after the stressful number of years I'd spent fishing for ideas out of thin air—a hit-and-miss scenario not entirely conducive to a steady freelance income. Upon final delivery of the requested graphic, Klein propositioned me for a few more at 600 dollars per design, an amount that bested the "top" World Industries rate by a good hundred bucks. The premise of less work for more cash was tempting, and I certainly didn't owe any loyalty to World—they were the ones who hobbled my income in the first place—so I simply ceased to do any more work for them and went full-speed on Birdhouse instead. I just neglected to tell anyone pertinent at World about this decision.

Skateboard phenomenon by night and office jockey by day, Rodney Mullen was the designated "graphic wrangler" at World Industries and it was his job to manage the production schedule and make sure the artists were up-to-date on all the new models coming from the woodshop. Having seen not a hide nor hair of a concept from me in over a month, Rodney finally asked around to see what I was up to. It wasn't necessarily a secret, just an unstated fact, and Rodney soon learned that I was now working for Birdhouse instead. This news came as a rude surprise—all the more so considering I was doing this from a World-leased office space that housed *Big Brother* magazine and the screening department—and Frank Messman immediately called me into a meeting to discuss this recent turn of events.

Normally I abhor any and all confrontational situations, but I felt my case was fairly cut and dry in this particular instance: Birdhouse offered to pay me more money per graphic, end of story. Frank's defense, however, was nothing short of offensive. He declared Birdhouse could not pay me 600 dollars per graphic on the grounds that World Industries paid their most prominent artists a rate of 500 dollars, thereby dictating the industry standard for all other companies to follow. Apparently, all logic had left the building, and following that absurd statement so did I.

When I relayed the details of my meeting to Klein that evening, he must've thought I was in a quandary about what to do because he immediately upped the Birdhouse rate by another hundred bucks. I honestly wasn't planning to negotiate for more, but the hell if I was going to complain and gladly accepted the bump. I did, however, make a personal vow to never stick my nose into any aspects of the business at Birdhouse other than those relating immediately to graphics. I was done being a meddlesome cog—no more concerns for the team riders, product, internal politics, marketing, sales girls—nothing. Virtually every time I'd deviated from my job description in the past, it never failed to end in trouble, so for my sanity and security I figured the less I knew and cared about the company the better.

World Industries / Jeremy Klein / by Marc McKee / 1990

World Industries / Jeremy Klein / by Marc McKee / 1991

World Industries / Jeremy Klein / by Marc McKee / 1991

World Industries / Jeremy Klein / by Marc McKee / 1992

I love Asian chicks, so the Dream Girl graphic pretty much reflects what I'm into. I remember Steve Rocco seeing the art, and I asked him if he liked it. He said, "I fucking love it, I want to marry that girl!" And you know what, I agree with him. This was a big-selling graphic for me, and I was able to buy a lot of video games and Red Vines with the checks I received. | Jeremy Klein

Birdhouse / Jeremy Klein / by Nancy Chiang / 1992

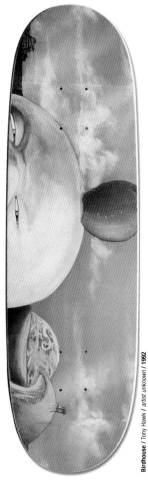

Birdhouse / Tony Hawk / artist unknown / 1992

Birdhouse / Tony Hawk / by Tim Malins and Per Welinder / 1992

Birdhouse / Tony Hawk / by V. Courtland Johnson / 1995

Birdhouse / Paul Zitzer / by Nancy Chiang / 1996

Birdhouse / Jeremy Klein / by Nancy Chiang / 1996

Birdhouse / Willy Santos / by Nancy Chiang / 1996

Birdhouse / Team / 1996 / by Nancy Chiang / 1996

There was a general feeling that starting our own company in 1992 was a bad idea, and I was considered a washed-up vert pro desperately hanging on to my skate career. I decided that a Titanic theme was appropriate: nobody thought the skate industry would sink, and my professional career seemed to be quickly drowning without warning. I figured it was my last try at a signature model and I wanted it to have meaning. I didn't have a model for two years after that until Per Welinder and Jeremy Klein decided that I was more effective as a pro skater than a CEO. I was still skating and learning new stuff regularly, so I felt it was justifiable. I have more fun skating than sitting behind a desk anyway. | Tony Hawk

Blind / Rudy Johnson / by Jeff Tremaine / 1993

Blind / Brian Lotti / by Jeff Tremaine / 1993

Plan B / Sean Sheffey / by Jeff Tremaine / 1993

Plan B / Sal Barbier (Bootleg) / by Jeff Tremaine / 2002 (original release 1993)

Jeff Tremaine

Prime / Kris Markovich / by Jeff Tremaine / 1995

Foundation / Steve Berra / by Jeff Tremaine / 1995

Birdhouse / Heath Kirchart / by Jeff Tremaine / 1998

Birdhouse / Steve Berra / by Jeff Tremaine / 1998

In 1992, Jeff Tremaine first met with novice publishers Steve Rocco and Mike Ternasky to interview for the position of art director on their newly formed skateboard magazine, *Big Brother*. During the highly informal proceedings, Tremaine let it not so casually be known to the industry magnates that not only was he a layout jockey, but a fine artist as well. His work consisted of large, uniquely textured acrylic paintings, and he'd stockpiled quite a few over the years. Both Rocco and Ternasky were sick of their artists wasting weeks on end to create a single graphic at the height of the slick bottom craze, so they seized upon the opportunity of readily available artwork at a fraction of the usual cost. At their request, Tremaine brought in an assortment of these old paintings, and the miscellaneous companies—namely Blind, Plan B, and 101—tore into them like a pack of Tasmanian devils feasting on the ass of a wallaby carcass. Since none of these paintings were created with the intent of being used on a skateboard, less than inventive measures were often taken to conform them to the long and skinny proportions of a deck. In addition to merely paying to use the art, Rocco bought up several of the paintings to hang in

the World Industries office space. Sometime later, the Jesus Frog painting that was used on a Brian Lotti slick for Blind was stolen from the reception area by Don Brown, the former Vision pro freestyler turned Sole Technologies shoe mogul—a crime that was openly admitted to yet never rectified.

Throughout his tenure with *Big Brother*, Tremaine became fairly prolific as a freelance artist and pumped out several new paintings on demand for use by companies in both the skate and snow industries (oftentimes milking his creative output for all its worth by first selling the rights to use the image before cashing out big with a final sale of the actual painting). In 1998, Birdhouse produced the last round of skateboards to feature Tremaine's artwork. These board graphics proved to be a fitting close to his haphazard stint as a deck artist, because all three were yet again the secondhand results of paintings created without the use of skateboards in mind and had to be stretched, cropped and abused to fit the slim confines of a modern-day popsicle stick. |Sean Cliver

flip
tom
penny

Flip / Tom Penny / by Daniel Dunphy / 2000

Flip / Tom Penny / by Daniel Dunphy / 2001

JEREMY KLEIN

Birdhouse / Jeremy Klein / by Sean Cliver / 1999

HEATH KIRCHART
B I R D H O U S E

Birdhouse / Heath Kirchart / by Sean Cliver / 1999

ESTABLISHED 1969
ORIGINAL
Carnie

BANQUET BOARD
BREWED BY SIDESHOW SKATEBOARDS
WITH ROCKY MOUNTAIN PEE PEE

Sideshow / Dave Carnie and Jeff Tremaine / 1998

This new modus operandi was made substantially easier for me in March 1997, when Rocco sold *Big Brother* to Larry Flynt Publications. In the transition of ownership, Marc McKee decided to resume his graphics position at World full-time, so I was catapulted into the role of editor in his stead. As a result, my work for Birdhouse became nothing more than a freelance night job with hardly any company interaction whatsoever aside from dealing with Klein.

Although Tony Hawk had briefly retired from the pro skateboard scene in 1993, he had since returned to the Birdhouse team with the advent of the ESPN X-Games in 1995, and I was now in the position to redeem myself for the Powell Peralta Toe Knee Hawk debacle. Some people have skeletons hidden in their closet, but me, I'm responsible for one of the worst skateboard graphics ever. Not only is it bad, it's latched onto the name of the most famous skateboarder ever, meaning this uninspired piece of crap isn't going to fall off the face of the Earth like so many other graphic flops are allowed to do. To my benefit, Klein was a big fan of the old "cool-ass-old-Powell-style" art, so I slipped into the familiar black line work that I'd abandoned in 1992 and created the first Hawk graphic I felt genuinely pleased with: a full skeletal rendition of the Screaming Chicken Skull. Sure, I stomped all over VCJ's figurative grave to do so, but aside from his trademark skull design there were plenty of other original bony elements going on to appease my artistic ego.

By the late '90s, the computer revolution was in full technological swing. This had a profound effect on reshaping the graphic face of skateboarding, although there were both positives and negatives to this computerized infiltration. The upside was an effective approach to color separations and production art; the downside was that any halfwit with enough RAM and resources could now swipe, scan, and stretch any image to the proportions of a deck. For some strange reason, I stubbornly refused to acknowledge this transition as it was happening right under my very nose, and years later I looked up from my drawing table only to find myself in a completely foreign world. My former artistic peers, Marc McKee and Daniel Dunphy*, were now scanning in rough sketches to click, point, plot, and color their way to finished art files—their original black-and-white inked artwork a curio of the past—while I was still scribbling away and hand-cutting my deck separations with an X-acto blade and Rubylith masking film.

Like any delusional romantic, I greeted the signal flares of obsolescence by fancying myself a modern-day John Henry, waging a noble battle against the encroachment of machines into a purist land. However, blind with denial and confident that I could achieve my goals faster and better by the power of my own hand, I failed to realize the computer was merely a more efficient means to an end—a tool no different than any other overpriced art material. I made a half-assed attempt to bridge this gap in my prehistoric skills, but the results were remarkably unsuccessful aside from the remedial task of manipulating type, and I've since given up on befriending this technology altogether.

---

* The last time I saw Dan Dunphy he'd fallen victim to carpal tunnel syndrome and was wearing wrist guards while working at the computer (imagine that—having to wear pads to draw skateboard graphics!), so I'm not entirely convinced the machines have won yet.

When the new millennium rolled around in 2000, I abdicated my editorial leadership of *Big Brother* after three bizarre years at Larry Flynt Publications. I passed the absurd torch on to the more able-minded Dave Carnie and returned to my graphic roots full-time for Birdhouse and Hook-Ups, a subsidiary company of Klein's sole creation and direction. The Birdhouse offices were based in Huntington Beach, but there was no way in hell I was defecting behind the Orange Curtain, so arrangements were made that enabled me to work from home in Los Angeles.

For the first several months I enjoyed my immersion in the graphics trade once again and put forth a tad more effort than in the preceding years. Klein kept requesting more and more illustrations in the style of VCJ, so I continued down this derivative path with several more Hawk graphics, like the Birdman and Crest, and the Andrew Reynolds Kosickutioner, a drawing that poked fun at the most famous skateboard photographer of all time. Although I'd worked closely with Rick Kosick on *Big Brother* for seven years, I was still slightly worried that he would take offense to the graphic, thinking I wanted him dead and therefore making him want me dead in return. But Kosick got a jovial kick out of it in the end and he even managed to squeeze some cash and product out of Birdhouse for the morbid liberties taken with his image.

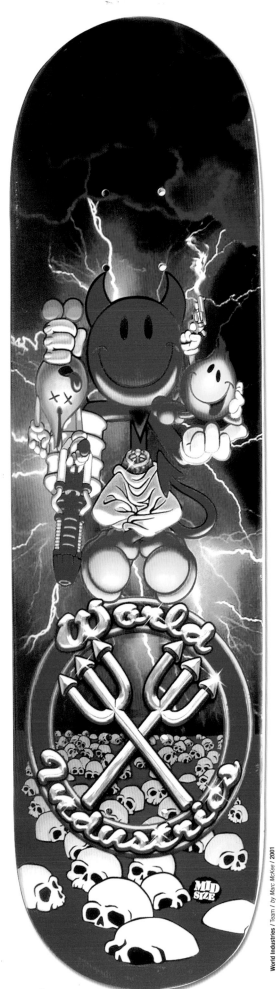

World Industries / Team / by Marc McKee / 2001

World Industries / Chad Fernandez / by Marc McKee / 1999

World Industries / Team / by Marc McKee / 2002

World Industries / Mike Maldonado / by Marc McKee / 2000

World Industries / Team / by Marc McKee / 2003

World Industries / Chad Fernandez / by Marc McKee / 1999

World Industries / Team / by Marc McKee / 1998

Blind / Team / by Marc McKee / 1997

Blind / Team / by Marc McKee / 1998

Blind / Team / by Marc McKee / 1998

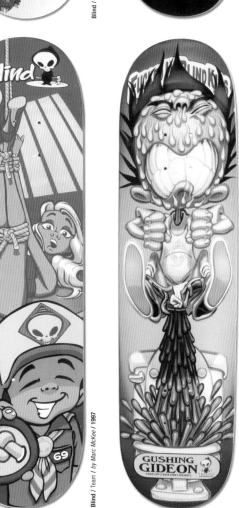

GUSHING GIDEON

Blind / Team / by Marc McKee / 1997

Blind / Gideon Choi / by Marc McKee / 2001

Blind / Team / by Marc McKee / 2002

4000 OUNCES

KASPER HOLICS BRAND "8000"

187% ALC/VOL

JOSH KASPER PRO MODEL

Blind / Josh Kasper / by Marc McKee / 2002

Hook-Ups / Team / by Jeremy Klein and Nancy Chiang / 1995

Hook-Ups / Team / by Jeremy Klein and Nancy Chiang / 1995

Hook-Ups / Team / by Jeremy Klein and Nancy Chiang / 1996

Hook-Ups / Team / by Jeremy Klein and Nancy Chiang / 1997

Hook-Ups / Team / by Jeremy Klein and Nancy Chiang / 1997

Hook-Ups / Team / by Jeremy Klein and Sean Cliver / 1997

Hook-Ups / Team / by Jeremy Klein and Sean Cliver / 1997

Hook-Ups / Team / by Jeremy Klein and Sean Cliver / 1998

Hook-Ups / Team / by Jeremy Klein and Sean Cliver / 2000

Hook-Ups / Team / by Jeremy Klein and Sean Cliver / 2000

When it came to doing graphics for Hook-Ups, I have to say I was leery at first. I wasn't an avid fan of Japanese animation, nor had I ever messed around with the "big-eyes-tiny-nose-slit-for-a-mouth" art style, but at Klein's behest I gave it a shot anyway. Aside from the first two Hook-Ups graphics I did, a 357 and Detonator-2, the ensuing girls weren't entirely of anime stock, I felt, but Klein seemed to like my loosely Americanized interpretation and ran with it. To the delight of some and dismay of others, the focus of Hook-Ups soon evolved from traditional anime artwork and characters to grossly T&A chicks with crazy boobs and mysteriously flapping skirts. Without a single sponsored pro-rider to its name, I'm sure many assumed this paper-doll approach to graphics would eventually run its course, but Hook-Ups remains an anomaly in the skateboard industry with consistent sales for well over a decade now.

The best and consequently worst thing about working from home was that it allowed me an amorphous schedule with ample time to procrastinate. Inevitably, I turned to the open arms of the Internet and it didn't take long before the packrat within me stumbled upon the sprawling online garage sale known as eBay. Through my various employers I'd acquired a tremendous amount of vintage skateboard memorabilia, all of which I'd squirreled away under my bed. My back, however, could no longer take the strain of moving 150-odd decks every two to three years (living in L.A. you develop a rather transient lifestyle chasing employers around the cement-plastered basin), and I came to the conclusion it was time to trade in their sentimental value for cold, hard cash.

Testing the waters, I placed a World Industries Randy Colvin Censorship model on the block, complete with black plastic bag, which sold for 152 dollars. I followed this auction up with a Blind Rudy Johnson Jock Skull, which garnered 112 dollars. These sales lead to a Biblical-sized flood of assorted Powell Peralta decks circa '89–91, most leaving my hands for an average of 75 dollars, but I did have a pristine condition mini Vato Rat model circa 1985 that blew up and out of my mailbox for 315 dollars*. However, when I went to grab a slightly used Steve Caballero Dragon deck from the early '80s, my engine of avarice seized up and brought the impetuous yard sale to a screeching halt. After all, the original Powell graphics drawn by VCJ were my whole reason for being involved with skateboarding in the first place.

Thus the auction process slowly reversed itself as nostalgia took control of the monetary reins and whipped me into joining all the other bidders clamoring for mementos of their old school past. Most of these people start out innocently enough by seeking their first deck, the board that kicked off their fascination with skateboarding, but they soon lose focus and start collecting anything and everything that haphazardly taps a sentimental chord. Others, like me, are pure graphic hounds, sniffing out the classic decks that miraculously escaped destruction over the years and are now being appraised as limited-edition lithographs, so to speak. Only after I mounted several prized acquisitions on the wall of my office years later did I realize the subconscious method to my collecting madness: I was trying in vain to recapture the momentous feeling experienced when I first walked into a skate shop in 1986.

---

*At the time, I couldn't believe people would pay such amounts for these outdated planks of wood. Currently, however, these decks have all substantially appreciated in value. The Vato Rat and Jock Skull, in particular, could both fetch a great deal more depending upon the idiotic depth of certain collectors' pockets, which in some cases are known to run as deep as the Mariana Trench in the South Pacific Ocean.

Collector Values

In recent years the number of collectors for skateboard memorabilia has grown substantially, leading to a fairly strong market for vintage old-school goods. Considering the vast majority of skateboards are destroyed in the very manner they were intended, the values now attributed to them aren't all that surprising—well, with a collector's tweaked mentality, that is—given the awkward supply and demand ratio with new buyers constantly joining the nostalgic fray.

Not every painting is a Picasso, nor is every deck a Ray "Bones" Rodriguez; the worth of an old skateboard is entirely subjective from person to person. There are, however, several desirable decks that command a hefty premium whenever they exchange hands. The following list is a sampling of noteworthy public and private sales recorded over the past several years*:

Powell Peralta Tony Hawk Bird (1983) $6,000.00
101 Natas Kaupas Devil Worship (1991) $5,366.69
Dogtown Wes Humpston Bigfoot (1978) $4,650.00
Blind Jason Lee Dodo Skull (1990) $3,500.00
Santa Cruz Jeff Grosso Wonderland (1988) $2,700.00
SMA Natas Kaupas Panther II (1985) $2,658.99
Blind Mark Gonzales Skull and Banana (1990) $2,600.00
Powell Peralta Mike McGill Jet Fighter (1980) $2,500.00
Dogtown Jim Muir Red Dog (1978) $2,412.00
Powell Peralta Alan Gelfand Tank (1980) $2,175.00
Dogtown Paul Constantineau Tail Tap (1978) $1,914.00
Schmitt Stix Joe Lopes Crystal Ball (1986) $1,872.00
Dogtown Shogo Kubo Airbeam (1978) $1,713.00
Zorlac Big Boys (1985) $1,698.00
Blind Jason Lee American Icons (1990) $1,675.00
Powell Peralta Tony Hawk Skull and Cross (1983) $1,500.00
Sims Bert Lamar Super-Ply Stinger (1980) $1,420.00
Schmitt Stix John Lucero X1 (1986) $1,410.99
Powell Peralta Steve Caballero Dragon (1980) $1,400.00
Zorlac Devil Fish 1st Edition (1986) $1,325.00
Powell Peralta Steve Steadham Spade (1985) $1,305.00
Zorlac Double Cut (1985) $1,250.00
Vision Agent Orange (1985) $1,200.00
Vision Mark Gonzales Gonz and Roses (1988) $1,136.00
Powell Peralta Tommy Guerrero V-8 Dagger (1985) $1,136.00
Skull Skates Social Distortion (1986) $1,033.00
Toy Machine Bam Margera Mullet (1999) $621.11

*Over the years, several of these values have fluctuated with the market as more and more models surfaced from random closets and storage boxes. It's also important to note there are many variations and release dates on certain graphics, especially the Powell Peralta decks (for example, the Tony Hawk Skull and Cross graphic was produced on a variety of shapes from 1983–1989). A number of rereleases, reproductions and bootlegs are also in circulation, so beware of frauds before committing to a diet of Top Ramen and toast for an extended period of time. For a better understanding of all these matters, consult artofskateboarding.com, where more detailed information on a deck's value, scarcity, and variations may be found.

Between this burgeoning collectors market for vintage skateboard memorabilia came the release of Stacy Peralta's documentary Dogtown and Z-Boys and the nationwide proliferation of Vans skate parks featuring reproductions of famous bowls from the '70s and '80s. A tremendous flood of old-school resurgence hit the marketplace with all the force of a proverbial concrete wave. Graphically speaking this spirit manifested itself in an abundance of reissued designs produced in the '80s by Vision, Powell, Santa Cruz, Skull, Schmitt Stix, and Madrid (sadly, many of the artists responsible for these designs did not receive any kind of royalty or token payment of appreciation). Another prevalent trend among many skateboard companies involved parodies and tributes to memorable designs of the past, like Christian Hosoi's trademark icons of the '80s, Mark Gonzales' self-drawn graphics, and the indefatigable line of "Skull-and-fill-in-the-blanks" produced by Powell Peralta.

I, too, capitulated to this groundswell of revivalism in 2003 with a series of Birdhouse graphics all based around decks and artists I found particularly influential. Granted, the sleek Popsicle shape of the decks certainly diminished their old-school flavor, but I genuinely enjoyed putting some quality time into all the illustrations, from rendering the tiny marijuana leaves on the Willy Santos Natas Panther spoof to including all the trivial details on the Vinny Vegas ode to Pushead with the oddly large copyright info Zorlac used to plaster on his legendary designs.

After fifteen years of continual participation in the fads and farces that have marched across the visual face of skateboarding, I still find myself harkening back to a comment made by VCJ during our initial meeting in 1988, when he said that a graphic with significant longevity is comprised of as few symbols as possible. Case in point, over 25 years later Court's designs still strike a resounding chord in subsequent generations of skaters. In the face of current computer-art software and four-color-process printing innovations, this remains the principle to which I subscribe, as friends continue to support my old-school habits with dusty rolls of Rubylith unearthed in forgotten corners of their workplaces.

Throughout all these professional escapades, though, my greatest triumph came in 2003 when I received a random email from a fourteen-year-old kid in Vermont who requested an interview with me for an English project. Apparently, the assignment was to create a presentation piece on a historical artist of their choice. While everyone else in the class selected famous dead people like Vincent Van Gogh and Pablo Picasso, he locked onto me through a profile on skateboard artists in Nickelodeon magazine. I responded to his questions, and a month or so later he wrote back saying that he'd received an A+ on the project.

His mother later thanked me in a personal letter—I guess it was one of the first times her son had really applied himself in his schoolwork—and enclosed a photo of him standing next to the final piece. Funnily enough, the focal point of his project was my first graphic, the Ray Barbee Ragdoll, and the whole thing was situated right next to another kid's presentation devoted to the undisputed Italian master, Leonardo da Vinci. Ha! |**Sean Cliver**

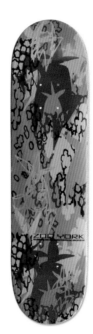

Dogtown / Wes Humpston / by Wes Humpston / 1978

Schmitt Stix / Joe Lopes (First Version) / by Neil Blender / 1987

Schmitt Stix / Chris Miller / by Chris Miller / 1988

Lucero Ltd. / John Lucero / by John Lucero / 1989

Part Five:
Skate and Create

Schmitt Stix / Andy Howell / 1990

Focus / Christian Hosoi / by Mark Gonzales / 1994

Toy Machine / Ed Templeton / by Ed Templeton / 1998

Anti Hero / Tim Upson / by Chris Johanson / 2002

Designarium / Swallow Tail / by Thomas Campbell / 2004

There exists a longstanding argument in skateboarding that graphics don't really matter. Those who harbor this glib opinion are shortsighted at best, because the importance of graphics runs far deeper than inconsequential kiddy trappings—perhaps even more so now that corporate America has seized upon the image of skateboarding and conveniently categorized, packaged, and produced it for the masses under the Madison Avenue-approved banner of "extreme sports."

In the past, one of the most integral functions of art in skateboarding was its ability to create an underground camaraderie with global reach. Such cryptic icons as the Dogtown Cross and Vato Rat managed to sum up the rebellious allure of skateboarding in but a few simple strokes. Varied renditions of the two designs were scrawled on lockers, notebooks, walls, ditches, ramps and griptape around the world, and regardless of the artistic outcome these hand-drawn graphics came to signify an unspoken bond between skateboarders everywhere. Best of all, to anyone not directly involved with the subculture these images were meaningless, sometimes even threatening. There were several laughable cases throughout the '80s, when local news officials picked up on the arcane symbols and issued stern warnings to be on the lookout for satanic practitioners lurking within the shadows of the community.

There is also the incontrovertible fact that skateboarding attracts a far more creative crowd than the usual raw jocks and so-called adrenalin junkies. Seminal artists such as Wes Humpston, Neil Blender, John Grigley, Pushead, Tod Swank, John Lucero, Chris Miller, and Mark Gonzales sparked the imagination of skateboarders worldwide with their thoughts, concepts, and drawings, and ultimately begat a whole new generation of accomplished artists. A few of those inspired were Ed Templeton, Ron Cameron, Andy Jenkins, Mike Hill, Thomas Campbell, Chris Johanson, and Andy Howell, all of whom would add their own distinct embellishments to the constantly evolving mythos of skateboard art.

This creative legacy remains to be the one true distinction between skateboarding and virtually every other jock-laden activity; strip the boards of their silk-screened soul and they become no better than any other performance-based sporting goods. So long after the companies, pros, and contest victories have faded into the sterile statistics of record books, the graphics will continue to live on as vibrant reminders of a time in any skateboarder's life when all that mattered was rolling across the ground on a board with four wheels attached to it.

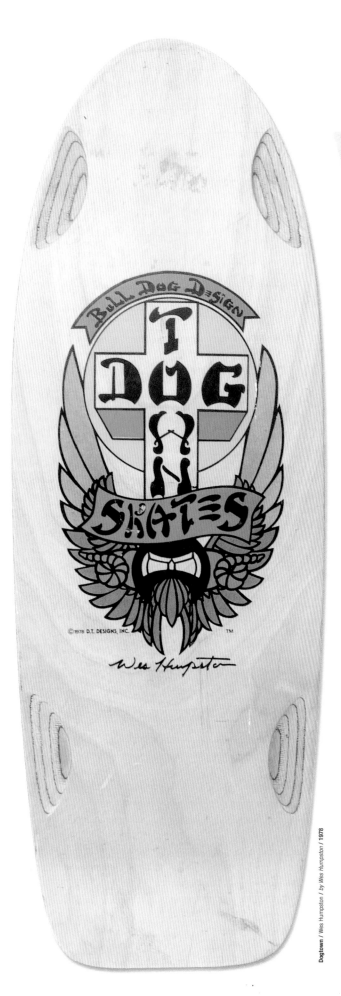

Wes

I started drawing on belly boards that Kevin Kaiser, Craig Hollingsworth, and were making in the late '60s. So when I started making skateboards by han around 1974 it was just a natural thing to do. We painted and drew them lik surfboards with whatever we could find: wings, skulls, Murfs, crossbones, flame dragons and anything else that influenced me from biker's jackets, pinstriped ho rods, "Big Daddy" Ed Roth's art, Creepy mags, sci-fi movies, Zap Comix, Mouse Kelly, and the king, Rick Griffin.

In 1978, when Jim Muir and I hooked up with Greg Clapper and Jeff Coope they wanted to make our hand-done Dogtown boards into production boards. get our models started, I first did the art for Jim's Red Dog nine-inch and m Bulldog ten-inch. Jim wanted a dragon, and I winged up the Murf for mine. Th Murf was the helmet in Rick Griffin's poster for the surf movie Pacific Vibration I saw it at the Santa Monica Civic Center around 1970 and always thought it wa an awesome painting.

Paul Constantineau's model was all ready to go, so just to get it out as soc as possible his graphic was worked up at the screeners by their artist off some my original drawings. During a mid- to late-'70s tour, the Rolling Stones had giant banner of an eagle with jet engines under its wings, and I tied that into Be "Bullet" Biniak's graphic. For Shogo Kubo's I was just thinking of a totem pole crazy stuff wrapped and hung on a cross. The Tri-Plane was based on a board th I was riding after we found some warped wood with a concave and made son skates out of it. Greg looked at the decks and said he could make them for m but Jim said I already had two models, so the Tri-Plane turned into his model. T graphic was just something I came up with after smoking a joint.

As far as other companies' and skaters' reactions, they just seemed to follo our lead. I didn't really care, but when I did look at the skate mags I'd laugh abo how other companies' boards were getting wider and had graphics and how th came up with a concave after we did it.

Dogtown took off and it was good and bad, but the cash flowed, the parti got better, and we had free passes at any park. Getting recognized when I was o with my girlfriend was weird. She used to give me shit like, "Oh, Mr. Big Shot!" a that's why I wore the gas mask in the photos with Glen [Friedman]. I wasn't in the rock-star thing!

In the '80s, Jim asked if I was into restarting Dogtown, but I wasn't. I w pissed and bummed about what happened to us with the crash of the skateboa industry. Jim and I were also on and off too many drugs, drinking, and I was ju in a shitty place and wanted no part of the business. But I was into doing art him and he would hook me up with whatever skater had a new model coming u

I was freelancing off and on while working a full-time job in printing tha hated. I missed making and drawing on boards. So I found a hardwood shop Solana Beach, grabbed some wood, and cranked out a few boards. I gave one Tony Alva and one to Ray Flores. This was around 1995 or 1996, and Ray was f ping that nobody was making boards like that anymore. He kept saying it was lost art." So Ray and I started Bulldog Skates with just a few boards that we lo to ride, like the '70s old-school shapes. Then we added longboards, and now so new-school boards are in our line, too. It's more like a quiver than the typical sk company, with 50 different paint jobs on one board. | **Wes Humpston**

Humpston

Hand drawn by Wes Humpston / 1975

Hand drawn by Wes Humpston / 1976

Hand drawn by Wes Humpston / 1977

Hand drawn by Wes Humpston / 1977

I met Wes Humpston on the beach in Santa Monica back in the early '70s. We became good friends back when Jim Muir and Wes were making boards in the garage. During this time, Dogtown was just a collective of creative surfers and skaters pushing the known limits of not just the sport, but also the images associated with skating and surfing. Both Wes and Muir would draw the Dogtown cross on the boards they made, but Wes could draw really well compared to Muir, and he was expressing his unique style way before Dogtown was a company.

We would shape all kinds of different boards, but only the ones we liked enough to ride would get the Sign of the Cross and the cryptic art by the master skate artist himself. I loved riding the boards with Wes' artwork. They were more than just planks, they were canvases with hidden messages and meanings. It was like the board wouldn't work right if it didn't bear Wes' hand-drawn art. After a while, not just the DT crew wanted Wes' board art. Everyone wanted them. So Dogtown Skateboards, the company, was created to satisfy the demand, but I always rode the hand-drawn, hand-shaped boards. | Ray Flores

Dogtown / Paul Constantineau / by Wes Humpston / 1978

Dogtown / Bob "Bullet" Biniak / by Wes Humpston / 1978

Dogtown / Shogo Kubo / by Wes Humpston / 1979

Dogtown / Jim Muir / by Wes Humpston / 1979

Dogtown / Jim Muir / by Wes Humpston / 1978

Dogtown / Prototype (Unauthorized) / by Craig Stecyk III / 1984

Suicidal Skates / Street Cycos / by Wes Humpston / 1984

Dogtown / Born Again / by Rick Clayton / 1985

Jim Muir

The first time the Cross was used in skateboarding was in Stecyk's [Skateboarder magazine] article "The Westside Style," where he spray-painted it on a wall. But as far as I know, the first time Dogtown was used in a cross, it was by a Hispanic gang down in East L.A. on the other side of the train station—if you go down there today you can still see it. But the first time we ever put Dogtown on a skateboard it was just the initials D.T.S. That was when we were just the Dogtown guys before the cross. You can see those first hand-drawn D.T.S boards on some shots of me in Stecyk's article "Sequential Overdrive"—these were also the first-ever skateboard sequences. Then Wes brought in a couple different influences, like Harley Davidson and Rick Griffin stuff, and applied it to the Cross.

When Wes and I were partners still, we did a licensing deal in the '70s, and that's where all the original graphics came from. But those business guys were just all about the money, and when skateboarding died they bailed out. I was in the process of getting all the rights back into my name and preparing to do skateboards again when I saw Nathan [Pratt] putting little quarter-page ads out with the [Dogtown] name and I watched what he did. Then I went to a trade show because I was putting everything together and getting ready to start the company again, when I saw Nathan had hooked up with Stacy [Peralta] and George Powell. They were trying to sell Dogtown decks, not realizing I still had the rights to it. I called George and was like, "Hey look, I still own the trademark. You don't have the rights, and I'm working on doing this thing again." Next thing you know I'm on a three-way call with Stacy and they claimed Nathan said it was okay and blamed it all on him.

From what I heard, George had to paint over a bunch of boards and lost a bunch of money on it. There are still a couple of those boards around, but not very many. I don't think they ever went into serious production. I went to Nathan afterward and said, "Look bro, I just live down the street from you, all you had to do was call me up—you could've saved yourself a lot of problems!" | Jim Muir

Dogtown / Eric Dressen / by Wes Humpston / 1988

Dogtown / Aaron Murray / by Wes Humpston / 1988

Dogtown / Aaron Murray / by Kevin Ancell / 1988

Dogtown / Micke Alba / by Wes Humpston / 1989

Dogtown / Eric Dressen / by Kevin Ancell / 1987

My first graphic was done by Kevin Ancell in the back of Con surf shop in Santa Monica. Ancell was like, "Come back in a week and I'll have your graphics." He really wanted it to impress Wes Humpston because the Dogtown cross art is his deal, and it meant a lot to all of us growing up in the town. The kanji mean, "Don't drink and crash," and the banners and cross make a "SM" for Santa Monica.

The gnarly part is that it's all done by hand, and my favorite part of the graphic is the half-toned hands. They've always blown me away. I wondered how Ancell did them, but I never asked. Ron from Black Flag silk-screened the boards, and my pop screened the T-shirts. We got back tons of broken boards because every-one thought you could jump ramp a building on one. I always rode the gray wood-stained boards and won my first pro contest on one.

|Eric Dressen

Dogtown / Ben Schroeder / by Lance Mountain and Wes Humpston / 1989

I remember giving a sketch to Ben Schroeder, and I don't think I even realized that Bulldog [Wes Humpston] redrew it for the longest time. Ben and I were just friends, so it was never official like Dogtown was licensing me to draw a graphic for them or anything. So when the deck first came out, I just saw it real quick, and I was like, "Oh, rad!" thinking I still drew the graphic. Then later on I asked if I could get a board or shirt, and I finally noticed "Bulldog Art" on the graphic, and that it was totally redrawn. Looking at it now, side by side, I'm like, "Of course they redrew the graphic, it's totally better!"

Lance Mountain

Ben Schroeder concept sketch / by Lance Mountain / 1989

Dogtown / Jim Muir / by Wes Humpston / 1989

Dogtown / Scott Oster / by Wes Humpston / 1989

Bulldog Skates / South Side (Limited Edition) / by Wes Humpston / 2002

Bulldog Skates / Saber-tooth (Limited Edition) / by Wes Humpston / 2002

Alva Skates

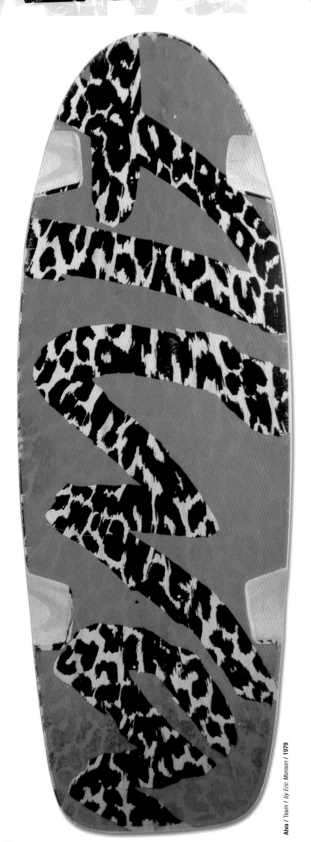

Alva / Team / by Eric Monson / 1979

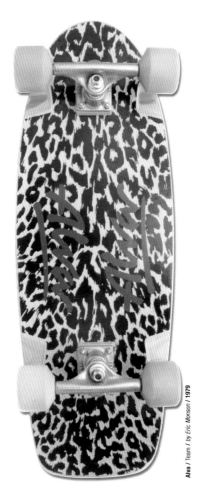

Alva / Team / by Eric Monson / 1979

Alva / Team / by Eric Monson / 1979

Alva / Litebeam / 1979

Alva / Team (Prototype) / by Tony Alva and Eric Monson / 1979

Alva / Christian Hosoi / artist unknown / 1983

Alva / Christian Hosoi / by Tony Alva and Mondo Beck / 1984

Alva / Scratch / by Mondo Beck / 1984

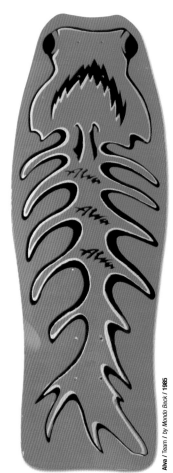

Alva / Team / by Mondo Beck / 1985

Alva / Mondo / by Mondo Beck / 1985

Alva / Dagger tail / by Mondo Beck / 1986

Alva / Eddie Reategui / by Mondo Beck / 1986

Alva / Fred Smith / by Sean McLean / 1987

Alva / Chris Cook / by Mondo Beck / 1987

Alva / John Thomas / by John Thomas / 1987

Alva / Jef Hartsel / by Jef Hartsel / 1988

Alva decks of the '80s marked a new era and the resurrection of Tony Alva's legacy as an innovative skater, artist, and brand owner. Tony's approach and method of riding, choosing, and marketing skateboards had already been well established in the '70s. "Alva Skates—Dominates" was the word once again in the '80s. Tony teamed up with the forever legendary Mondo Beck, an OG artist, surf bum, and skate anarchist from the shores of Jersey. Mondo pretty much came up with all of the cool shit that was being produced from Alva at the time.

These decks resembled nothing at all like the corporately produced deck of any era to this day. These decks sported Fish, Minnow, Dolphin, and Dagger shapes, all hand-screened by skaters, team riders, musicians, or surfers who either knew Tony or Mondo, or just needed cash. These cues were individually customized, with never—and I mean never—two sticks alike. A lot like buying a surfboard. They were all hand-airbrushed in neo-tribal and abstract transitions of contrasting patterns and markings.

Check this out, the Alva Scratch logo of the '80s was inspired from Enter the Dragon on choke buddha. It was Bruce and surfers on acid! Shit, this had an effect on me. I was nineteen at the time, skating on these Fishes and Dolphins in Waikiki, when I first got sponsored by Alva. I think it was still one of the only companies of that time that didn't have a pro model. You rode for Alva Skates and you were stoked. Eddie Reategui became the first pro with a model on Alva, when he took over the dolphin shape and popularized it. The rest is history.

Even when Alva started producing and marketing our boards as pro models, Tony always allowed us maximum freedom in the design and shapes of our boards. I've seen Tony use every one of his pro's decks in his quiver. With probably the most diverse team to date in terms of the riders' background in origin, personalities, and riding styles, we traveled and rode these skates to the four corners of this Earth and back. Our shapes and graphics meant something to us. They were our "colors."

Jef Hartsel

Alva / Bill Danforth (Second Version) / by Marc Rude / 1988

Alva / John Gibson / by Marc Rude / 1987

Alva / Craig Johnson / by Gary "Gul" Frayer / 1987

Alva / Dave Duncan / by Gary "Gul" Frayer / 1988

Alva / Jef Hartsel / by Jef Hartsel and Gary "Gul" Frayer / 1988

Alva / Jim Murphy / by Gary "Gul" Frayer / 1988

Alva / Alva Posse / by Gary "Gul" Frayer / 1989

Alva / Mario Rubalcaba / by Gary "Gul" Frayer / 1990

Bernie Tostenson

I'm a surfer at heart, so I was right in the middle of the "sidewalk surfin'" fad in 1963, when we made our own decks out of two-by-fours and modified metal shoe skates. Since I was from a coastal community, we made them long—about 36 inches—so we could practice our surfboard maneuvers, like "walking the nose," "hanging ten," "spinners," "handstands," "360s," etc., and we'd find freshly paved mountain roads and casually carve our way down all day. The metal wheels were loud and would stop dead if you so much as ran over a pebble, turning you into Superman with only your elbows as brakes.

My first job was at a sign shop in 1967 at the age of seventeen. I learned just about every skill they had to offer: hand lettering, gold leafing, hand-cutting stencils, making and exposing the silk-screens, and mixing my own inks from fluorescent and metallic powders. I also learned every advanced screening trick in the book: hand-pulled color blends, split fountains, transparent inks, tints, etc. I split in 1970 to form a company with Steve Krajewski in the San Fernando Valley. We had some huge customers, including MGM Studios and Bally pinball machines—I screened a lot of those upright glass plates with lights behind them using transparent inks.

That all came to an end, though, when I moved to the jungles of Kaua'i to avoid the draft. Paradise is great for honeymoons and vacations, but it gets old really fast. So eighteen months later—after surviving Hurricane Doreen while trapped in a 1959 Rambler station wagon with no back window—I moved back to the San Fernando Valley to start up the sign shop again.

In 1976, I met a girl, fell in love, and left everything behind to live in Santa Barbara. The only job in town for a silk screener was at Sims Skateboards, and I started working there for six dollars an hour. Interestingly, all the employees Tom hired were the best surfers in Santa Barbara (it was rumored he did it to get more waves at Rincon because nobody would dare to snake the boss).

Silk-screening then was easy. The graphics were just company logos printed on the top and bottom in one-color passes, which was really boring considering the skills I'd picked up at the sign shop. So in my spare time, I showed Tom Sims that I could draw by designing two logos for Sims in 1976, one being the oval logo with the three striped wings on each side. I only got 185 dollars, but I got job security and was soon doing the ads and brochures, as well as spending my days screening hundreds of 44-inch and 36-inch Taperkicks.

The next phase in skateboard graphics was pro-signature models. The problem was that since the pros were only fourteen to sixteen years old, they had the typical signatures that all eighth graders have. So it became

Sims / Winged Logo / by Bernie Tostenson / 1976

my job to create stylized "dynamic" signatures for these guys that were printed in a second color below the Sims logo. Skateboards were still considered toys at this time, so Tom, an expert skier (he was a stunt double in a James Bond film), stressed making skateboarding a legitimate sport. He wanted to make the boards look like racing equipment, and began doing so by having me do the ads and brochures featuring action shots with clean blueprint-style spec-sheet drawings using millimeters and centimeters instead of inches.

Sims soon became one of the most popular skate companies, and as a consequence, big money and big greed stepped in. Counterfeit, broken decks started flooding in. We'd usually get three or four broken returns a month, but then we started getting twenty to 30—we didn't know it at the time, but they were being made in Canada and distributed by an East Coast distributor.

At first, Tom and Mike Streff, my manager, started reprimanding me for inferior silk-screening, but I vindicated myself by laying the film positive on top of the graphics to prove the boards were not screened by me or with my screens—the logo was sloppy and the color was way off, and they were also using enamels, while I was using lacquers. They apologized, and I convinced Tom to let me do multicolor graphics to complicate things for the counterfeiters—an idea he reluctantly agreed to under certain conditions. He stressed that the graphics must have the Euro high-tech look, and I was given a stack of European ski catalogs to emulate. I did so, as evident in the Mike Folmer, Dave Andrecht, and Bert Lamar pro models. He also had me devise a "tilt jig" so I would be able to screen on the curved kick tail of a skateboard, making it even harder to counterfeit (the tilt jig and variations of it are used in every skateboard screening shop today).

Everybody was stoked until those designs were counterfeited, too. So Tom then hired Chuck Barfoot, an expert carpenter and surfer. Tom didn't trust anybody at this point, not even his friends, and Chuck was given his own shop with strict orders that no one was to go in there except for him. There Chuck devised a custom wheel-well machine that was outstanding. Still, the counterfeiters figured out a way to pull off a half-assed version, and the rural mom and pop skate shops still had no idea between the original and the fakes. According to management, this distributor would advertise they distributed our product, but then fulfill 90 percent of a shop's order with their manufactured fakes. Years later they did the same thing to Skull Skates with fake Hosoi decks.

Out of desperation, Tom had Chuck rout shallow shapes on the bottom of the board. It then became my job to somehow put graphics in these holes to make them look cool. Since graphics couldn't be screened

Sims / Super Ply / by Bernie Tostenson / 1978

Sims / Gregg Ayers / by Bernie Tostenson / 1978

Sims / Snake (Prototype) / by Bernie Tostenson / 1978

Sims / Street Stik / by Bernie Tostenson / 1980

Sims / Dave Andrecht / by Bernie Tostenson / 1980

Sims / Bert Lamar / by Bernie Tostenson / 1980

Sims / Mike Folmer / by Bernie Tostenson / 1981

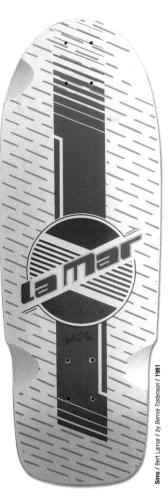

Sims / Bert Lamar / by Bernie Tostenson / 1981

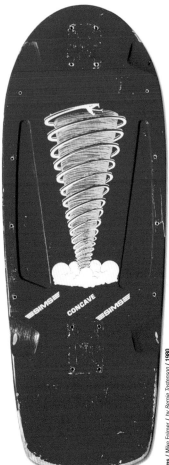

Sims / Brad Bowman / by Bernie Tostenson / **1980**

Sims / Brad Bowman / by Bernie Tostenson / **1980**

Sims / Brad Bowman / by Bernie Tostenson / **1981**

Sims / Mike Follmer / by Bernie Tostenson / **1980**

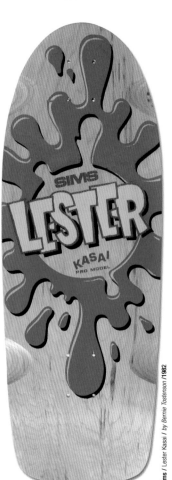

Sims / Steve Rocco / by Bernie Tostenson / **1982**

Sims / Brad Bowman / by Bernie Tostenson / **1981**

Sims / Lester Kasai / by Bernie Tostenson / **1982**

Sims / Screamer / by Bud Fawcett and Bernie Tostenson / **1983**

in these routed holes, I designed some logo graphics that could be screened onto metallic decal paper, die-cut to the exact shape, and then inserted into the hole. The first two were the Lamar and Andrecht models. The one I am most proud of, though, is the Brad Bowman Superman logo, where the routing was designed around the graphic, making it part of the graphic. In the ads, we told the public that we did the routing for "lightness," but that wasn't the case at all. We just tried to make it harder to prevent the counterfeiting.

In 1979, I got fed up and moved to Aspen for a year. I got back to my roots and landed a cool job at a sign shop that catered to the seasonal, super expensive restaurants: Western-style graphics with lots of gold leafing. But surfing soon brought me back to Santa Barbara. Skiing just doesn't compare, and the women are frigid in more ways than one—unless you are a millionaire.

When I moved back to Santa Barbara things had drastically changed. Most of the people were gone at Sims. There was no more laughter. Gloom was in the air. There wasn't even a woodshop or silkscreen area anymore, so Tom offered me freelance work to screen the decks out of my garage. During this time I developed some innovative racking systems and screening jigs that allowed me to do four runs per minute—30 cents a run then equaling $1.20 a minute. That doesn't sound like much today, but 23 years ago that was like five dollars a minute in today's economy.

But then a new problem arose: the Zoning Commissioner. They were on to me. Even though I was living and working in the sleaziest part of Santa Barbara with all the gangs, prostitutes, and drug dealers, they wanted to pick on me. Luckily, I had the best alarm system that money could buy. His name was Kane, a 120-pound dog that hated suits after they'd hauled his ass away to the pound twice. So whenever he barked, I looked under the door. And if I saw shiny shoes, I'd tiptoe to the back of the house and pretend nobody was home. Then I discovered a chink in their armor: the bureaucratic system closes down at 5:00 p.m. So I'd start working at 7:00 p.m until 3:00 a.m.

Sims then licensed his name to Brad Dorfman, who owned Vision Sports Inc., in Newport Beach, California. Bud Fawcett, a friend, photographer, and sales rep for Sims, moved to Newport to work for Brad. I continued screening piecework in Santa Barbara and delivered the finished boards to Vision on Thursdays, partied with Bud that night, and then went surfing at the Huntington Beach Pier Friday morning before going back home.

All of my notable Sims graphics were done during this transition. I don't know what was going on, but I seemed to have free rein for a very short period of time. Brad wanted a product that would appeal to the skaters rather than the clueless sporting-goods shop buyers. His vision was to make skateboarding "rad," and he wanted me to do "fresh" new graphics. I had no clue what "rad" was, but I'd met this little 21-year-old, blue-haired Filipina girl, with ripped clothing and a wicked spiky dog necklace and wristband, who introduced me to punk and new wave music. She made me go to these punk shows in San Francisco at the Mabuhay Gardens, which was a restaurant during the day and a punk club at night. Little did I know it, but I saw some of the most legendary punk bands in history: Fear, X, The Avengers, Nico, Black Flag, The Dead Kennedys, The Germs, and The Cramps, and it was really weird seeing this little Filipino girl jump into these mosh pits and start kicking ass (I eventually married her for awhile and we have a six-year-old daughter now).

I couldn't always relate to the punk shows, so I'd wander around collecting the punk Xerox flyers stapled to telephone poles. These flyers turned out to be very valuable to me in 1983, when I contracted Bud to photograph some skate punk. Using the flyers for the authentic look, I tortured the photo on a Xerox machine to come up with the Sims Screamer.

I was a lot older than the average skater so I had to be very careful about producing corny graphics. So whenever I got into a bind, I'd find out what the popular songs and bands were, and I bought the albums to emulate the cover art. For instance, on the Steve Rocco freestyle model, the lettering was from the first Blondie album and the checkerboard background was from The Specials. The Brad Bowman Digital was inspired by Devo.

Sims / Christian Hosoi / by Bernie Tostenson / 1982

Around the time Brad was telling me about this red-hot Japanese [American] skater, Christian Hosoi. There was a song released called "I'm Turning Japanese." There wasn't an album cover, so I just used graphic Japanese cliches. Brad disagreed with Bud and I over the graphic. He said that the modified Wonton font was offensive to the Japanese and that the rising sun flag would offend some of the American sporting-goods storeowners who still held a grudge over Pearl Harbor and World War II. But Bud convinced him otherwise. I kept the graphics simple on the Hosoi, because I still made most of my money screening them on piece-work. At the time I didn't know if it was my design, the song, or Hosoi's skating talents, but I was screening 500 of these decks alone per week. My motivation for graphics at this time wasn't to be recognized as some "art guru." I just realized that the better my graphics sold, the more money I'd make silk-screening them.

Since there were very few skate shops then, we were encouraged to cater our graphics to the elderly, clueless buyers of the sporting-goods stores. The popularity of skateboarding rose as a result of contests, magazines, and pros. One contest promoter even held a seminar attended by representatives from all the skateboard companies, and the topics of discussion were suggested guidelines for fair market pricing, corporate image, graphic content, amount of colors screened, and the wholesome image of skateboarding for the advancement of the sport. Therefore, "skull and crossbones" and "tattoo-style" designs were discouraged, even though all the pros and skaters were craving these types of graphics.

Bud and I didn't know what was going on between Brad and Sims, but the atmosphere changed drastically. Then Brad pulled the plug and I

Brand-X / Knucklehead / by Bernie Tostenson / 1983

Brand-X / X-Con / by Bernie Tostenson / 1984

Brand-X / Phase 3 / by Bernie Tostenson / 1984

Brand-X / Weirdo / by Bernie Tostenson / 1984

was told that he was going to start his own silk-screening department. Bud and I were both fired. We couldn't get mad about losing our jobs. Another recession hit, just like the one in 1979, and companies were going out of business left and right. While Brad was picking up the screens at my garage in Santa Barbara, he was examining my tilt jigs, and the next thing you know he hired Tom Mallard to make his own version of it—he had to since all my graphics at the time required a tilt jig (Tom Mallard and I remain good friends to this day out of mutual respect).

So here was the situation: Bud, a top photographer and salesman with the list of every shop and distributor in the U.S. and Europe, was out of work; and I was an artist with a fully stocked art department and silkscreen shop with 500 dollars' worth of printing inks who was now out of work as well. So what are you gonna do, get a job at Uncle Steve's Radiator Shop? I don't think so. Our destiny was obvious, and Brand-X was born. I did all the graphics, silk-screening, and ads, so our overhead was almost zero. Work suddenly became fun.

Basically, Brand-X was started as a kamikaze company destined to die. We just wanted to go out in a blaze of glory—and use up all my inks in the process. We had no faith in the economy or the future of the sport, and we just wanted to piss everybody off. For eleven years in various industries I just got sick and tired of the phrase, "No, you can't do that," so we obtained the official "suggested guideline list for skateboard companies" to break every rule. Skeletons were considered "okay," but "skull and crossbones" were discouraged. So we not only did a skull and crossbones deck, we made the skull and crossbones our logo.

It was also suggested that only two to three colors be screened on the bottom of a deck, and one color on top. So in 1984 Brand-X came out with the Weirdo. Inspired by R. Crumb's abstract graphics, I went ape shit and used every silk-screen trick in the book: hand-pulled color blends, transparent inks, split fountains, and I even mixed my own inks using clear binder inks and pigments for brighter colors. I advertised it as being twelve colors, but it was actually a lot more when you consider I was blending colors on every pass and the transparent tint doubled the colors.

This made the old farts and Taiwanese skateboard manufacturers look really cheap in comparison, but my revenge took its toll. Silk-screening is very physical work and I soon realized that I'd created a monster. We received thousands of orders for the Weirdo and I was the only one who knew how to screen them. Completely miserable and sore, I got these massive Hulk Hogan arms from screening that made me look awkward with my thin body. But I showed them! And let me tell you this: There is nothing, and I mean nothing more satisfying than silk-screening your own graphics. It makes you giggle. You put the finished product next to the TV and just stare at it in disbelief saying, "Did I do that?" All of the early Brand-X graphics were designed to display my silk-screening techniques and skills. I was more proud of my advanced silkscreen innovations and inventions than I was of my art at the time.

Brand-X was a true underground company, because when you own your own company there are no rules or restrictions. Not to mention we were still conducting a business illegally by running a commercial business in a residential area. So we spent our days surfing, skating, having fun, and working all night in my cracker-box garage. If we were to try and do that today, the SWAT team in haz-mat space uniforms would evacuate the neighborhood thinking we had a meth lab. This went on for five years until we outgrew the garage. Those were the happiest years of my life.

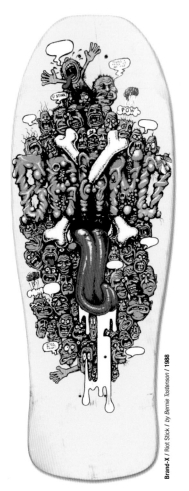

We then got an industrial space in Ventura, and a big house on the beach—the rents in this area were half of those in Santa Barbara. We were now legal and no longer had to keep looking over our shoulders. The house turned into a hospice for European skaters with loud music, TV, beer, and lots of people hanging out. Brand-X was a family of friends supporting each other, and it became very graphic/skater-oriented towards the end. I invited artists from all over the world to participate. Two of the people I most respected were Steve Krajewski, who did the Max Ray Man and the first Sean Goff model, and Ken Sigafoos, who did the art on all of his models, as well as Dan Tag and Chris May's. John Lucero did Bob Schmelzer's decks.

I drew the Eddy Gein model in 1986. Gein wasn't a skater, he was a taxidermist and the original ghoul/cannibal/necrophiliac/grave robber/transvestite loosely portrayed in the movies Psycho and The Texas Chainsaw Massacre. Brand X couldn't afford a pro at the time due to a lack of financing, but there were hundreds of unknown pros at the time, so what the hell, we gave Eddy his own model. I thought he was ancient history and that nobody would remember the guy, but they did, and I've never received so much hate mail in my life. According to some, I now have a one-way ticket to Hell for doing so.

Just like the Eddy Gein model, the second Sean Goff model was based on a true story. Brand-X became very popular in England and Europe, as a result of my European team captain Jeremy Fox, and I had four Euro Brand-X riders living downstairs at my house on the beach in Oxnard, including Sean Goff (our only pro and England's number one skater). Well, word got around that we let European skaters stay at our house, and pretty soon our house was swarming with non-Brand-X skaters that asked to stay a few days but then refused to leave. It started

getting out of hand and I had to lock my bedroom because a lot of my personal stuff was getting stolen.

Nobody would tell me who the thief was, so I finally asked Jeremy and Sean to get rid of these guys. Then one night someone pounded on my bedroom door at 3:00 a.m screaming, "Sean has been stabbed!" I went downstairs to find that one of the uninvited skaters had broken a long neck beer bottle, snuck up on Sean and gutted him in the stomach outside the house. I looked at the wound and it wasn't bleeding that much—it looked like a nasty scratch—until he spread it apart to reveal a gaping hole. I almost fainted. So I rushed him to the emergency hospital where the nurse also thought it was just a scratch. Then Sean spread it apart for her and she almost fainted, too.

Throughout his treatment and stitches, Sean was cracking jokes and showing no pain. After he was all bandaged up, we walked out and found the lobby filled with police officers all pumped up to get the would-be assailant. Now we all knew it was this skater who rode for Zorlac, but to my complete amazement Sean told the cops that some bum tried to rob him on the beach and he didn't see the guy's face. On the way home I asked him why he didn't turn the guy in. He said, "I'll just handle this in my own way." The next morning the skater was gone—never to be seen again. Fearing the worst, I thought the others had killed and buried him on the beach, but years later I found out that he'd given up skateboarding entirely and was a junkie living in Germany). So I put the story on a skateboard as a graphic for Sean—the freaked-out guy is me when I saw the wound.

The graphic industry became real competitive, so we were constantly listening to the shop owners on what was selling and why, and to our amateurs and pros on how to make a more desirable product. We had silk-

Flip / Tom Penny / by Bernie Tostenson / 1997

Flip / Andy Scott / by Bernie Tostenson / 1997

Flip / Tom Penny / by Bernie Tostenson / 1998

Flip / Tom Penny / by Bernie Tostenson / 1998

Flip / Tom Penny / by Bernie Tostenson / 1998

screening down to a science, but the unexpected desire for super con-caves threw me for a loop. The bigger companies stayed with the flatter and easier-to-screen deck—maybe because of the popularity of their pros—but we were a small company that needed an edge, so we chose monster concaves and kicks to compete. My nose-to-tail tilt jig handled normal decks with rail-to-rail graphics just fine, but the super concaves now made it impossible for me to do these full-length rail-to-tail graphics. But as a silk-screener and artist, I had the ability to spot the problem areas for screening and design my graphics around them.

Take the Riot Stick, for example. It had a really concave shape, and as you can see by the shape of the graphic, I avoided all of the problem areas by giving it a weird-shaped graphic. This deck was not only super con-cave with a nose kick, the tail was a "V" kick and I completely avoided a tip-to-tail graphic on that one. But with the Riot Stick I learned to have some fun with the new limitations due to the ever-evolving shapes, con-caves, and kicks. I guess you could even call it the "first interactive skate-board graphic" for a couple of reasons. A lot of the characters had little "cartoon word bubbles" that had messages that only a skateboarder could relate to, and I left a lot of those word bubbles empty so the skate-boarder could personalize it with their own sayings.

I still think the Riot Stick was an ugly shelf board, but when assembled it was at its best—the little characters by the top truck looked like they were being squished by it, and the saliva near the bottom looked like it was actually flowing around the riser pads and trucks. This was our sec-ond best-selling board ever, right after the Weirdo.

All went well until we got huge in Europe and couldn't finance the mas-sive orders. The banks wouldn't lend us the money. We'd show up with 25,000 dollars in Postal Orders and they would deny us because we did-n't have any credit history—no bad credit, but no good credit, either. So we couldn't buy the blank boards necessary to fulfill our orders. It was frustrating as hell.

So in 1988, we met one of our distributors, who wanted to form a part-nership, and signed a three-year contract. That first year we kicked ass and made 175,000 dollars according to his bookkeeper's ledgers. However, when we went for our profits, he wouldn't give us our share. He also told us that he'd secretly trademarked Brand-X in his own name and now owned the company. Then he fired us. We tried to sue but found out the hard way that you can't win a civil lawsuit against a millionaire and went bankrupt in the process. We definitely would have won—we had massive evidence—but we lost because you're only entitled to the amount of justice you can afford In civil law, no matter how strong your case is the millionaires will always win because they'll counter-sue and complicate things until you finally run out of money for lawyers.

In his mind, the investor's evil plans seemed to have been successful with his "hostile takeover," but his greed soon killed the company. He hired bottom-of-the-barrel artists and screeners. He also underestimated the power of the international Brand-X amateur team, which he'd cut off as well. Amateurs will ride your product and say nice things about the com-pany, but if you fire them they'll do everything they can to destroy a com-pany's image out of pride. Soon every shop owner knew about this guy's morals and ethics and what he had done. Brand-X took six years to build, but with his management practices it took only six months for it to die.

I've done over 100 deck graphics since then, but the early days were my glory days. I was very lucky to witness the birth and evolution of skate-boarding. |**Bernie Tostenson**

John Grigley

I started skating for Sims while I was in Florida. At that time I was doing this spay-paint artwork on clothing I would paint in my front yard. Around 1983, a store in NYC was buying the stuff, and I started sending some of the artwork on paper to Brad Dorfman in California. Brad really liked the art, and I switched from Sims to Vision when I moved to Newport Beach with Paul Schmitt and Chuck Hults.

It was really difficult trying to print the spray-paint stuff using a silkscreen on skateboards, and I think we may have been the first company to print on skateboards using halftones. The first board was an experiment, but Brad ended up printing and selling around 300 of them—it was on a Christian Hosoi Rising Sun shape, the Sims deck I was riding at the time. After we got the printing down, I started working on what was to become the Guardian skateboard. I didn't want a pro model—I wanted a series of boards without my name on them—so we had to come up with names for the boards in the Old Ghosts series. The Guardian was the first, and it was designed in the spray-paint style. The second board was the Hippie-Stik. It had an odd shape with hips on the tail and we made the graphics kind of psychedelic. The inside joke was that "you could beat a hippie with this stick." The third board of the series was named the Street Ghost. I'm right-handed, and this board was designed when I had a broken right arm, which explains a lot.

| John Grigley

Vision / Old Ghost / by John Grigley / 1984

John Grigley / 1986 / Photo by Grant Brittain

Vision / Guardian / by *John Grigley* / **1985**

Vision / Hippie Stick / by *John Grigley* / **1985**

Vision / Street Ghost / by *John Grigley* / **1985**

Vision / John Grigley / by *John Grigley* / **1987**

Vision / John Grigley / by *John Grigley* / **1987**

Vision / John Grigley / by *John Grigley* / **1988**

Vision / John Grigley / by *John Grigley* / **1988**

Vision / John Grigley / by *John Grigley* / **1989**

Tom Groholski sent us this 8.5" x 14" Xerox of a Jersey Devil that was so badly drawn Tom Sims refused to print them. Sims was still into high-tech graphics then and tried to talk him out of it, but Groholski prevailed. Sims still decided it needed to look more professional and that it should be huge and strong—Groholski sent this bony, nerdy version of the Tasmanian Devil—so Sims told me to redraw it with huge muscles and a screaming face. I'm not sure what it was with Tom's screaming faces, but every action shot in his ads and brochures featured a close up of him doing a huge backside turn with a screaming face. I guess he wanted to look intense and aggressive, and he transferred this trademark face of his to the graphics.

I think 50 decks were produced before Groholski saw it and flipped out. He wanted his graphic on the deck exactly as it was drawn, so Sims had me redraw it again, using the same character but with a better pose. Once again it was rejected. Finally, I had to take a piece of vellum and trace his original drawing in ink for production. I don't know what went on behind the scenes, but I heard it got pretty intense. I just got caught in the middle of the conflict. This was very important to skate-art history, though. Not only did Groholski force a manufacturer into producing one of the first cartoon graphics, he forced them into doing his own exact drawing. | **Bernie Tostenson**

The Agent Orange boards by Vision were designed by the band. Brad Dorfman cut us a great deal and the board sold thousands in the early '80s. Agent Orange was also featured in Vision's landmark skate video Skate Visions and at one time the band received more royalties from the skate decks than from record sales.

The first design was created by using a "spin art" toy set that gave the appearance of motion to a static graphic design. The second Agent Orange skateboard utilized printed circuits we xeroxed out of library books. I think it was our answer to what was going on in music in the mid '80s. Synthesized "electronic" music was big—Gary Numan, Ultravox, Kraftwerk—as well as the birth of personal computers, like Apple. We wanted to "electrify" or "computerize" a very unsophisticated piece of wood. Scott Miller, the drummer of Agent Orange, would come up with concepts for deck designs that were not of this earth or humanly possible. While Mike Palm and I listened to his ideas, we knew he was from an alternate universe and would someday return to his home planet. Scott only used his skateboard as a dolly to move his drum cases anyway—any other use would've been catastrophic.

James Levesque,
Bass Player of Agent Orange

Vision / Agent Orange / by Mike Palm and James Levesque / 1985

Vision / Agent Orange / by Mike Palm and James Levesque / 1987

Vision / Joe Johnson / by Joe Johnson and Greg Evans / 1986

Sims / Jeff Phillips (First Version) / by Greg Evans / 1984

Sims / Jeff Phillips (Second Version) / by Greg Evans / 1986

Sims / Jeff Phillips (First Version) / by Marty Jimenez and Greg Evans / 1987

I came out from England in late '84 to check out the skate scene in the U.S. with some friends. We came out on a one-way ticket and a five-day Greyhound ticket. We went down to Texas to hang out with the Zorlac crew and that's where we met up with Jeff Phillips. Jeff liked the way I skated and hooked me up with Sims. We then made our way out to the West Coast to pick up some boards and check out the scene, where I got down to my last dollar and ended up working at Vision/Sims in the warehouse, along with John Grigley and a bunch of other spackers. He mentioned that he'd spoke to Brad Dorfman and if I won the next three freestyle contests Brad would turn me pro. So I won the next three contests and then John told me he really didn't talk to Brad. Fucker. Either way, Vision turned me pro and my first board was in the works.

Keith Butterfield was the last pro freestyler for Vision—he went missing in action—and his board shape was a little wacky, so I created something that had a better nose and tail. Back then, the board companies had more say in what your graphics would be, so I just went along with what the art director, Greg Evans, whipped up for me. He threw down this big arse Vision logo over the top of a photo of me from a TransWorld "Check Out," where I was simulating pissing on a lamppost. I'm not sure what he was thinking, and I didn't really care, so all kinds of crap was thrown on the board. A good friend of mine, and fellow freestyler from the U.K., Mac, did the little cockroach looking things. There was also a pig on the board, which is in honor of being from the best skate scene in the world, Brighton, England, which was also know as "Pig City" due to the hassle that skaters got from the police.

In retrospect, I wish I cared about what the graphics were, but all I cared about was skating and didn't care about what it took to do it. If I had to design a graphic for my board today, I'd have a tweaked pentagram and change my name to Bam so I could make some money! |Don Brown

Variflex / Stuart Singer / artist unknown / 1980

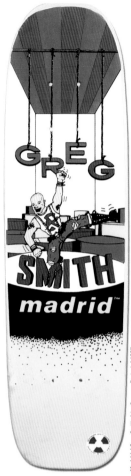

Zorlac / Jeff Newton / by Jeff Newton / 1982

Madrid / Greg Smith / by Spencer Bartsch / 1987

Vision / Keith Butterfield / artist unknown / 1982

Vision / Don Brown / by Greg Evans / 1986

Vision / Don Brown / artist unknown / 1989

Santa Cruz / Ray Meyer (Prototype) / *by Jim Phillips* / **1985**

Santa Cruz / Ray Meyer / *by Jim Phillips* / **1986**

Tracker / Per Holkneckt / *artist unknown* / **1986**

Titus / Christian Seewaldt / *artist unknown* / **1987**

Schmitt Stix / Hans Lindgren / *artist unknown* / **1987**

Sims / Pierre Andre / *by Greg Evans* / **1987**

Circle A / Fabian Kravetz / *by Kevin Marburg* / **1989**

Circle A / Bob Schmelzer / *by John Lucero* / **1989**

World Industries / Rodney Mullen / *by W.T. Lageose* / **1989**

World Industries / Rodney Mullen / *by Marc McKee* / **1990**

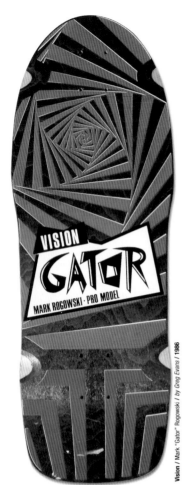

Vision / Mark "Gator" Rogowski / *by Greg Evans* / **1986**

Vision / Mark "Gator" Rogowski (Prototype) / *by Greg Evans* / **1987**

Vision / Mark "Gator" Rogowski / *by Greg Evans* / **1988**

Vision / Mark "Gator" Rogowski / *by Greg Evans* / **1988**

Vision / Mark "Gator" Rogowski / by Greg Evans / 1988

Vision / Mark "Gator" Rogowski / by Greg Evans / 1988

Vision / Mark "Gator" Rogowski / by Greg Evans / 1989

Vision / Mark "Gator" Rogowski / by Greg Evans / 1989

Vision / Gator Mark Anthony / by Gator Mark Anthony and Greg Evans / 1989

Vision / Gator Mark Anthony / by Gator Mark Anthony and Greg Evans / 1989

Vision / Gator Mark Anthony / by Gator Mark Anthony and Bernie Tostenson / 1989

The Mark "Gator" Anthony model was one of his last models before turning himself in for that tragic murder that will probably keep him confined for the rest of his life. It took me an entire week to do this graphic with Gator by my side making suggestions. He wanted total involvement, so he sat next to me for three hours a day while we slowly developed that deck. It showed a street scene with every crime imaginable going on, but the only ones the cops were chasing were the skating monkeys. At the time he seemed like a nice, honest, religious guy with very strong convictions on what was right and wrong in the world.

Bernie Tostenson

Andy Takakjian

In 1985 I got a phone call from either Marty Jimenez or Greg Evans, asking if I wanted to do art for a skateboard—I think they found out about me from Safari Sam's in Huntington Beach, somehow. I said I'd take a look and went across the swamp to [Vision's] "illustrious" offices: a crummy, little, concrete-slab industrial building located on the bluffs in Costa Mesa. The inside was decorated in "early American trailer trash," and everything seemed to have either Plastisol or an undifferentiated dark, colorless guck stuck to it; the gum-encrusted shag carpet smelled of mildew and cat pee— very sad-looking. I think Greg Evans was the "acting" art director, but there didn't seem to be any real structure, just the owner, Brad Dorfman, Greg, Marty, and a few "rescued" farm-workers running the shop. I think Mark Gonzales was there for this initial meeting, but he didn't say much—he was just a kid then. It was impossible to tell he was this magnificent, brilliant skateboard rider.

My first graphic was Mark's board. I just went home that day after the vague tour and meeting, and slapped the art together out of old leftovers from my Ocean Pacific and freelance days with a little Scotch tape and a Sharpie marker.

That was it. The Mark Gonzales board was born. I got a check for 150 bucks. That's it. Ever. Of course it looked like that was all Vision had, too, and it was certainly more than I had. Who knew?

Mark never really said a lot [with regard to his first graphic], in fact there really wasn't any direction at all from anyone, other than, "Do something cool, dude." I remember there were a lot of Xerox experiments colored with highlighter markers piled around and taped to the walls and furniture. I can't remember if some were Mark's. I think Vision was toying with the idea of him doing the design, but then for some reason they all just liked what I did. After the initial Gonzales deck, Mark did his own art, which was very wise. His popularity was growing, and the decks carried his personal touch. The effect being, he was there with the kids, it was the real Mark, not some imagery "the company" cooked up to promote him. Marty, Greg, and I would give him a hand with placement and specs, but that's about it.

The Psycho Stick was another slap-bang-dash piece. When I finished the Mark board, they showed me the blank template for the Psycho Stick. This

Vision / Mark Gonzales / by Andy Takakjian / 1985

Vision / Mark Gonzales / by Andy Takakjian / 1987

Vision / Psycho Stick / by Andy Takakjian / 1986

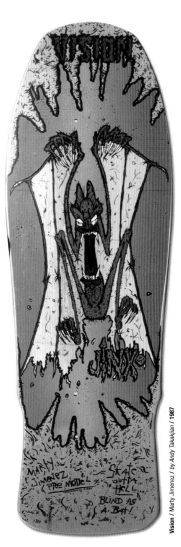

Vision / Marty Jimenez / by Andy Takakjian / 1987

Sims / Eric Nash / by Andy Takakjian / 1988

Sims / Eric Nash / by Andy Takakjian / 1988

When I was fourteen years old I had a pair of orange Vision Psycho Stick shorts that I wore every day. I remember meeting a girl who was 24 years old who knew people who worked in Vision's art department. She told me about the guy who did the Psycho Stick and how he looked exactly like the guy on the board because it was a self-portrait. I was fascinated and lost my virginity to her. | Ed Templeton

obliquely shaped piece of wood held high in the air and cradled in artifi purple velvet, revered like the Holy Grail: the deck of all decks, the Buddha board-dom. I went home with "Psycho Stick" ringing in my ears, and look around my desk for something suitable. There was a photo a friend had tak of another friend, and I scrawled on some swirly eyeballs, more marke Scotch tape and boom—Psycho Stick, the accompanying Psycho M device, and another 150 bucks. Never got a deck.

I had no idea the Psycho Stick or the Gonzales deck would have effect on anything except my back rent. I think my friend who was "Psycho Man" still suffers trauma from the monikerization—I know hair fell out.

The Sims Eric Nash was a big surprise. He told me what he wante bandito with smoking guns, where the smoke spells his name. I did the a was approved, and it went through the production mill. A few months la get a call from the marketing director telling me all the decks say "fuck y in the smoke—apparently some Amish kid in Pennsylvania bought the d and his momma spotted it and called the company screaming, "Law lawyer, lawyer!" I said, "WHAT?! I have to see this." I looked at my art couldn't see it. So I went to the office, where Greg and Marty pointed it ou me. Honestly, I couldn't see it until they pointed it out. Then it wouldn' away. That's all I could see. So of course I had to redo the art, and all was in Skateville again. I think about 500 boards made it to market before the

Generally speaking, there really isn't a lot of time or money for wea subliminal content into commercial art. Deadlines are hard and fast. By 1980s people had pretty much abandoned subliminal gadgetry, and just v ahead and put the coochie on the cover. It's still like that: show it or don't.

Sims / Pharaoh / by Andy Takakjian / 1987

Vision / Lee Ralph / by Andy Takakjian / 1988

Vision / Ken Park / by Andy Takakjian / 1988

Vision / Johnee Kop / by Andy Takakjian / 1988

bat on the original drawings for the Jinx board included, by posture, an anatomically correct bat. Simply put, it had a little bat-pecker. This was, of course, ixnayed by family-market-concious Brad for good reason, and it went through several revisions in progressively reduced sizes until it was ultimately just a dot. I believe the board sold well even without god's input.

Then there was the Harley badge scare, when I had replaced the words "Harley-Davidson" with "Vision," and "motor" "cycles" with "skate" "boards" on the Harley logo. Somehow this got out of the company—I don't know if the boards even made it to market—and we got a call from Willie G., or one of his attorneys, and were promptly slapped with a cease-and-desist.

The most interesting thing about the Vision art department then was that it grew—and grew and grew with exponential rapidity. It outsized itself eventually, and I think overwhelmed Dorfman's mind to the point where he couldn't make a decision anymore. As sole ruler and final art czar, there came an impasse, a point at which no art could move forward because no decision could be made—there was just so much art to wade through. There were literally hundreds and hundreds of great designs sitting in the morgue file screaming to be used. Between running the ever-expanding and diversifying companies and swimming through this sea of art being generated by the art department, Dorfman was reduced to "eenie-mee-nie-miney-moe" every other two weeks every other Sunday regarding art selection.

Vision had over grown itself to Jovian capacity with the tiny Dorfman as a fulcrum, and it got to where I could no longer ascertain who to call to

book an appointment to book an appointment to book an appointment to book an appointment to find the key to the bathroom. So I pretty much just faded from the company, evaporating into the ether of Los Angeles smog, where I remain growing cancer cells, benign polyps, and more hair. There was a brief attempt through a pal to do something with Santa Monica Airlines, but alas, no pay dirt.

I had no idea about the Vision "anniversary" stuff until someone sent me a website showing the products in early 2003. Damn, I thought ... 150 bucks. All the skaters bought houses—plural—while I bought Top Ramen. A lot of the stuff I did made it into movies, televison, magazines, etc. The Psycho Stick was on popular album covers and huge billboards all over town—and I mean everywhere—advertising Cigna health insurance. You couldn't go anywhere and not see it. Sixteen-foot tall Psycho Sticks! I'd look up at these huge billboards and realize: I'm jobless and broke.

One night I saw a prostitute being arrested on the evening news wearing one of my Vision shirts. So big and obvious, like a staged advertisement for Vision—now there's royalty! **|Andy Takakjian**

VISION

Mark Gon

zales

Vision / Mark Gonzales / by Mark Gonzales / 1988

Vision / Mark Gonzales / by Mark Gonzales / 1989

Vision / Mark Gonzales / by Mark Gonzales / 1989

GET INTO THE GROVE YOU'VE GOT TO PROVE YOUR LOVE TO ME
STEP UP TO THE GET INTO THE GROVE BOY YOU'VE GOT GET IT RIGHT
SEAN DON'T SKATE   I KNOW I ASKED HIM

John Gibson

My first model on Zorlac came out in '82 or early '83. Previous to that I rode for Caster out of San Diego—I was about to turn pro for them and get a model, but the whole skate industry collapsed. Then I was approached by Jeff Newton of Zorlac, and he wanted to put my boards out. So I took the concept of the Chris Strople model on Caster and combined it with some of my ideas and Newton's, thus coming out with that shape. As far as graphics were concerned, all I wanted to have was a cow skull involved. Newton took that idea and came up with these scary-looking dudes in the back. The board was out for nine months. There were probably only five- to six-hundred made. Nobody was selling boards back then. That's what was so cool, because all the so-called "big companies" were fading just as we were coming out of the underground and beginning to make a difference.

One time when I was in the band Barkhard, I was at my drummer's house, and his roommate came in with one of my brand-new boards with the Pushead graphic. The deck was black with yellow and red graphics, and it was really cool. I asked him where he got it, and he said from a thrift store in Pasadena for five dollars. I thought, "Who would give a brand-new board to a thrift store?" He said the guy behind the counter told him an angry lady and her son came in. She'd said that he worked all summer mowing yards to save money to buy a skateboard, and when he came home with my board she told him there was no way he was keeping this satanic, evil board. She dragged him in tears to the thrift store and made him give it up.

I really loved Pushead's work. That's why I never changed the graphics on Zorlac. Skating was supposedly dead at that time, and his artwork was a true representation of skating in the underground. | John Gibson

Pushead

Zorlac / Double Cut (Third Version) / by Pushead / 1985

Being both an artist and a skateboarder, it was natural to try and combine these two abilities together. While in high school in Boise, Idaho, during the mid 1970s, I created two designs for T-shirts that were just for the local area. It wasn't until a short move to the Gulf Coast area of Alabama in early 1977 that the idea of creating skate graphics would actually begin.

I was lucky enough that one of my cousins had all these electrical tools and a huge woodshop, so the task of cutting out and shaping skateboard decks became a regular occurrence. Buying birch, ash, or certain types of lightweight hardwood, I would hone the wood down to a shape that was wider than most decks. My main concern at that time was the weight, so to get it as light as possible was the goal. Once the wood was cut and sanded, the process of actually drawing on the wood began. The lines would be inked in India ink, and then the areas would be colored with Pelikan colored inks. When the inks saturated into the wood, there would be this brilliant transparent tone, keeping the wood grain visible. Once finished, it would get a couple of coats of Varathane, then it was taped and ready to skate. Quite a few of these decks were made for friends and family.

I then moved back to Boise in late 1977, losing that great woodshop, but laminated decks were becoming the rage and you could buy blanks. So I basically just did the same process as before. All the graphics would be based around a brand-name-type logo. This was a lot of fun. During that time there was some minor communication in trying to do actual skate-deck graphics, but no one was really interested in anything besides a logo-type image on a skateboard.

When I moved to North San Diego County in 1978, I became a local at the Del Mar Skate Ranch. This opened up a few more doors to get product, but it was still a hard sell to get an illustration on a deck. During this time, I went up to El Segundo to have a meeting with these two guys who owned Dogtown. My intention was to sell them on skate graphics, since it seemed Dogtown was the only company that had something more than a logo. I ended up doing deck and wheel designs for them, but never graphics. Losing a job and not being able to find another one forced me back to Boise at the end of the summer in 1979. I had plenty of Dogtown unpainted prototypes from working with them, and I'd do graphics on those for personal use as the ramp era began.

A friend of mine in Boise was doing his own type of underground skate shop since he had a dealer's license. He would purchase skate stuff at wholesale and provide the area with cheap equipment. He regularly did business with Santa Cruz, and I know he always asked them about doing graphics. Then one day, probably late 1980 or early 1981, I got a call from him. He said that Santa Cruz was making this new skateboard magazine called *Thrasher*, and they wanted to know if we were interested in doing some type of write-up on the Boise skate scene. So I illustrated a large page and left the areas blank for the photo placements—this was when *Thrasher* was in the larger format. This "League of Wimpy Skaters" illustrated article was accepted and printed, and it opened up the door to start doing work with *Thrasher*. It started out slowly, but I gradually became a regular contributor.

It must have been 1983 when I got a call from Kevin Thatcher, the editor of *Thrasher*. He said this guy Jeff Newton, a regular contributing photographer to *Thrasher*, had talked with him about the possibility of having me do some artwork for his skateboard company Zorlac. I really didn't know much about Zorlac except that it was a Texas-based company and had ads in *Thrasher*, but I told KT, "Sure, have Jeff give me a call."

Zorlac / John Gibson / by Pushead / 1983

Zorlac / Craig Johnson (First Version) / by Pushead / 1984

Zorlac / Craig Johnson / by Pushead / 1986

Plan 9 / Misfits Evil Eye / by Pushead / 1986

Jeff was really cool, and it was something to look forward to, finally doing graphics for skate decks. Jeff sent over the new John Gibson deck so I could check it out. He wanted a revamped version of that image, so that was my first Zorlac illustration. It was cool to be able to do this graphic for John since I had met him at Del Mar years before, when he was riding for Caster and a Strople protege. He was really shy, but had a clean, fluid style. In conversations with Jeff, we decided to make the theme for Zorlac based on voodoo images, since he felt this was something that related to the South. So at the same time the new John Gibson was being illustrated, work was being done on a Shrunken Head design.

The original Shrunken Head illustration had a stake coming up through the chin and piercing out through the top of the head. The stake was short, since the idea I had was to have it fit between the trucks. That image was printed on the Double Cut deck. Jeff either couldn't make the image work, or he had personal difficulties with it, because he removed the stake. The Shrunken Head without the stake would become the image that represented Zorlac, with not only the skate deck, but T-shirts, stickers, banners, etc. For lettering, the "cactus" letters were created, and there was a whole alphabet I drew out. From that the first Zorlac logo was born. When these two skateboards were released to the public it changed the path of Zorlac forever.

The one thing you never thought you would hear—especially during this time when skateboarding was underground—was that shops would be complaining about the graphics. But Jeff was getting flack from people who thought the images were "satanic" or for "devil worshippers" or some nonsense like that. Jeff thought this type of reaction was great, but some stores wouldn't carry the products, and a few others would hide the decks under the

Craig Johnson / Dallas, TX / 1986 / photo by Grant Brittain

We all skated—and had been skating well before punk rock—so we knew Jeff Newton and the Zorlac crew. Jeff approached us about having a board, so me and Chris and Biscuit decided on a shape for the board. Tom Smith and his friend in San Antonio were making these homemade boards, where they would take a square blank and put a quarter down on each corner, trace that and then cut. They were these really great pig boards, and we wanted to do something like that. Of course, you have three people designing, so the final result was a sort of compromise.

The graphic was also a combination of the three of us. The banner and sacred heart were drawn on every board of Chris' and mine that a friend of ours made—Dogtown was a very big influence—and Biscuit had the two-headed baby skeleton. The anarchy skate symbol pretty much summed the Big Boys up. Plus, it was easy and quick to spray-paint instead of writing out "Big Boys." |Tim Kerr

Zorlac / Big Boys / by Tim Kerr and Randy "Biscuit" Turner / 1984

Zorlac / Metallica / by Pushead / 1987

Zorlac / Metallica / by Pushead / 1988

counter. To me, it was hard to believe this type of thought process still existed as well as the power struggle to try and control something as harmless as skateboarding.

So here I am, living in Idaho, sitting at a really small, round table doing these graphics, and someplace in the Bible-Belted South people are getting upset. When Jeff called up and said he had this new rider, Craig Johnson, who needed a graphic, I had already thought out that the next Zorlac graphic was going to be a voodoo doll—even before Zorlac was creating a bit of controversy. Jeff never said that we needed to tone it down, and personally, there are plenty of people in the world with opinions, and I would just do what I had been doing, not going toward either side.

The concept behind the voodoo doll was to make it look like the type that used a piece of fruit carved to be the head, with the fabric body, and have an anonymous hand holding it outward. I finished the illustration and sent it down, but didn't do a logo for Craig's name. So it was first printed with his name in type. When I received samples of that deck, I felt it needed a better name logo, but I just couldn't get it to match up. Not only was that bothersome, but I was starting to have my own issues with the whole way the head was looking when it was printed. Finally, a name logo was created, and it appeared on later runs of Craig's deck. I also did a new head to go over the original head.

Sometime after this graphic was finished, the move to San Francisco happened in late summer of 1984. Once in SF, the first new Zorlac graphic I created was the second Craig Johnson illustration, the Fire Demon—probably one of my favorite Zorlac designs.

With Jeff doing the three-and four-color spot screening process, I don't know if the colors ever really worked the way they should have, but then again, when Zorlac was based in Texas, colors were a whole other story. Some of the samples that were sent out, when you looked at them, the color balance was all off. It wasn't a registration problem, just unusual color matchings. I made some comments to Jeff about this, but he didn't say much. It wasn't until a little while later that I found out he was colorblind.

Not only were there illustrations being created for skateboards, T-shirts, stickers, etc., I also got the okay from Jeff to create ads for *Thrasher*. I'm not sure how many different ones were made, but during this time I met James [Hetfield] and Kirk [Hammet] from Metallica, and they asked me to do work for their band. Hanging out with them off and on, between tours and whatnot, James mentioned that while they were on tour he was bored, with nothing really to do before the show. Kirk agreed. We were talking about stuff they could do, and I suggested skateboarding. James got really excited about the idea. "Mannn, I love skateboarding!" he said. I told them I might be able to get some decks, and I called up Jeff to ask if he would send out boards for them. Metallica was still an underground band at this time in 1986, but Jeff was thrilled to do it.

One night I was fortunate enough to be able to ride with the guys in their tour bus to a gig here in SF with Ozzy. When the bus pulled into the dock, James and Kirk just hopped out of the bus and started skating all over the place. The crew there really had no idea these were actual band members. That night was a memorable experience.

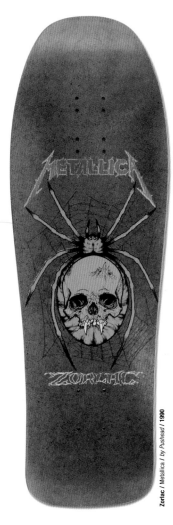

Zorlac / Metallica / by Pushead / 1989

Zorlac / Metallica / by Pushead / 1990

Zorlac / Gargoyle / by Pushead / 1987

Zorlac / Mark and Barry Abrook / by Pushead / 1989

Soon after that I mentioned the idea of Metallica having their own model, since they really skated and skaters were digging their music. They were into it, so I mentioned it to Jeff, who had already released the Big Boys deck, and he loved the idea. So the hookup was made for Jeff to meet the band when the tour took them into Dallas. Metallica's management worked out the contract so that I was in control of design and graphics—it specifically stated the work could not be done by anyone else.

Since I was already doing Zorlac ads, I asked James and Kirk if they would be interested in doing an ad. They were, and they came by my house for a photo shoot. There were two main areas the photos were shot, the first being this ten-inch mantle above the fireplace, where the two stood holding decks, dangling downward, tied by string to their fingers— a play on their latest *Master of Puppets* album. The other was shot in the bathroom, where I asked them to simulate skating in a bathtub. They grabbed some toothbrushes and toilet brushes and just started going at it. The John Gibson, Craig Johnson Fire Demon, and the Shrunken Head decks were placed inside the bathtub behind them. This turned out to be the ad "Hella Clean," based on the fact James said "hella" to anything!

The first Metallica deck was the Pirate—also known as the Damaged Pirate—a variation of the Damaged skull turned into a pirate. But skateboarding and Metallica took an unexpected turn when James broke his wrist on a downhill run somewhere out on tour. Time went by, James healed, and went back to skating. Then one day I got a call from Kirk asking if I wanted to go skating with him and James at the Blood Bowl pool over in Oakland. This would be their first time in a pool, and I was actually more concerned about Kirk skating in the pool, since I'd already seen

that James had better control of his board than Kirk. In the beginning, I was showing them lines in the pool, how to hit the wall, carve, hit tile, coping, and whatnot, but when James saw a grind, he really wanted to get that high up and do that.

Basically, for them it was just a session of hitting the front wall and getting the feel. Kirk was doing more carves in the bottom, and James was going for kick-turns on tile. I was showing Kirk something in the shallow end, when James took off to hit the front wall. When he came down, though, his weight was centered towards the back of the board and he fell backward. Naturally, he stuck his arms out to break his fall, and even though he was wearing the super heavy-duty wrist guards, he broke his wrist and the bone went through the wrist guard. He was screaming. After that, the management supposedly said he was done as a skater. I would do four more Metallica Zorlac decks after this.

As Zorlac's business was picking up, the company grew and skateboards became an inventory of unusual shapes. I threw my hat into the pile with the Gargoyle, a board that was created for the way I skated. I liked the big, round nose on the Jay Smith Powell Peralta deck, and I also liked a wide tail. Other than that, there really wasn't a need for much width, so it was cut down with a shape for grabbing. It was a functional design, but it also turned out to have a phallic shape, which was not done on purpose. There was a regular size and also a mini.

Around this time, Jeff sent me some contracts. He wanted Zorlac to become more of a legitimate business, in the professional sense, as the company grew bigger. I had my lawyer look over them, and he made a lot of changes. So no contracts were ever signed in the end. Soon after the

Zorlac / Scott Stanton / by Pushead / 1989

Zorlac / Aaron Deeter (Version 1) / by Pushead / 1990

Zorlac / Mark and Barry Abrook / by Pushead / 1990

Zorlac / Donny Myhre / by Pushead / 1991

Gargoyle deck was released, maybe I wasn't paying attention, or just focusing on doing more work, but there was a problem in Dallas. Payments were not arriving and it was becoming harder and harder to get Jeff on the phone. The debt to me was high and I was getting frustrated. I heard Jeff was trying to sell Zorlac, but each time the deal would fall through. Then for me, Jeff disappeared.

A call then came from a skate/music shop in Japan that I'd created the name and logo for, Violent Grind, and they informed me Zorlac had been sold to some unknown company in San Diego. At that stage, I was done with Zorlac, and started trying to see if I could work with another company, but the reality was most of these skateboard companies didn't pay much, if anything at all. It took awhile, but I received a call from one of the new owners of Zorlac, who wanted to fly up to SF to meet. I later learned they had acquired Zorlac and the license for the Metallica skateboards, but couldn't do the Metallica line without me, as they thought they could use someone else. Having no idea who these people were, there was a sense of hesitation, but they offered to pay all the money owed by Zorlac Texas, plus up the amount paid by Zorlac Texas per graphic. For this and the sake of continuity, I continued with Zorlac, since this was already an established identity I'd created. It was easy at first, but over time there was something different, and that something became frustrating.

The first real exposure to this was in Japan: while I was visiting the Violent Grind shop in Tokyo, I saw a Metallica board with the colors so far out of registration it should have been a reject. I checked over all the Zorlac decks in this shop and others in Japan, and they were all what would be considered rejects. This was infuriating to me, seeing something so butchered and pawned off. More problems continued to surface, from

salespeople starting to make suggestions on what designs should be based on shop requests—which were not of the Zorlac identity—to a bizarre type of alienation.

Since one of the owners was always making these statements that he hoped to one day pay me this large sum of money, I decided to start another company with Matt Barker, who was a screener there. Museum was created in 1991/1992, with the basic concept that this company would make limited-edition decks that came with a signed and numbered certificate, and rotate simple graphics at first, so as not to confuse anything with the work I was doing for Zorlac. At first, everything seemed to be going well, but then became one thing after another and I learned too much about who I was dealing with.

Once again, I was in Japan, and walked into a random shop that wasn't even skateboard related, where I saw a piece of clothing that had an embroidered image of one of my designs—not for either of the two skateboard companies—that was never authorized. I asked the shop owner where these garments came from, and in the most courteous manner this person brought out the actual invoice for me to look at. I should have been surprised, but I wasn't. Everything crumbled soon after that. Frustrated with Zorlac, Metallica sent them a cease-and-desist letter to stop producing anything related to the Metallica designs or name. Museum ended, and I stopped illustrating for Zorlac, basically just getting away from the skateboard industry for awhile, burnt out on the scams.

It wasn't until many years later that I would get a call from my old friend Matt [Barker], who was now working with Tod Swank at Tum Yeto. They were interested in a graphic for Josh Beagle, but the idea was way over the top and it never happened. Some more time would go by, and again

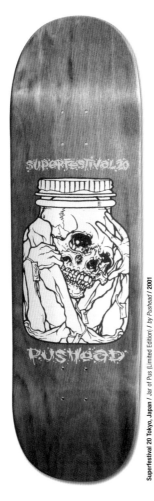

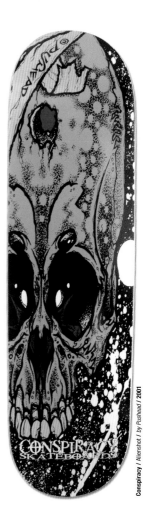

Museum / Fire Girl (Limited Edition) / by Pushead / 1992

Superfestival 20 Tokyo, Japan / Jar of Pus (Limited Edition) / by Pushead / 2001

Zero / Adrian Lopez / by Pushead / 2000

Zero / Adrian Lopez / by Pushead / 1999

Conspiracy / Alienshot / by Pushead / 2001

Matt called, this time for a pro skater named Adrian Lopez, who was riding for Zero, a brand distributed by Tum Yeto. He was a fan of the artwork, in part due to his late father. So it was a great thrill to be able to do skate graphics again in a new environment. From there it was over to Conspiracy, a company being run by my friend Lindsey [Kuhn], who I had worked with in getting silk-screened prints made by him.

The market has changed, as well as the strategy. There is a vintage market based on memories, while people try to capitalize on graphics without proper authorization. Skaters really don't know the difference—they're just fans, and they get excited when they see things they like. It's easy to be bitter, after having your work abused again and again with stories that would make people turn red with anger, but there is always that desire to create. And when you have skateboarding in your blood, you wish to be a part, to continue creating and feeling that excitement. At a trade show recently, the two guys who bought Zorlac—and now have a totally new operation—said to me, almost in unison, "We would have none of this if it wasn't for Pushead." Disposable? I don't think so! **| Pushead**

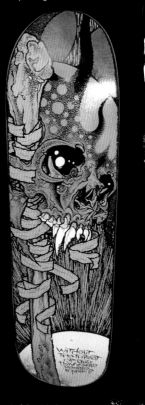

"Without the fear of god, how would people think?"

This is a one-of-a-kind deck created for the Canvas Exhibition, a charity event, with proceeds going to "Skaters for Portland Skateparks" on August 1, 2003. I chose to participate in this project due to the fact the Portland area represents a special place to me for skateboarding. It goes back to 1976, when on a high school contest trip to Portland from Boise, Idaho, I skated what seemed like ten miles to a surf shop to get my first set of sealed-bearing wheels—Road Rider 4s. From that moment on, skating was always kind to me in this great Northwest corner of the world.

When asked for a price to place on this deck, I insisted it be sold via an auction, so the bidders could decide the outcome. All money made from the winning bid I specifically requested be given to this charity. I was disappointed when I heard other artists wanted their cut and didn't care about the cause, especially when every artist was told in advance this was a charity exhibition.

| Pushead

Rip City / Black Flag / by Raymond Pettibon / 1984

Rip City / Black Flag / by Raymond Pettibon / 1984

Rip City / Black Flag / by Raymond Pettibon / 1984

Rip City / Black Flag / by Raymond Pettibon / 1985

The Black Flag decks were made in the early '80s, and I believe it was right at the time Henry Rollins joined the band. One of the guys who came into the store regularly was way into the punk scene. He'd become friends with Greg Ginn, and they came up with this idea Black Flag should make a skateboard. Our first meeting was in an apartment down in Lawndale, and we started talking to Greg about what kind of artwork they wanted to put on the boards.

We were sitting in this big double living room and at one end of the room there was a gray, industrial metal desk. So we're talking and I'm looking over there and I see someone is under the desk, kind of in a fetal position. I'm like, "Who is that?" Greg says, "Well, that's Henry. Henry's not talking today." Greg's brother was Raymond Pettibon, who did all the artwork for the band, and we had several meetings with him as far as doing art for the boards. He had definite ideas as to what should be on them and he could provide the artwork ready for production. We were just a shop at the time and weren't into production at all, so this was new for us.

The first run we did like 150 boards, and they were all hand-shaped and screened by Skip Engblom of Santa Monica Airlines fame. Skip brought them over to the shop, and he was so proud of himself because they were so beautifully painted and screened—unfortunately he put the Black Flag bars on backwards on the tail. My partner blew a fuse because we were under some pressure to get these things done, and here they were, all done wrong. So Skip scratches his head, takes them all back, and returns them to us where he'd taken a template and spray-painted them. So on all the original boards you can see over-spray on them—they're just ghetto looking.

Wes Humpston did the top logo for the decks. In 1979, we opened up here at the same time Dogtown had their own store on Barrington, so they obviously hated us. But Wes was somewhat disenchanted with the whole deal at that time, so we got a hold of him because we loved his art. He came in and was the nicest guy. The original logo was a checkerboard design, and he did about four or five more after that. | Jim, Owner of Rip City Skates, Santa Monica, California

JFA / JFA / *artist unknown* / 1985

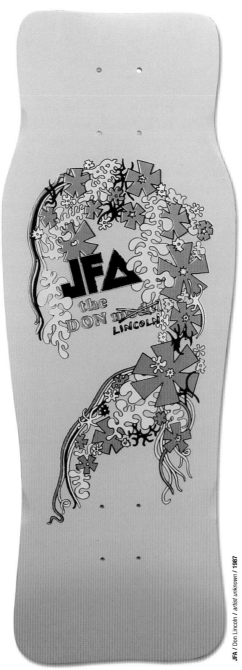

JFA / Don Lincoln / *artist unknown* / 1987

We came up with the idea of doing boards between the '84 and '86 tours. Up until then the whole band was riding either Duane Peters boards or Salba Bevels. We talked to Zorlac about putting them out, but ended up doing it ourselves. Even though we worked with Placebo, our record label, to put them out, we had to get somebody to build them. Initially it was Madrid, but they couldn't keep up in both quality and quantity, so we went with an outfit in Arkansas called Skateboard Plus that also made furniture. This kid did good quality wood. We wanted a stinger fishtail that was wide and had a long wheelbase—for big desert pipes and pools—and this board became the Paisley JFA model. The Don Lincoln was my attempt at having a board with two tails, but I screwed up and didn't leave enough nose—almost like a Ray "Bones"—but I don't go backward that much anyway. Alva told me it ruins your bearings. The graphics remind me of a Matisse cut-paper poster I had at the time and the Lincoln thing was from a Thrasher story I'd written where I replaced all of the key verbs and nouns in the story with the word Lincoln. I guess you had to be there. **Don Redondo, guitarist for JFA**

I've always preferred Indy 215s because of the maximum grindage they allow in backyard pools. So when we decided to make our own boards, I made sure we had one that was wide enough at eleven inches to handle those extra-large Indys. I was really into wearing thrift-store paisley shirts at the time, hence the graphics—the artist was the drummer for a Phoenix band called the Zany Guys. JFA has always carved a different line than most other bands. We've always played fast music, but when everyone else played nothing but generic hardcore, we threw in some funk and surf. When everyone was into leather jackets and black T-shirts, I took the paisley route. In a world where people buy punk regalia at the mall to be different like everyone else, what's more punk than paisley? **Brian Brannon, vocals of JFA**

Skull Skates

The Hosoi Hammerhead shape was designed by Christian, and the logo was designed by his father Ivan. The combination of the two was an original concept that, at the time, completely captured people's imaginations. It also didn't hurt that Christian was one of the best skaters ever. We eventually made the Hammerhead in three sizes—mini, mid, and max—and in countless color combinations. This was Skull's best selling model ever.

The Steve Olson with the checkers falling apart signified the ending of his longtime relationship with NHS. It was kind of a jab at them, because of the checkerboard designs that graced many of his Santa Cruz models.

The Dead Guys coffin shape and concept came from my brother Rick Ducommun, who gave me a ballpoint pen sketch on a napkin. I went to work the next day and banged out the shape and graphic. Rick was a comedian—actually more like a comedian's comedian—and the concept came straight from his personality.

We were living in Los Angeles at the time and he was doing the Hollywood routine. I think he started to notice some things about fame and the commodity of talent, and struck upon this idea that once a person reaches an iconic status in show business, there ceases to be any interest in the person as an individual and the industry turns humans into characters of their former selves. These icons don't even have to be living beings anymore, and the characters they constructed continue to live after the individuals are dead and gone.

The juxtaposition of players for the Dead Guys board was purposely chosen to illustrate the absurdity of fame: John Belushi, the coked-up comic who went out in a storm of excess; Elvis Presley, the hip-shaking, pill-popping superhero who finally had "left the building"; James Dean, the troubled, introspective youth who apparently couldn't drive worth a shit; Albert Einstein, the "genie's ass" who invented the most destructive scientific advances in the planet's history and is still loved by millions; Jimi Hendrix, who took his art and lifestyle to extremes that have yet to be matched; and Sid Vicious, the junkie punk poster boy who proved once and for all that he really didn't give a fuck. I think the universal appeal of the Dead Guys board is due to people's admiration of fame and the knowledge that no matter how famous one becomes, none of us can escape death, but by building a character we can extend our existence in the memories of others.

One time I was talking with the original guitar player for the Red Hot Chili Peppers, shortly after we began making the Uplift Mofo deck, and I asked what he thought of the boards. He said, "Something has to be changed," but unfortunately he couldn't tell me what exactly. We made boards for several bands, but we had to blow off one group because the graphics they sent us were full-color separations on film of these horrendous war atrocities. I told the dude we weren't gonna produce crap like that, and he got all bummed. **PD, owner of Skull Skates**

Skull Skates / Diehard / by PD / 1984

Skull Skates / Christian Hosoi / by Ivan Hosoi / 1985

Skull Skates / Dead Guys / by Rick Ducommun and PD / 1989

Skull Skates / Johnny Ray / by Johnny Ray / 1986

HACKETT
iron cross

HACKETT
street sicle

STEVE
OLSON
SKATES

SKATES

DUANE PETERS

TUB

SKATES

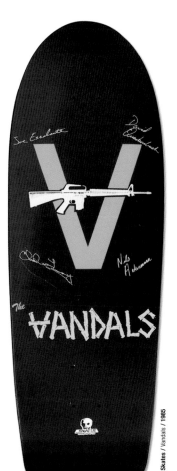

The VANDALS

GangGreen
KING OF BANDS

GENUINE   GENUINE

SKATE ALL DAY, DRINK ALL NIGHT
DRUNK AND DISORDERLY IN BOSTON,MA

SOCIAL

DISTORTION

RED HOT CHILI PEPPERS

Jim Phillips

Graphic art is an integral part of skateboarding. No other sport has embraced art as much. Skateboarding has inspired me and stretched my imagination more than anything else during my 40 years as an artist. This work provided a reward beyond the ability to make a living, and that's the interest and appreciation I'm fortunate to experience from skateboarders around the world on a daily basis. Many of these fans go to the lengths of having their favorite images tattooed on their bodies, a compliment that many of the world's greatest artists don't receive. It has also been one of my greatest pleasures to work with some of the best skateboarders of all time, especially during the golden years of transition from "sidewalk surfing" to its own unique sport, distinct and separate from surfing. My life and work continues to draw inspiration from my many years of skateboarding.

Art and skateboarding began for me as a child in the 1950s, when I skated a two-by-four with an orange crate nailed to the top and old metal roller-skate trucks and wheels nailed to the bottom. As a teenager, I began surfing, and two of my friends in the '70s, Rich Novak and Jay Shuirman, distributed polymer resin to surf shops. Because of their connections, they were the first to know of the development of urethane, which revolutionized skate-board wheels and became an industry.

As NHS, they contracted me to create art and advertising for Road Rider Wheels and Santa Cruz Skateboards. My first jobs were T-shirt designs and logos. The solid-wood decks of the time were simply branded, like cattle, with the Santa Cruz lettering, but silk-screening shortly became the state-of-the-art application and I created a slant-lettered logo that was double printed one color upon another as if it had a shadow.

Since my early teenage years, I instinctually put art on everything; my bedroom walls and schoolbook covers were canvases. Later when I could drive, my cars got the treatment: pinstripes, scallops, "Big Daddy" Ed Roth monsters, and psychedelic crazy-color. I also freelanced on the side, doing rock posters for outrageous bands like The Tubes, and was able to create intense designs for them. So I naturally saw the skate deck as potential art space. But the industry was steeped in the surf industry, and my suggestions were not embraced (since most skateboarders were

surfers, design trends followed surfboard styles and in the mid-'70s surf-boards usually employed a simple sticker-logo and not much else). There just weren't any graphics being done, and companies tend not to want to take risks or break down any doors without solid incontrovertible evidence of a market.

In the late '70s, Tim Piumarta, who started out at NHS as a shipper and deck screener and worked his way up to management, dabbled with the idea of an early graphic attempt and asked me to create something on the narrow wooden boards. So I created a one-color design of a winged dragon holding a sphere of the Santa Cruz logo. Although it was limited in production, the "Dragon" was definitely the first graphic for Santa Cruz decks, but it was ungloriously assigned as a mop-up piece.

In recent years, I heard a rumor that the graphic was an attempt by NHS to sell off some obsolete decks, because the market was moving into laminated wood and fiberglass decks like the five-ply. That may help explain the scarcity of those decks. A few boards have shown up with that design, but they're a latter day re-usage of the graphic years later. After the inevitably lackluster sales of these obsolete decks, the whole project was seen as a failure and it took a few years before NHS was ready to do more graphics.

Santa Cruz soon began to attract some of the best skate-boarders in the world, like Steve Olson and Duane Peters, who were among the new breed of "punk" skaters to emerge. Heavy metal music gave way to new-wave music and culminated in punk rock. Punks have been with us since Cain and Abel, but this modern rock brought with it an aggressive trend of Day-Glo jagged-geo pop art.

Steve Olson was formerly a clean-cut Adonis of several Santa Cruz ads, but he came in a few years older, sporting punkish sunglasses and spiky hair, and asked me to design his new nine-inch deck with a checker-board motif. Duane Peters was the consummate punker of the day and is recognized as a pioneer in skate punk-rock trends. He had particular ideas also and had me create his graphic consisting of several shredded Day-Glo diagonal bands with his name in Choc lettering. Unknown at the time, these were momentous events that ushered in a world of graphic art wild-ness that knows no limits.

Santa Cruz / 1976

Santa Cruz / Street Skate / by Jim Phillips / 1978

Santa Cruz / Steve Olson / by Jim Phillips / 1978

Santa Cruz / Team / by Jim Phillips / 1979

Santa Cruz / Stinger / by Jim Phillips / 1979

Santa Cruz / Steve Olson / by Jim Phillips / 1979

Santa Cruz / Steve Olson / by Jim Phillips / 1983

Santa Cruz / Steve Olson / by Jim Phillips / 1983

Santa Cruz / Duane Peters (Bootleg) / by Jim Phillips / 1980

Santa Cruz / Duane Peters / by Jim Phillips / 1985

Santa Cruz / Steve Alba / by Jim Phillips / 1981

I was really into Duane Peters' first Santa Cruz graphic, both the green and black and red and black stripe versions. At the time it was sort of dangerous looking in its simplicity. There were no traces of a hippy, soft-edge, surf-culture, nature-boy influence. It looked like a no-entry sign at a nuclear power plant. Gavin O'Brien

Duane Peters / Upland, CA / 1980 / photo by Jim Goodrich

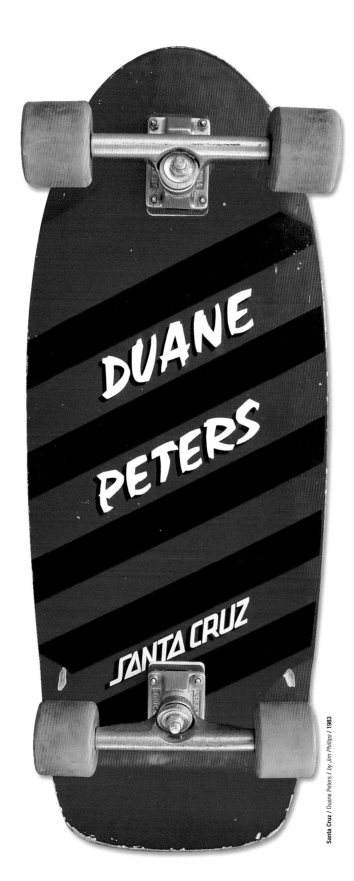

DUANE

PETERS

SANTA CRUZ

Santa Cruz / Duane Peters / by Jim Phillips / 1983

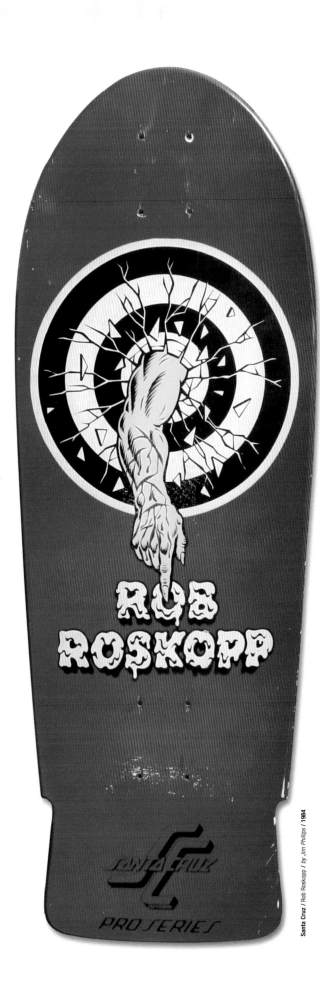

Santa Cruz / Rob Roskopp / by Jim Phillips / 1984

Santa Cruz / Rob Roskopp / by Jim Phillips / 1985

Santa Cruz / Rob Roskopp / by Jim Phillips / 1986

Rob Roskopp was a local young skater who was a good-looking-enough kid to fit into the NHS magazine ad-model mold, and he became sort of a protégé of Rich Novak. When the bosses nodded to a pro model, Rob asked me for a target with an arm popping out of the center all cut up and the finger pointing to his name at bottom. This deck was a turning point for Santa Cruz. Roskopp was a good skater and the graphic turned out to be a grabber.

By the following year, sales were impressive enough to feature another Roskopp model. Tim Piumarta called me to his office and said, "You know the target and the arm? Can you give it more, like more of the arm coming out or something?" I knew this was the beginning of something more for me, where I could finally cut loose with my imagination. I gave them some monster hands and feet breaking out from behind the target. Sales records began to shatter, and so did the target on the next model after that one, with a glimpse of a monster peering out behind the pieces, his arm extending down and grabbing and stretching the melting name. This was fun! I was able to feel free, and my artistic judgment became more respected by the management.

By the mid '80s, the market was heating to white hot, and it was time to pull out all the stops to stay on top. I gave the Roskopp IV the full treatment. The monster was getting aggro, and his flesh was beginning to break away with the target to reveal his inner robotic workings (no doubt an influence of my lifelong obsession with science-fiction books and movies). His arm, at this point in the sequence, had stretched and dragged Roskopp's name into an unreadable, melting oblivion.

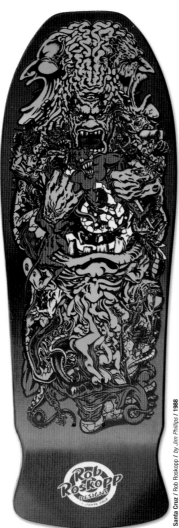

Santa Cruz / Rob Roskopp / by Jim Phillips / 1987

Santa Cruz / Rob Roskopp / by Jim Phillips / 1988

Santa Cruz / Rob Roskopp / by Jim Phillips / 1988

Santa Cruz / Rob Roskopp / by Jimbo Phillips / 1989

The pace was set, and many of the Santa Cruz models were selling at a rate of about 5,000 a month. Our skaters received a dollar per board and were getting wealthy. Some bought houses and Porsches and more than a few got in trouble with the IRS for bookkeeping naïveté. The NHS salesmen would come back from the trade shows with smiles, thanking me for "making their jobs easy." The pressure was on, but it was my medium and my life purpose fulfilled.

So for the Roskopp V I went all out, paling all my other efforts by comparison. I began by working much larger than before. Most of my deck art was done at actual size, because the size of a deck was the maximum size for a drawing table, top to bottom. When an artist draws on art board measuring 30-inches, the lower end is pushed into his abdomen as he leans across to draw or ink at the top, and it creates a limit. To overcome this, I cut the sketch in half and transferred it to two pieces of art board to draw the graphic oversize. I then reattached the final inking together for camerawork. The Roskopp V contained worlds within worlds, body parts, and surrealistic fantasy, the centerpiece of which was a face that turned into an altogether different face when looked at upside down. I considered this graphic to be my masterpiece in the sense of being a masterwork, one that I would continue on late at night after working on ads, logos, T-shirts, stickers, and a hundred other things that were done during the day. On top of this Roskopp series was the street model. This series began with the Face and it remained on the product list for many years. Eventually, in my studio, my son Jim Phillips Jr., or "Jimbo" as he soon became known, created a mini Roskopp with a deteriorated face.

My first graphic was a big departure from all the graphics Santa Cruz previously had. Ed "Big Daddy" Roth appealed most to me when I was growing up. I always admired his crazy monsters driving crazy looking hot rod cars. So when I first started thinking about graphics for my first deck I wanted to incorporate his type of style. I came up with the bullseye idea, and it was a local artist named Ray Garst who actually drew up the first graphic with the hand coming out and pointing to my name. Ray and I met a number of times before we got to that point. Then Santa Cruz wanted Jim Phillips to put his style to it because he was doing everything related to artwork for them. After I met with Jim, he redrew it by making it more cartoon-like, along the lines of Ed Roth's style. Jim suggested we continue to have the creature come out of the bullseye, making it a graphic series, and each time I was blown away at how well the progression turned out. After time went on, I learned it was just better to let Jim take over because he'd come up with the wildest things. Rob Roskopp

Santa Cruz / Jeff Kendall / by Jim Phillips / 1986

Santa Cruz / Jeff Kendall / by Jim Phillips / 1988

Santa Cruz / Jeff Kendall / by Jim Phillips / 1987

Santa Cruz / Jeff Kendall / by Jim Phillips / 1989

Jeff Kendall's series began around 1986, when NHS was picking up many new riders, and they made efforts to let the skaters decide what their graphic would be. Jeff was obsessed with this apocalyptic vision of technology and destruction of earth, as did Aldous Huxley in his 1932 novel *Brave New World*, which portrays a grim future where technology submerges human values. Jeff began his series by asking for these "hands of technology" breaking open earth like an egg, with an atomic mushroom cloud coming out, and it became a bright, colorful design that was relevant to many.

For his next deck, he wanted a freeway overpass with the retaining wall showing some graffiti. There were many cases where I would steer the art in another direction in an effort to make it better, and this was one instance. I suggested that a large scene of the freeway on a deck might not work well, and that the graffiti was the part we should build a graphic out of (I don't think there were any graffiti-style decks yet, whereas today there are lots of them). He asked for the "hands of technology" again, breaking through with the spray can. It was a popular deck and sold well.

The one skater who really got to me was Rick "Spidey" Demontrond. He was into the Sex Pistols art, which was fine, "God Save the Queen" and all that, and for his graphic he gave me a list of details, like a portrait of him holding a cup with this and that, leopard skin with safety pins, and so on. I always prided myself on satisfying the skater's requests, and I worked hard to fulfill each of his ideas, taking extra pains to make it as good as the idea would allow. I thought the finished design would stoke him, but when we met he wanted to redesign it with all kinds of little arbitrary changes. I was right in the factory office and I just stood up and said

loudly to his face, "NO!" The bosses were there and they knew I was right, so we just went straight to production with it.

Phillips Studios came into being in 1987. After working single-handedly at NHS for thirteen years off of my living room drawing board, I was cranking day and night with work stacked up to my eyeballs. I could only work on one design at a time, so when the bosses at NHS piled more work on my plate I would just add it to my list—and the list was running at about two-dozen items. So I went to the office and asked if there was room for a studio, but there wasn't. I then set out to find something to rent. I looked all day, but nothing turned up that was suitable.

That night there was a lot of noise going on next door. It was a small house my stepfather owned, and the tenant had moved out and sublet it to a bunch of UCSC students. They were busy partying, music was blaring, and then it struck me: why not get that place! I offered 100 dollars more to my stepfather. He thought about it and said, 'Well, the former tenant broke the lease to sublet, so why not make a 100 dollars more?' So he kicked out those idiots and I cleaned it up, painted, and installed a bunch of drawing boards and light tables. I went to yard sales that weekend and picked up a bunch of bar stools. Then I needed to hire some artists.

I wanted skateboarders, and I knew I couldn't run the bills up too much by offering high salaries, so I decided to get young kids who liked to draw and I would train them. I didn't realize then how much effort that training would take, but it worked out okay, even though it added a lot of extra time to my already overburdened schedule. First I asked Jimbo, but he was already working for a guy who did marbling on fabric.

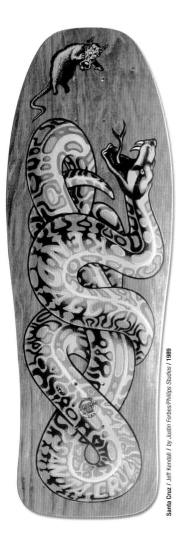

Santa Cruz / Jeff Kendall / by Justin Forbes/Phillips Studios / 1989

Santa Cruz / Jeff Kendall / by Kevin Marburg / 1990

Santa Cruz / Rick "Spidey" Demontrond / by Jim Phillips / 1987

Santa Cruz / Micke Alba / by Jim Phillips / 1986

I'd recently created a skateboard comic book titled "Road Rash," and used contributions from several young skate artists. Justin Forbes was the best of the bunch that I published, so I called him. He was available, as he'd washed out in his freshman year at UCSC. Justin and I worked together for a while, and I discovered he had exceptional talent for his age. I would do some drawing and have him ink, then I'd let him pencil and I'd ink. It was amazing to have a helper, and he gave me hope. I worked with Justin to create the Kendall Snake model. Jeff wanted it ready to eat a mouse, so we drew a guy's head on there like in the movie, The Fly. I had Justin trip out on the snakeskin pattern, and in it we spelled Kendall with Santa Cruz on the tail. Justin was good, and I began to trust and depend on him more, with guidance, to turn out a decent graphic.

I used to hang out with Spidey, and he was a Pistols fan. I think his whole idea was that he was going to "swindle a board out of Santa Cruz." I don't know what that was about, like if it was because he shouldn't have a board or if it was because they were swindling him or what. Anyway, I was just messing around, drawing something for this little book I made called The Book of Spide—I just collected stories about him, like stuff he had said—and I did a little drawing of him as Johnny Rotten on the mic. I don't know if he told me that's what he wanted or if I just drew it, but Spidey then took it to Jim Phillips. The final graphic was basically the same idea, but Phillips drew the face really good, like where it looked exactly like Spidey. Before it was more just a character. | Lance Mountain

Spidey sketch / 1986 / by Lance Mountain

Hosoi / Christian Hosoi / by Justin Forbes/Phillips Studios / **1986**

Hosoi / Christian Hosoi / by Phillips Studios / **1986**

Hosoi / Christian Hosoi / by Phillips Studios / **1987**

Hosoi / Christian Hosoi / by Phillips Studios / **1987**

Hosoi / Christian Hosoi / by Jimbo Phillips / **1988**

Hosoi / Christian Hosoi / by Phillips Studios / **1988**

Hosoi / Christian Hosoi / by Phillips Studios / **1989**

Hosoi / Christian Hosoi (Reproduction) / by Jim Phillips / **1990**

Christian Hosoi was another fantastic rider who came to NHS. His father, Ivan, ran a family skateboard company and asked Novak to produce the Hosoi line. We produced their existing V-Dot graphic in several variations, along with a few others dictated by Christian, like the Rising Sun design and a street photo of him at Venice Beach. When the order came down for a full-on Hosoi graphic, I was given free rein on the project and I wanted to create an abstract image, something worthy of Christian's abilities. So I laid out an oversized template and penciled in an outline of Hosoi grabbing air. I told Justin about a drawing game my grandfather and I used to play, where we would combine our talents and take turns adding elements. Justin worked on the graphic during the day as I worked on other projects, and then at night I would go into it with new stuff. It was fun, and we went on like that for about a week.

When Jimbo saw that deck, he could see we were having fun and he quit his other job to work for me. Jimbo already had a lot of drawing experience and some art knowledge learned from watching Dad. Next we had orders for the Hosoi street model, and I wanted to take the abstract idea to the next level with a Picasso-looking skater. I put Jimbo on that one; he did a good job of inking it, and it came out pretty cool. We created a few other Hosoi models, like the Stained Glass graphic, a series of color images divided by letters of his name. It was great to work with Christian, and my artists were thrilled to meet such a superstar skater and work on his projects.

With three studio artists there was more good spirit and a great flow of ideas. Things were looking up, but I was still losing ground with the extra burden of training, so I hired a few more guys. Andreas Ginghofer was one of Jimbo's friends and lived just down the street. He couldn't draw very well, but he cut Rubylith overlays very precisely, so I made him the studio color-overlay cutter, and there was enough of that work to keep him busy full-time. That was a tedious job that had taken a lot of my time, so it was a step forward.

Another "Road Rash" comic artist, Johnny "Mojo" Munnerlyn, applied to NHS, and I gave him a test to design a comp sticker. He did a pretty good job of it, so he was hired. He had some good ideas and proved to be a consistent, quality worker. He knew another kid named Kevin Marburg who

was able to draw, and I took him in. Keith Meek was a Santa Cruz skater who wanted to get out of the deck-printing shop over at the factory, so I also hired him, thinking it would be good to have a pro skater's input. Keith actually had some talent and created a few good pieces, probably the most well known was the Oops deck. My wife Dolly was doing my typesetting and bookkeeping.

We were finally making headway, everybody got in the groove, and it was beginning to work. The spirits of these young studio artists was high. Ideas flew around the room constantly, and they would flow and grow as each took his turn adding to it, and always with great humor. I put them under pressure, and in return, they stretched their abilities beyond my expectations in an amazing display of team effort. There were squabbles, and someone even got punched in the nose, but they soon got over it and pulled together. It was one of the best experiences of my life to train and work with these talented kids, and the creative spirit alive in there was a great consolation to the stress I was under.

Some of the riders would come into Phillips Studios not knowing exactly what they wanted, but wanted to control it. So we would send them into our extensive art book library. I had a decent pile of art books to begin with, but after I opened the studio I started buying many more at the flea market or yard sales: books of all sorts of art, reference books on various subjects, or anything that was graphically stimulating.

Out of the book and scrap file archive, Jeff Grosso found a sketch of a vampire bat drawn from a pulp science-fiction story illustration by Virgil Finlay and ordered it up. To balance out the evil he wanted an angel flying overhead carrying a banner with a heart on it. After the bat, Jeff reverted, I guess. That is, he started wanting toys on his graphics, starting with a blue stuffed toy donkey and progressing into the Goofy-Face Grosso logo. Now to me the Goofy-Face was anti-art, and it was fodder for jokes around the studio, but I tried to both give the rider what they wanted and keep the management happy. I put Jimbo on the Goofy-Face deck and he did as good as could be expected, with a sort of tripped-out border. Then Jimbo did the classic Grosso Evolution, showing the rise and fall of Jeff's skating career. That was cool.

Hosoi / Christian Hosoi / by Jim Phillips and Justin Forbes / 1988

Schmitt Stix / Jeff Grosso / *by John Lucero* / **1986**

Santa Cruz / Jeff Grosso (Prototype) / *by Jim Phillips* / **1987**

Santa Cruz / Jeff Grosso / *by Jim Phillips* / **1987**

Santa Cruz / Jeff Grosso / *by Jim Phillips* / **1987**

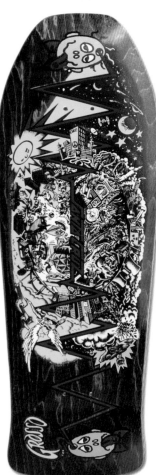

Santa Cruz / Jeff Grosso / *by Jeff Grosso and Jimbo Phillips* / **1988**

Santa Cruz / Jeff Grosso / *by Jim Phillips* / **1988**

Santa Cruz / Jeff Grosso / *by Jimbo Phillips* / **1989**

Santa Cruz / Jeff Grosso / *by Justin Forbes and Andreas Ginghofer* / **1989**

disposable|

Jeff Grosso

My Schmitt Stix graphic is my favorite. The Baby Doll was my first pro graphic, and it was just a real special time in my life to turn pro and have my dreams realized. I wish I'd appreciated it a lot more while I was in it. I was real proud of my first Santa Cruz graphic, too. The idea was mine. I was caught up in the whole yin and yang, good and evil trip, because I was completely fucked at seventeen.

I tried to get John Lucero to do my Santa Cruz art, but I was bumping heads with [NHS] because they had exclusivity with Jim Phillips. So whenever I got with Phillips, I nitpicked everything he did. The graphic was supposed to be satanic and evil, but it looked like something out of Walt Disney. The original Demon drawing was pretty rough—one of the wings was totally lopsided—and there were only four to six boards made before I had the graphic changed. I was a real asshole to Phillips ... I was upset

that I'd left Schmitt Stix. Well, what I wanted to do was ride for Schmitt Stix, but I wanted to be treated the way Santa Cruz treated me. I couldn't have the best of everything, so there was just no pleasing me.

I hated the Toy Box graphic. I had long hair back then, and I hated the way Phillips tried to make me into the baby doll, when John had already made me into the baby doll. I didn't like the way it was drawn, and I hated the way the doll was all patchwork-quilted like it was made by a loving grandmother. The baby doll wasn't supposed to be like that. He was supposed to be like this "jester of love I'm gonna blow everything up" bratty thing, but whatever ... we're getting way too in-depth about the theories behind people's graphics. I'm not here to bash on Phillips, he's a great artist; he did make up the Indy logo and all kinds of really cool graphics, but once you have John Lucero draw a graphic for you these other guys don't really suffice. It's like getting a shot of smack and going back to weed—it doesn't really work. I hate using that as an analogy, but since I'm in rehab right now I will.

The Alice in Wonderland graphic came about after smoking cocaine for three days with a friend. We had one of those old hippie stickers you get out of the bong shops on our refrigerator door, and we'd spilled a bunch of freebase cocaine on the kitchen floor. We were scraping it back out from underneath the refrigerator

Santa Cruz / Jeff Grosso Top Logo / by Jimbo Phillips / 1989

when he looked up and saw that sticker. He goes, "You should do that as a graphic with like your baby doll running with Alice 'cause they're in love." He hassled me for weeks afterward, insisting that I have that as a graphic. So I did it as a "tribute/shut the hell up" thing.

There was never a cease-and-desist order for the Alice graphic. I don't know who came up with that, but it's a total fabrication. There was a cease-and-desist order from Coke, and that graphic came out before the Alice, so maybe there was fear of retaliation from Disney. But I can't see this deck being worth thousands of dollars today if everyone knew there wasn't a cease-and-desist order. A large amount of them were made, and no one really cared because it was a mini-model and the only people who bought them were little kids. My Coke board meant a lot to me, though, because I actually got Santa Cruz to do something that was wholeheartedly me. It was my way of sending a message about being a disposable hero and to enjoy the laughs because I'm gonna die.

It was trippy back then ... skateboard graphics were a way of communicating with your sponsors and the skateboarding public in general. The Baby Doll, Demon, and Coke graphics all had meanings behind them. One, I was a punk; two, I was trying to figure out if I was gonna remain a bratty, little stuck-up kid; and three, I caved in and stayed the punk I became in later years. That's the tale of those three graphics. | Jeff Grosso

What is referred to as the Santa Cruz Skull deck was created sometime around '88-'89. It was an experiment by NHS to see if a deck without a pro-rider could cut it on the market. (Prior to this model—after the early '80s, that is—a board was always attached to a rider for his endorsement to be accepted by "skate star-crazed" buyers.) I was called into the office and it was proposed to me as a "Red Dot" generic board. I was quite willing to develop a graphic idea from scratch, and for once be free of the yoke of trying to please riders by interpreting their ideas and transforming them into something I thought was viable. So I went back to my studio to work up my first idea.

For quite a few years I kept away from skulls on decks, since our biggest competitor, Powell Peralta, had so much of that, and artists like V.C. Johnson and Pushead had covered that genre pretty well. But I had a good-sized skull collection on display at my studio, for anatomical and inspirational purposes, and we had a few human skulls, including a 200 year-old woman, and Jimbo's fetus skull, which was about the size of a tennis ball. We also had plenty of animal skulls, some of which we cleaned from dead animals formerly living under the studio. Anyway, that night I noticed a lamp shining on the 200 year-old skull, with most of its left eye socket in shadow. I sketched out a thumbnail and thought it was unlike any of the other skulls on the market. I considered my self-imposed policy of no skeletal depictions, but the image seemed to beckon to me. I thought, "Well nobody has a corner on skull images, they've been rendered by artists for thousands of years." So I started sketching it out oversize.

I first began messing around with contouring and shading with little skulls. The idea was to simulate bone texture, so they had to be small and plentiful, and by the hundreds. There was no way I could portray the overall effect for review in a pencil sketch, so I decided to go straight to ink and shine getting final approval. So after I sketched the contour blue-line and began inking tiny skulls, I got the idea to include faces, ghouls, and monsters. I went to our archive and found our box of Famous Monsters of Filmland magazines that Jimbo and I collected when he was growing up. We were big fans of sci-fi and monster movies. It was one our biggest thrills to see every horror movie that was available on our half dozen channels, and I'd make a list on Friday for each weekend. We always decorated the list by drawing monsters from the list around the border—it was a fun father/son thing. I began thumbing through these old raggedy copies, and after a few hours of getting hung up in them, realized that it was going to take forever to render all of them. I looked fondly over to my studio copier, a large 17-inch bed with a wide arrange of functions. It was hard won from the management, but it was the best machine available at the time. I turned the project into a combination pen & ink and collage, which by no means made easy work of it. I copied and recopied, reduced and adjusted contrast on the faded grey images. From Lon Chaney to Peter Cushing, King Kong to Dr. Jeckyl, they're all in there. From my pile of little faces I pasted up a few and then connected them with ink. It was one of those designs where the time goes away and suddenly the sun is coming up. I repeated the skull medley into the five color separation layers, deciding on bone tones as the base color scheme—later, Mike Nyder, the screen printer, came up with using the reds and yellows which looks the best. For identity, I created a degenerated image of the red dot by moving it on the copier as it scanned. It was designed for under the jaw at first but was eventually moved to the tail to be larger.

My original idea was to keep the light and shadow effect in force by ordering them on black decks. Often, once the design was turned in to the printing department, there was no controlling what colors of ink or deck was used. They liked to mix up the colors and sometimes it worked. But in this case I was dismayed that many were printed on clear wood, purple, or whatever. The light color decks not only dissipated the lighting effect I was pursuing, but with my keyline border now showing, it turned the skull shape into an oblong. It was an unintended look but I didn't bother crabbing about it, I was too busy to worry about graphics that were out the door.

Over time the Skull deck became one of NHS's biggest sellers and more than held its own against rider-based models (the sales response was good enough to create a sequel, which turned out to be what we called The Creep). The T-shirt version is still being produced 15 years later. I've probably received more comments about the Skull than any of my other skate graphics.

Santa Cruz / Skull / by Jim Phillips / 1988

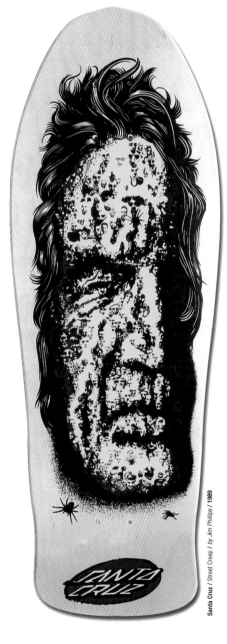

Santa Cruz / Street Creep / by Jim Phillips / 1989

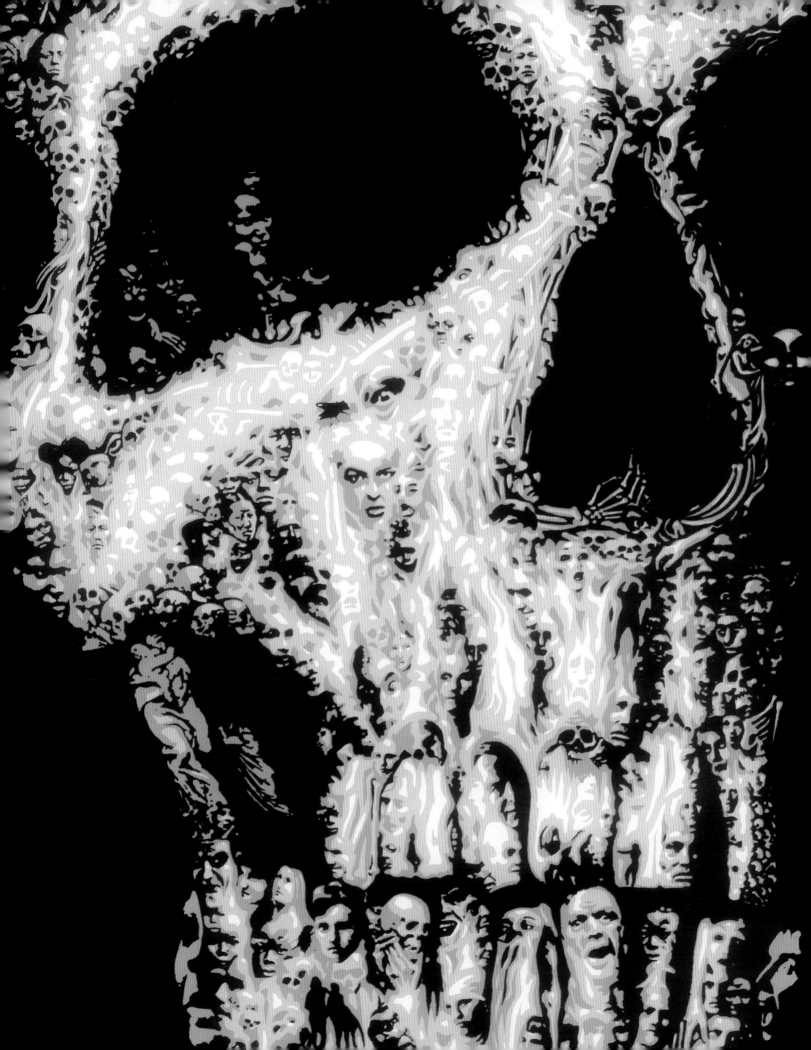

Santa Cruz / Steve Alba / by Steve Alba and Jim Phillips / 1987

The witchdoctor deal came specifically from me. I was getting into indigenous people's roots, and reading a lot about slaves from Africa and how voodoo arose. I was also into the blues and how the song of protest came about in dance, singing, and rhythms as a form of getting back at the boss man by keeping their traditions alive, which the slave traders tried to suppress. This, in turn, lead me to American Indians and their social and religious ceremonies that gave thanks to the gods of various things, like food, hunting, and creation. This brought a spiritual awakening in me that seemed way out of place in my prediction of the future, and how people and society today shunned many of the beliefs of pure living the way people used to. That seemed the way to go instead of certain religions where missionaries deemed the savages were into the Devil because of the way they lived. This was ludicrous to me— live and let live.

All this inspired me to draw up my witch doctor tattoo, which went through various stages, but the mask was always the integral part. I was never very good at drawing bodies, but tried anyhow. I then took the design to Bob Roberts, a famous tattoo artist who did all the musicians I looked up to. Bob fixed up the body, and from there my thought was to incorporate it into a graphic. I came up with the pot, the girl was stolen out of a Playboy magazine, the heart was a voodoo "veve" I got out of a book—the voodoo people drew these on the ground in white chalk when they made their spells—and I drew it all up.

John Lucero did the letters and the stuff coming out of the flames. He was going to fix it more but never got around to it, so I redid it one more time and then gave it to Jim Phillips, who changed things a bit. I was bummed because it took the original meaning away, and he put eyeballs on it because he knew I always wore "evil eyes" to ward off evil spirits. He did make the chick look better, because I suck at faces.

So the whole idea took off from there and ended up on the top graphic for my Tiger model, too. That idea came from an old pre-Civil War story about the slave traders who brought slaves and animals from Africa to the South and Eastern seaboard. Black panthers came from these ships and escaped, bred in the wild, and in turn started killing livestock and humans. The populace tried to kill these panthers by cornering them in the cane fields and setting them on fire to kill off the evil spirits that made the panthers kill other animals and people for taking them from Africa to America. So the graphic reflected that, and Phillips did that one, too. I think he drew some of the most influential graphics. Nobody even came close to his level of professionalism.

Steve Alba

Santa Cruz / Steve Alba / by Steve Alba and Jim Phillips / 1989

Santa Cruz / Jason Jessee / by Jim Phillips / 1988

Santa Cruz / Jason Jessee / by Jim Phillips / 1988

Santa Cruz / Gregor Rankine / by Jim Phillips / 1989

Santa Cruz / Claus Grabke / by Jim Phillips / 1987

Santa Cruz / Claus Grabke / by Jim Phillips / 1988

Whenever Jason Jessee came to the studio, he would ride his Harley with his skateboard strapped on the back. He'd show the boys his tats, and they'd make sketches and then go skate up and down the street until they were sweaty, then bust out the Dews from the stickered-up studio refrigerator. Some of the Jessee graphics were inspired by his tattoos, like the Neptune and Sun God. Jason liked art, and he liked our work. He was an inspiration to our studio.

Claus Grabke was Santa Cruz's premier European skater and a true gentleman. He would come to the studio on his trips from Germany and always skate out in the street with the boys from the studio. Claus loves clocks, and he told us of his clock collection in his ramp-filled Gothic castle. I suggested an exploding clock, and Claus loved the idea. I drew him into the design falling out from the gears. After that model, he asked for the nightmarish and Dali-esque melting clocks trying to get him. I took some Polaroids of him skating to sketch from. A while later, Grabke asked for a skating alarm clock, which we had fun with. Working with skaters from around the world, like Claus, Toyoda of Japan, Gregor Rankin from Australia, Bo Ikeda from Hawaii, and others broadened our awareness of skating around the planet and brought the world a little closer.

I parted with NHS in 1990. It had to do with being asked to relocate my studio to creatively restricting confines, which I rebelled toward at first and was given 365-day notice, but after which I asked to stay on. I really couldn't understand why I was let go, and no one could tell me. I was forced to fight for quality work, progressive graphics, and to bring innovations as I did by introducing computers and copiers. Maybe I cared too much. There's a lot of water under the bridge now, and I don't want to dwell on the negatives, but I did love to create skateboard art, and I felt that I was an asset to the company and to skateboarding.

Jim Phillips

Santa Cruz / Sergie Ventura / by Johnny "Mojo" Munnerlyn / 1989

Santa Monica Airlines / Mike Conroy / by Johnny "Mojo" Munnerlyn / 1989

Santa Cruz / Jeff "Ffej" Hedges / by Johnny "Mojo" Munnerlyn / 1989

Santa Cruz / Jeff Kendall / by Johnny "Mojo" Munnerlyn / 1991

Johnny "Mojo" Munnerlyn

A friend of mine who worked for Santa Cruz told me Jim Phillips was looking for artists to help out in his studio. I tried out for a job in November 1988 and was lucky enough to get to work for him. He hired several other young artists around that time because there was getting to be too much Santa Cruz work for him to handle. I really enjoyed working with him. He was my art hero at the time, so it was the ultimate dream job. Just getting to see him do his work was amazing. We all looked up to him and were big fans of his Santa Cruz graphics.

The first deck graphic I got to do was for Sergie Ventura. He rode for Hosoi, and Christian and his dad Ivan came in to discuss the graphic with Phillips. Ivan brought a napkin that he had scribbled the basic idea on. It was a big fork, which was something Sergie was into—I guess he and his friends actually branded themselves with hot forks, and it represented East Coast pride.

Jimmy asked me if I'd like to do it, and I was so stoked to actually get to do a graphic. All said and done, I ended up doing four deck graphics and a lot of wheels, T-shirts, decals, ad artwork, etc. while I worked for Phillips: Sergie Ventura, Mike Conroy, Jeff "Ffej" Hedges, and Jason Jessee's second Neptune graphic with the mermaid.

When Jason Jessee came in to talk to Jimmy about a new graphic, he didn't have any ideas and he still liked his Neptune graphic. So he asked if we could just make it gnarlier. Jimmy said yes and asked me to

do it, so I redrew it with tattoos and more skulls and stuff, but it was very similar to the original graphic. The thing I came up with was doing a mermaid for the tail art. Jason really liked it—he even got the mermaid tattooed on his leg—and we made the mermaid a decal and T-shirt. Looking back, I think we should have replaced the whole Neptune graphic with the mermaid, but we didn't think of that then.

To make a long story short, things between Phillips and Santa Cruz deteriorated until they went their separate ways in 1990. I ended up working in-house for Santa Cruz with Kevin Marburg. We started a new art department and handled all the Santa Cruz art. There was a time in the early '90s that we tried to get away from that Phillips style and change the image of Santa Cruz, because it really wasn't what was happening anymore. Also, slick-bottom boards came out, and suddenly we could do photos and full-color artwork. It got us through that period, but the brand lost its focus.

That was a difficult time, with graphics changing very fast. No matter how hard we tried to shake it, Santa Cruz continued to be defined by Phillips' artwork. I can appreciate it all now, but at the time it was frustrating as an artist not being able to escape his influence. Kevin stayed for several years and then left to help form Sonic Skateboards and do their graphics. I stayed until 1999, when I left to work freelance. **Johnny "Mojo" Munnerlyn**

I was twelve when I scored a Thrasher from my brother, and there was a Neil Blender interview. It was just a one-page interview, but it was the best interview ever. I was reading it in church, and I remember getting so fired up my mom told me put the magazine down. I looked at her and said, "I have to go to the bathroom," so I finished it in the men's room because moms don't go in there. Anyway, it fucked me up. Then I went to Del Mar and met Neil. I was twelve, and then everything went nuts. He was an adult, way intimidating. I told him I just read his interview, and he said, "Oh great." Then I told him my dad was coming back and I had to drop in. He said, "All right, roll in frontside." He wins ever since. That's all I ever really cared about was his stuff and Mark Gonzales'.

In 1988 I wanted to get this whole ocean scene on my back, and I got the first tattoo from Mark Mahoney. Then I went to NHS and they're like, "Okay, you get a board. You got any ideas for graphics?" I'm like, "Holy shit! No, but my back is all tatted." Well, I had one tattoo on my back, so Jim Phillips came over to NHS, and I showed him my back. He said, "Great, jump up on the copy machine. We'll copy your back and go from there." He was very cool and didn't fuck around. So they sent me some sketches, and it was great. They printed it, I got it—I was seventeen and ready to destroy my body with it. I was fired up, so I went to Neil to show him the board. "Look what I brought you, Neil, my board. Don't you fuckin' love it?" He looked at it and just said, "Not at all." I'm still suffering post-trauma syndrome, it was so great.

Steve Keenan or Bob Denike said it was cool if me and John Schuler went to Phillips' house, his studio, and it was way cool. He was really neat. We were blown away. The Neptune graphic was the only one that he and I actually were in direct communication on. The rest just got filtered through the studio. They were all somewhat my ideas. The Flames graphic—my friend John drew it on a blank deck. I was way stoked, and then Johnny [Mojo] redrew it perfect. But if it were now, I would have the flag upside down and backward and it would say "Jesus died, eat shit." | **Jason Jessee**

Santa Cruz / Tom Knox / by Kevin Marburg / 1989

Santa Cruz / Eric Dressen / by Kevin Marburg / 1989

Santa Cruz / Hugh "Bod" Boyle / by Kevin Marburg / 1989

Santa Cruz / Tom Knox / by Kevin Marburg / 1990

Daniel Clowes lived in Chicago, and my friend Dan Field knew him, so I flew out there and went to his house and told him I wanted something like the Thee Headcoats album cover he did. He also had a three-legged turtle at his house, so I told him to put that in there, too, but that's all I told him. I was just stoked having him do my name in that cool lettering he does. It took eight months to print those decks because NHS had their woodshop in Wisconsin print the wood plies before they laminated the boards, and it took way longer than they thought. Clowes didn't like how dark the colors came out. I think we paid him 500 dollars for it, but I used to send him tons of the boards, stickers, and shirts, and he'd sell them at comic-book conventions. | Corev O'Brien

Santa Cruz / Corey O'Brien / by Daniel Clowes / 1991

Santa Cruz / Tom Knox / by Johnny "Mojo" Mannerlyn / 1991

When my first board was going to come out on Powell Peralta I was still pretty much in dreamland. It was the only team I had ever wanted to skate for, and I was always waiting for them to call me in the office and say, "Okay Jim, the gig is up. You're nowhere good enough to be on the team." But then when Powell showed me the graphics concept for my first board, I was so disappointed. It was this terrible snake thing that I just wasn't into at all. I wanted my first board to mean something, almost like a tattoo that would last forever. I can't remember the exact chain of events, but I think it went like this: saw weird snake graphics, Powell starts to lose focus on skating, George not looking at me when I tried to talk to him at a meeting, and finally Natas calling me up and asking me what the hell I was doing and offering me a spot on SMA.

But the SMA Joker board was a weird one, too. Natas and I were at the premiere for Public Domain—I hadn't summoned up the courage to quit Powell yet—and during an intermission he asked me if I wanted to see some graphic ideas for my first board. I was really into comics at the time, and Natas had these great drawings of this morose superhero sitting on a gravestone with this evil character looking down on him. Obviously tongue-in-cheek, the main guy had like a "Super T" on his chest for Thiebaud. This was clearly funny to us, but I guess they took it pretty literally at NHS. Later, when we saw what Phillips Studios did for the actual art, we were a bit surprised. Using the Joker on the board may have been a little of our idea, but the case may still be open as far as statutes of limitations go, so for the record it was 100 percent NHS's doing.

For my last SMA board I wanted to do something a little looser. I was going through a rough time, feeling a little alienated, out of step with what was going on around me. I was touring my ass off nonstop and I would come home to find things different. People had changed, spots were gone, and all I could think about was the next trip.

I was really crazy about Natas's art, so I asked him to draw the main guy drinking some coffee, pondering his next move. Andy Howell did a little drawing for it, too. The robber dropping the fish tank was a weird, arty way of how I sort of felt at the time, like a thief who wasn't really pulling it. The giraffe with the slingshot was just something funny I wanted on there. I think Natas actually wrote the poem about sanity, possibly while listening to some Bad Religion. I was real happy with the board because all the pieces meant so much to me. Unfortunately I don't think it went over real well in shops. Should have stuck with the Joker motif.

Jim Thiebaud

Santa Monica Airlines / Jim Thiebaud / by Justin Forbes / 1989

Santa Monica Airlines / Jim Thiebaud / by Justin Forbes / 1989

Santa Monica Airlines / Jim Thiebaud / by Natas Kaupas and Andy Howell / 1990

Santa Monica Airlines / Julien Stranger / by Julien Stranger and Natas Kaupas / 1990

Santa Cruz / Jaya Bonderov / by Kevin Marburg / 1992

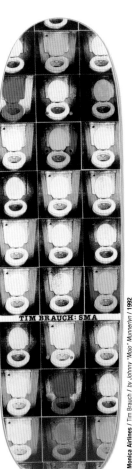

Santa Monica Airlines / Tim Brauch / by Johnny "Mojo" Munnerlyn / 1992

Santa Monica Airlines / Tim Brauch / by Johnny "Mojo" Munnerlyn / 1992

Santa Cruz / Tom Knox / by Gavin O'Brien, Tom Knox and Johnny "Mojo" Munnerlyn / 1992

Santa Cruz / Tom Knox / by Nathan Carrico / 1992

Santa Monica Airlines / Jason Adams / by Nathan Carrico / 1992

Santa Cruz / Ryan Aningalan / by Kevin Marburg / 1994

Santa Cruz / Team / by Johnny "Mojo" Munnerlyn / 1996

Santa Cruz / Ron Whaley / by Johnny "Mojo" Munnerlyn / 1996

Santa Cruz / Ron Whaley / by Johnny "Mojo" Munnerlyn / 1997

Santa Monica Airlines / Tim Brauch / by Johnny "Mojo" Munnerlyn / 1994

Santa Cruz / Chet Thomas / by Johnny "Mojo" Munnerlyn / 1992

Creature / Darren Navarrette / by Johnny "Mojo" Munnerlyn / 1996

BARKER
BARRETT
CREATURE

Creature / Barker Barrett / by Johnny "Mojo" Munnerlyn / 1994

That Sonic board was my whole skateboarding life summed up in one graphic: the clown on that board was me. On skateboard tours I literally drank myself to the point where I was physically sick and mentally ill. I had put a balloon animal gun to my head that I had wished was a real gun many times.

If you look in the background, the circus tent is burning down and all of the animals are running away; the circus is destroyed. During the course of my skateboard "career," I somehow managed to burn nearly every bridge I had made with every sponsor I had. If you ask most of my former sponsors, they will tell you that I was the worst rider they'd ever sponsored. I went into the skateboarding scene as a happy-go-lucky clown who loved to skate and make friends. I left the scene as a sad, depressed, and drunken clown who wanted nothing more than to die. That graphic depicted the way my entire journey through skateboarding happened to pan out. For the record, I'm doing much better now. I'm an assistant pastor at a church, and I'm feeling pretty good these days.

| Simon Woodstock

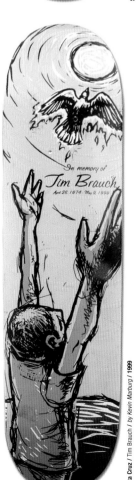

In memory of
Tim Brauch
April 26, 1974 - May 9, 1999

Santa Cruz / Tim Brauch / by Kevin Marburg / 1999

Sonic / Simon Woodstock / by Mike Prosenko and Kevin Marburg / 1995

simon woodstock - sonic

Sonic / Simon Woodstock / by Kevin Marburg / 1994

When Sonic was kicking I really pushed for an anti-tagging graphic, because I hate that crap and I wanted to piss off all the knuckleheads in skateboarding who condoned it. The result was the Simon Woodstock Model Citizens deck that featured clowns catching taggers in the act and pounding their faces in. Ha-ha, take that, yo!

Simon was great to work with when he was with Sonic. We sold about seventeen-gazillion of his signature boards, especially the Circus deck. Simon was unique, and skateboarders at the time, especially other pros, couldn't understand that uniqueness. Wearing your own clothes and doing your own tricks was not in the '90s rulebook of skateboarding. I hope people are more relaxed now.

| Gavin O'Brien

Garry Davis

In 1984, I made a fictitious pro model deck for a cartoon character of mine named Kent Watson. This deck measured 9 3/8" x 30" and gradually curved inward on the sides going back toward the tail, abruptly curving out just before the rise of the kick—giving the overall shape the vague appearance of a bomb. I spray-painted the deck yellow, then stenciled and Magic-Markered on a simple eyeball graphic with cartoony lettering in white and blue—all topped off with Kent's signature at the bottom. I don't remember what inspired the eyeball graphic, I probably just thought, "That would look hot!" Plus, no one else had done it. I made the Kent Watson deck mainly because I thought it would be funny to skate around on a pro model for a pro who didn't even exist. I ended up riding it for quite a few months at Del Mar Skate Ranch and many other places.

Hand drawn by Garry S. Davis / 1984

Tracker / GSD / by Garry S. Davis / 1985

Tracker / GSD / by Garry S. Davis / 1986

The following year, Tracker—who I had been skating for since 1982—asked me if I wanted a pro model. Who would say no to such an offer? I shrunk down the Kent Watson shape a bit to 9" x 29 1/2" and refined the eyeball graphic—with rub-down line screen, no less—replacing Kent Watson's name with my initials, GSD, in the same cartoony lettering—all supported by a Tracker logo that I designed exclusively for this deck, plus the words "Banks/Curbs" and my signature. As it turned out, this became the first-ever signature-model street deck.

In 1986, I changed my graphics with an enlarged close-up photo of part of my face covered with drawings of pterodactyls flying around, which was inspired by my lifelong love of prehistoric life. I drew a couple Tyrannosaurus deck graphics for fellow Tracker pro, Dan Wilkes, who also loved dinosaurs. Since fish shapes were becoming all the rage, I completely redesigned the GSD model into more of a fish shape in 1987 with a really pointy nose and pointy tail corners—just trying to be different again. Back in the '80s, it was really important for each pro model shape to be quite different from the others. My 1987 graphics were inspired by the drawings inside an airplane safety pamphlet, because I flew to a lot of contests in those years.

Nineteen-eighty-eight brought one more graphic change on the fish shape GSD deck—this time a rough line drawing of, appropriately, a fish spanning the entire bottom of the board. My pro model fizzled away sometime the following year without much fanfare. Over the years, many guys I don't even know have told me they bought several GSD decks, that they were really psyched on the graphics and that they had the best tails for ollies.

Fast forward to 2001. I was paying a visit to a longtime friend from the early Del Mar days, Tod Swank, at his nice, swanky house overlooking Mission Valley in San Diego. We were in his garage, looking through a stack of old decks, when all of a sudden and without warning, he whipped out my original one-and-only Kent Watson deck from 1984. Needless to say, I was totally surprised, yet psyched to see it. Since it has so much sentimental value to me, I asked Tod if I could have it back, but of course he just laughed and said no. End of story? Not yet.

I didn't think about the Kent Watson deck a ton until recently, when I received an email from Sean Cliver regarding this book on skateboard graphics he was putting together. The fire was rekindled and I soon found myself driving back down to Swank's house for a surprise visit. To make an already long story a little shorter, Tod gave me hell for having the gall to ask for the deck again, but for a trade of a couple of my drawings and GSD decks, he finally gave up the ghost. I'm happy to say that the Kent Watson model is finally back home where it belongs. | **Garry Davis**

Tracker / GSD / by Garry S. Davis / 1987

Tracker / GSD / by Garry S. Davis / 1988

Tracker / Dan Wilkes / by Garry S. Davis / 1986

Tracker / Dan Wilkes / by Garry S. Davis / 1987

Blockhead / Notch Nose / by Dave Bergthold and Ron Cameron / 1986

Blockhead / Sam Cunningham / by Ron Cameron / 1986

Blockhead / Jim Gray / by Ron Cameron / 1987

Blockhead / Jim Gray (Second Version) / by Ron Cameron / 1988

By the time sixth grade came around, my life was pretty much laid out. I started skateboarding in second grade, writing funny stories and drawing hot rods and KISS in fourth grade, and discovered new wave and my mom's '50s jazz-record cover art by sixth grade. That was it for me. I even figured out the four-color printing process on my own that year.

My bible was *Skateboarder* magazine, and in one of those mags was a Sims ad with Tom Sims in a backyard going over blueprints for skateboard designs. I then decided, in sixth grade, that I needed to own, operate, and design a skateboard company. Sims brought other forms of enlightenment to me by way of Brad Bowman's models, like the Superman, Fingerprint, and Digital graphics. Little did I know this would all set up for a weird, vicious circle of drive later in my life.

More new and exciting ideas came in junior high via *Thrasher* magazine and the punk-rock scene in general. A little later, *TransWorld SKATEboarding* magazine started up, unleashing another unexpected blast of life-changing stimuli. Neil Blender, Garry Davis, and Lance Mountain seemed to have the green light from *TWS* to draw anything they damn well pleased and write some of the most free-minded fictional stories to ever seep into my fragile, eggshell mind.

These new ideas seriously changed my life and finally showed me that I could draw my own drawings, instead of copying pictures, and be a "good drawer." This also helped reinforce my idea that school was nothing but an elaborate babysitting service with stupid art teachers telling me how to draw and ridiculous English teachers telling me the rules of writing. Fuck that shit!

The last big inspiration came years down the road in the strange grouping of Mark Gonzales, Chris Miller, Jason Jessee, Steve Claar and Lee Ralph. There was a "movement" there, I swear to god. Someone needs to document that. Something was going on there. I still smell it!

My first graphic ever screenprinted on a skateboard for mass consumption was the Blockhead Sam Cunningham model in 1985. It started

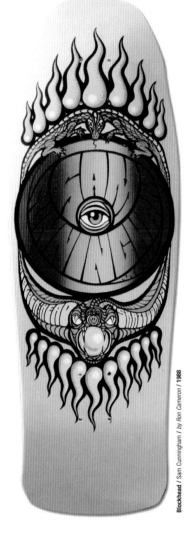

Blockhead / Sam Cunningham / by Ron Cameron / 1988

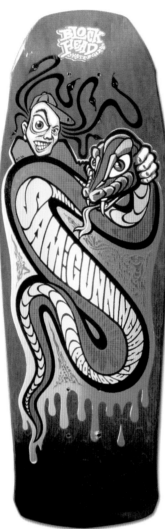

Blockhead / Sam Cunningham / by Ron Cameron / 1989

Blockhead / Sam Cunningham / by Dave Bergthold and Ron Cameron / 1988

Blockhead / Mark Partain / by Ron Cameron / 1988

with the face, and then became a collage of ideas that were added upon. I was only a sophomore at Encina High School at the time, working in the commercial art field at a food marketing agency designing and illustrating food labels, hand lettering, etc. Blockhead sponsored me a few months before this—at a demo in Stockton with Rick Windsor and Mark Gonzales—and owner Dave Bergthold was doing all the art up to this time. I started doing most of the art thereafter. So this was truly the beginning of my tiny chance at the big time.

Jim Gray was our first So Cal hook-up into the skateboard industry. I had no idea what to do for his graphic, but luckily he had all kinds of ideas and was very easy to work with. He would cut out things from magazines, packaging, etc., and the background part was the style he saw in a graphic that he really liked. I tried to make it look like the sample, but it ended up looking like my style, or the "Blockhead look." Then I added a black and white sketch I had done to give some impact on top of the chaotic mess in the background. Look for an "S" in the art chaos; it

stands for Sandy Gutierrez, my longtime girl infatuation. My first car, a 1963 Ford Falcon, is in the background too. I'm sentimentally flawed.

In 1988, I looked at my second Sam Cunningham graphic as my finest moment—up until that point, at least. I really thought it was great, but nobody else seemed to notice it as much as I thought they would— maybe because I was coming dangerously close to flat-out ripping off Wes Wilson's '60s San Francisco psychedelic poster art style. It was an early experiment for me in layering transparent ink colors. Keep in mind all these Blockhead graphics were done with repro-blue pencils, Sharpie pens, and leak-proof butcher paper from the grocery store. At the moment, if I remember right, I was hoping that John Lucero would be impressed by it. I still think it's a classic graphic; durable, clean, long-lasting—go ahead, kick the tires.

To this day I think the Tragicomic was my most personal of graphics. I was just out of high school in 1988, beginning to realize there was never going to be any sort of "adult world" to enter into, and still living in my mom's apartment in Sacto (most of the Blockhead graphics were completed on my mom's coffee table while watching TV). This graphic is important on three levels: one, I was trying to communicate a new way of "living and thinking" ideal; two, me toying with the idea of turning pro; and three, the top graphic becoming my most popular piece of art I have ever done. The bottom graphic was completely under the inspirational influence of Love (Arthur Lee), Jimi Hendrix, Clash's funk reggae stuff, Wes Wilson, graffiti art, and the Blender/Miller/GSD/Gonzales skateboard artist camp. Nowadays it strangely seems to be a visual for the Neil Young song "Thrasher." This was also when I decided that I wanted to move away from civilization when I turned 30 (look at the smaller color graphic area for the "you choose" theme).

Blockhead / Trajicomic (Top Graphic) / by Ron Cameron / 1988

This board also got me in trouble with the NSA and CASL contest organizations because of my name being on the bottom and Blockhead claiming that I wasn't quite pro yet (I soon thereafter broke my ankle and never did officially go pro). The top graphic was drawn with a Sharpie pen on the Blockhead office shipping table, and it got so many snickers that I put it on the top of this board in just one color. Since then I have become the "Nothing Is Cool" guy and may never be able to live it down. It was simply a play on words, as in, "Hey, what's up?" "Oh, nothing." "Up" was replaced by "cool," because I seriously wanted to destroy anything "cool" at the time. A big lesson in worrying about if something you are doing, saying, or thinking is cool or not—go for uncool every time!

The Blockhead Hard Times was more of my sloppy art style direction. The term "Hard Times" came from Joe Lopes, J.J. Rogers, and Jay West from San Leandro. They would come visit Dave and I in our new Oceanside apartment in So Cal, usually with little or no money. Examples of this phrase would be: "Hard Times Spaghetti"—Top Ramen with ketchup, or "Hard Times Sandwich"—white bread with lettuce. In 1989, Dave, being the entrepreneurial mastermind that he is, decided that this would be a great marketing idea for price-cutting skateboards. No fancy wood stains and one-color, sloppy, retarded art—simplicity with attitude. These sold better than anything Blockhead ever made, so skaters obviously dug the shit.

The H-Street Colby Carter was my first board graphic for a company outside of Blockhead, because Carl Hyndman wanted me to do some cameo art for them. Jeff Klindt had done the Matt Hensley and Ron Allen boards with art similar to that of Blockhead, and instigators were always ribbing me about it, trying to start shit. I never really thought Jeff was biting my style—or if he was I didn't care—so I decided to do this graphic to smother any possible fires. You know, a nod to H-Street saying, "Everything's mellow." It was strange, because I didn't know Colby at the time, so it was difficult to figure out what should be on the bottom of his board. Instead of worrying about it, I just did "my" art, which looked 100 percent like Blockhead stuff. Even though I had quit the company by this time, I hoped Dave wasn't too bummed about me slutting out the Blockhead look.

Blockhead / Simple Simon (Ron Cameron) / by Ron Cameron / 1987

Blockhead / Trajicomic (Ron Cameron) / by Ron Cameron / 1988

Blockhead / Sick Sense / by Ron Cameron / 1989

Blockhead / Hard Times / by Ron Cameron / 1989

Blockhead / Omar Hassan / by Ron Cameron and Andy Jenkins / 1990

H-Street / Colby Carter / by Ron Cameron / 1991

Acme / Classic / by Ron Cameron / 1991

Acme / Dork / by Ron Cameron / 1992

Acme / Happy Face / by Ron Cameron / 1992

After a failed business attempt at trying to start a skateboard company called Sector 3 just after I quit Blockhead, I decided to hook up with Jim Gray to start Acme Skateboards in Orange County. This was to become an experiment in drastically trying to change my graphic style from my known Blockhead look. It was now going to be all racing stripes, clean geometric shapes, and bold colors. It's nice to know that you may not have peaked your graphic style at the ripe old age of 21.

Around 1994, I quit Acme to start a company with Ed Templeton and Mike Vallely over at the World Industries camp under Steve Rocco. That company never happened, so I ended up doing some World Industries and Blind graphics. Those were fun times. Met some damn good people, and I got paid well in the skateboard industry for the first time! All good things come to an end, so when Templeton took Television to Brad Dorfman, I tried to start a new company with him at the same time as well. That whole thing was destined to fall apart from the beginning, so Ed and I headed to Tod Swank, who was looking to launch the Foundation empire. Ed had already changed his company name to Toy Machine, and I had gotten to know his team guys, Jamie Thomas being one of them. I had done two similar-style paintings for Foundation family members Matt Barker and Garris, one cat and one kid. Jamie liked the kid one, so I just reconfigured it to fit as a board graphic.

The Templeton Consume graphic was a variation of a graphic that I'd done for Donny Barley, the Smoker, which was a modified version of a poster made in the '50s. This new graphic was 100 percent my creation but done in the style of the first one. This graphic was part of a whole series for Toy Machine, but I like Ed's the best because I feel it caught his image the most out of all of them. This is me still trying not to do "my" style, but as everyone keeps telling me, "Oh, I can totally tell that you did this artwork." So much for trying to elude everyone for ten years—just be proud of who you are, what you are known for, and get the fuck on with it. | **Ron Cameron**

Toy Machine / Jamie Thomas / by Ron Cameron / 1994

Toy Machine / Ed Templeton / by Ron Cameron / 1999

Chris Miller

Schmitt Stix / Chris Miller I / by Chris Miller / 1988

Even though I was into drawing and doing art, my first two graphics were done by G&S. It never occurred to me to do my own graphic. On my first model, I wanted something that was Dali-influenced and I told them what I had in mind, but the graphics just didn't work out the way I envisioned and I hated them. They were new-wave '80s-style, definitely not Dali.

For my next graphic, I worked more closely with them and tried to describe how I wanted an abstract portrait of me set against a Mondrian color-blocked background with this silhouette of me falling through space. But each time they came back to me with something, it was so far from what I wanted. The portraits of me looked more like the Joker from Batman, and the whole thing was just way more comic-book style than Warhol or Mondrian. The problem for me was that I couldn't articulate what I wanted, so finally I came in with a sketch and showed it to someone in the art department. She was like, "Why don't we just use this?" It wasn't my intention for that to be the actual graphic, and in the end it didn't turn out exactly how I wanted because they "cleaned it up." I didn't know what it took to turn a sketch into production artwork, so that's just the way it went.

Almost all my other graphics were from my sketchbooks. I didn't necessarily plan on them becoming board graphics. There was a G&S board with a lizard on it that was a good example of this. It was from a woodblock print that I had done, and then later turned into a graphic.

G&S was pretty good about letting us influence or even dictate what graphics we were going to have. In a lot of ways it was great that we weren't very calculated in our graphic choices. There was no market research, it was just art on a skateboard. I am not sure if that was a marketing philosophy of theirs or if it just worked out that way. My feeling was that other companies at the time were less open to riders having graphics that deviated from their themes. For example, Powell and Santa Cruz were pretty set to a specific style; I think their riders had a choice on graphics, but not the style of art.

Neil Blender was the first pro to really start doing his own graphics. He drew them, they were whatever he wanted, and they obviously reflected his personality. If it weren't for Neil, I don't think graphics designed by the riders would have been as prominent as they became in skateboarding. He was my biggest influence in doing my own graphics and in even thinking it was possible at all. I also believe he opened the door for people like Natas Kaupas, Mark Gonzales, and Ed Templeton to do what they did.

Graphics such as these have a deeper meaning that makes them more than just commercial art on another product, and I believe this is one of the qualities that makes skateboarding more than just a "sport" or an "industry," and it is important for the integrity and character of skateboarding to continue to nurture this connection to art. | **Chris Miller**

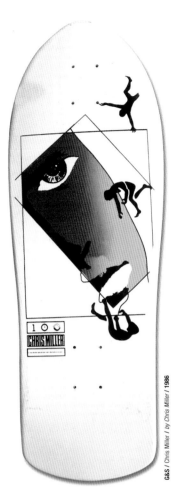

G&S / Neil Blender / by Neil Blender / 1982

G&S / Neil Blender / by Neil Blender / 1983

G&S / Neil Blender / by Neil Blender / 1985

G&S / Neil Blender / by Neil Blender / 1987

The first graphic—that's the hottest one, that one was hilarious. Steve Cathey was like, "Hey, you guys need to come up with graphics because you're turning pro and getting models." We were just like, "What?" But he goes, "If you guys do art or whatever, do your own, because no one does their own." So we just drew our own, and that was the first thing I came up with, the little ramp guy thing. Really retarded. **Neil Blender**

I'll take it to the grave, I consider Neil Blender to be the first great skate artist. He single-handedly changed the face of G&S when his first pro board came out. It had a single line drawing of his with like three or four guys falling off a ramp that was collapsing. The graphic was printed in white on a navy blue board, and it was just so simple and so cool.

Up until that time, everything was designed, executed, and produced—but Neil had no plans. The drawing wasn't derived from anything, it didn't have to be technically profound or perfect, and it could've been entirely different ten minutes later. It just came straight from his gut without any care or worry about the marketing or longevity of the board. It was meant for nobody else but skateboarding, and I felt very stoked to be a part of some sort of underground society where this could exist and we could be putting this stuff out. Neil's art was one of the first things in my generation to set the tone for freedom in artwork. **John Lucero**

G&S / Neil Blender / by Neil Blender / 1988

G&S / Neil Blender / by Neil Blender / 1988

G&S / Neil Blender / by Neil Blender / 1989

G&S / Neil Blender / by Billy Waldman / 1990

G&S / Steve Claar / by Neil Blender / 1989

G&S / Neil Blender / by Neil Blender / 1990

G&S / Neil Blender / by Neil Blender / 1990

G&S / Neil Blender / by Neil Blender / 1990

Mike Hill

Alien Workshop / Visitor / by Mike Hill / 1990

Alien Workshop was formed in October 1990 by Chris Carter, Neil Blender, and myself. The idea was to start a company that operated on its own terms and didn't look or feel like any other skateboard company that was or had been in existence. I always liked the period of skateboarding where each brand had its own aura through their team, products, and visual image, and you would align yourself with whichever fit your personality or style. Like Santa Cruz was punk with Olson and Peters, Powell and Vision had their trip, G&S was clean and stylish. Then, in the early '90s, it moved to more of a "copy whatever was successful" mode, which made for one or two leaders, with the rest switching their images to whatever was popular at the moment, leaving little diversification between brands.

There was also a movement of using known existing graphics from the mass-market world and knocking them off to fit a rider or brand, which was actually quite original and shocking when first done by World Industries, but then other unimaginative brands had to jump on and ruin it. We were determined to try and plow our own path and not jump on what was successful for others. It didn't make any sense to not do something as differently as possible.

The fact that we were in Ohio made it effortless to isolate ourselves from the influences of the industry. I wanted Alien Workshop to become its own entity that would be recognizable by its style, content, and ideas, and to have a depth that wasn't normally associated with skateboard companies. I like pictograms, logotypes, and simple shapes that convey information, and Neil obviously had his own artistic identity, so the two were intermixed to form unique, opposing styles.

The formation of Alien Workshop was acknowledging what we didn't want to do as much as what we were planning to do. We were young and did not have a clue what was involved in running a company, but it consumed our lives; nothing else could penetrate them. We were bunkered down in basements and raw warehouses, living the transformation. There wasn't much thought of being successful, just surviving to release the next project or product. Carter, to his credit, kept the company alive during this period of conceptual development in which the concern for sales to pay bills was way down on the list of importance.

Alien Workshop / Xenia / by Mike Hill and Neil Blender / 1990

Alien Workshop / Neil Blender / by Mike Hill / 1990

Alien Workshop / Steve Claar / by Mike Hill / 1991

Alien Workshop / Neil Blender / by Neil Blender / 1991

Alien Workshop / Neil Blender / by Neil Blender / 1991

For me, it was to be much more than just a skateboard company. I wanted Alien Workshop to be an organization that itself was the origin of the concepts, products, and graphics that came from it, not human beings. Alien Workshop was the entity, not the individuals working on it. Treating it as an institution, I had delusions that it would eventually grow into a school/cult in South Dakota with different things practiced and taught: film, art, music, graphic design, subculture, skateboarding, private self-sufficient living. This was how the "SECT" idea originated. Turns out I was the only one with this delusion of grandeur.

We had very little press, no catalogs, and deliberately made it hard for people to obtain information on the brand. Some of our early ads were obscure to the degree of confusing people to what we even were. This allowed for something that is hard to achieve today: imagination. People used their imagination to fill in the gaps around Alien Workshop. Too much information kills imagination. People have always read things into the graphics, like there were hidden messages built in some of the logos, so it made for interesting dialog.

The team riders were the only ones who would speak on behalf of the company then, and Rob Dyrdek would always talk to me about what people would say to him. It was amusing. The idea of overly simple, almost childlike graphics having a somewhat sinister or thought-provoking idea behind them is at the root of a lot of those early logos. Religious overtones in some of the alien graphics bothered those that you would expect. The early clone stuff really touched nerves with some skate-shop owners. Now it's nightly news. The mind-control graphic had a jumbled word message "r u god?" that took years for someone to write and ask about.

Alien Workshop / Team / by Mike Hill / 1994

Alien Workshop / Team / by Mike Hill / 1994

Alien Workshop / Team / by Mike Hill / 1995

Alien Workshop / Team / by Mike Hill / 1996

The idea of being visited by aliens at night and waking to think you saw owls influenced the replacing of the aliens for owls in the Triad logo. Same with the praying mantis being connected to aliens screening your memory, and you dreaming of having giant insects in your bedroom. It made it fun to work on things, having vague overtones beyond just a deck or T-shirt graphic. It was a way to communicate with like-minded people without having to actually talk to them.

The use of alien-based icons grew out of my hypothetical thinking that if there were to be universal pictogram symbols for extraterrestrial themes such as abductions, mind control, reproduction, etc., then the Alien Workshop would be commissioned as the creators of these icons and they would, in turn, become part of the imagery of the company as well. In my mind, I was making icons that would be established for future use by government agencies, the same way Olympic pictograms are used for various sports. This was all before The *X-Files* or other mainstream acceptance of aliens. The subject was still very much a tabloid parody, so for the people out there who were interested in this stuff, they really became our legion of loyal fans alongside Midwestern skateboarders. We would receive mail from professors and freaks worldwide that would talk about being into a T-shirt design or decal, and it was cool because they were not part of the skateboarding circle, just some guy or girl who was into the implied concept.

The success of the alien graphics came gradually. It started out as a cult following but then developed into a trendy nightmare. People would tell me how our shirts were really popular with ravers. This was the last thing the Alien Workshop was about—a bunch of overly social people dancing to techno while dressed for year-round trick-or-treating—and it was quite devastating.

One day a shop account called and said Madonna had just been in their store and bought one of our shirts. He was all excited and thought we should be, too. I remember going berserk and screaming about why would they sell it to her, that they should have

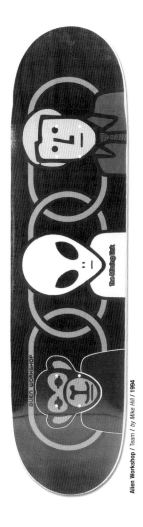

In the heyday of conspiracy we were all dead serious about it. It was no joke to us—food, weapons, and gold were being stocked. Of course it pretty much peaked out at Y2K and has since faded. Alien was the first company outside of California to ever rise to the top, and it was the first company to create an image through its graphics. All of today's skateboard graphics are directly influenced by the style Mike Hill pioneered. Rob Dyrdek

denied her. But you can't control these things. It happens to bands all the time: the people who drove you away to the point of making something yourself out of frustration end up your customers.

I had a running timeline of logo icons that touched on various alien/conspiracy theories over the years that was somewhat derailed after seeing one too many alien-head lollipops at a Sunoco in the middle of Hicksville, Ohio. Many people decided for us that when the alien imagery phenomenon blew over we would be done and out of business. They would tell us it was the only reason for our success up to that point and that aliens were played out. These are the same people who were swept up in the latest nostalgia ripple and wanted you to rerelease all the old alien-based graphics.

When we first started the Workshop, we would sit around, talk about ideas, and make these papier-mâché sculptures. I was really into being in my basement, listening to music, watching with the sound off the way television is edited, making sculptures and lamps from papier-mâché. Since it is a long process of layering strips of newspaper on top of shapes using paste, there was a lot of time to think, and it was how much of the visual direction for the Workshop were formed.

A couple years later, the sublimation process for slick decks allowed a photograph to be printed cleanly on a board, so I started making the dioramas for deck graphics. I liked the idea of making a three-dimensional sculpture for a skateboard graphic, since most up to that point had been drawn art or halftones of photos. The creatures were usually made in segments that assembled together when finished. This allowed you to work on different areas as various components dried—many were built with movable appendages with the thinking they could be animated for videos later. When finished, they would be painted and arranged in the setup for the photo shoot.

Some of the finished slick decks printed really dark, because Professor Schmitt was still ironing out the sublimation technology. It made me paranoid to have spent that much time on a puppet to have it print like crap, so I kept painting them brighter and brighter, hoping that would help them from coming out dark on the deck. The Duane Pitre Aardvark graphic was one that printed horrible on a deck, but the 4 x 5 photograph was fine. The Bo Turner Stabbing graphic was a tribute to J Mascis. I wanted to try and make something that visually looked the way the album *Your Living All Over Me* sounded to me.

One of the slick graphics was a photo of colored mice that had hatched from corresponding colored eggs. This was before we had computers, and I tried to dye the fur of the mice by dunking them in a can of food coloring, but the natural oils on the fur repelled the dye. So I had to resort to RIT dye and handpaint it on the mice. It felt lame holding them and brushing on the color, but at the time, bringing these graphic ideas to fruition was above all. The mice never took the color very well, so they

Alien Workshop / Bo Turner / by Mike Hill / 1993

Alien Workshop / John Drake / by Mike Hill / 1994

Alien Workshop / Bo Turner / by Mike Hill / 1996

Alien Workshop / Rob Dyrdek / by Mike Hill / 1996

were pastel looking. We had several people hold the mice by their tails over the colored eggshells and the photographer would snap the photo as soon as we released them, before they could hide under the eggs. I kept the mice in my basement afterward and they started eating each other. I finally let them go in a park by the Workshop and wondered if anybody ever happened upon one of those pastel-colored mice in the woods.

Another slick graphic was a papier-mâché creature that was to appear to be eating goldfish. I had put the fish in the freezer to kill them and then pulled them out right before the photo shoot to finish the diorama. One was stuck on this piece of thin wire coming out of a section of sod, and as the photographer was taking light readings, the fish thawed out, came back to life, and started thrashing around on the end of this little piece of wire. It was an unplanned, creepy cryogenics success. I eventually dropped the fish in boiling water, and their fins and tails stiffened nicely for a life-like effect. This incident marked the end of the use of animals for the dioramas.

The team has always been a huge part of the depth of Alien Workshop. They understood how much energy went into the whole visual aspect of the company, so they seemed to respect our ability to decide how the graphics came together. Sometimes they would talk about an idea or colors they liked or didn't like, but for the most part they left the decisions to us. Their pro models were usually non-alien related; those were designated for the team/logo decks.

There has always been room to work as far as deck graphics, but if it wanders too far out of the original idea of how things should look, the consistency starts to suffer. It takes an overall long-range vision for things that aren't tainted by influences that change on a weekly basis. One of the most rewarding things is having team riders who understand and appreciate the effort that goes into making the company unique visually. |**Mike Hill**

exalt the new God ®

I was very honored to have graphics done by Neil Blender. Funny thing is, the first board I ever wanted was the G&S Blender Snake, but the mail-order place was out of it, so I got a G&S Foil Tail instead. Funny again, because G&S was my first full-blown sponsor, and Blender and I later became friends. Once I started to play music, Blender made me a graphic called Fret Face. It has a drawing of a guy's face with a fret board from a guitar instead of a forehead—it ruled.

The Workshop graphics are still my favorite. They're the most original graphics to date. I mean, I have one tattooed on me—my dedication to AWS was deep. They were like my older brothers, not just the owners of the company I skated for. |Duane Pitre

Alien Workshop / Duane Pitre / by Neil Blender / 1991

Alien Workshop / Duane Pitre / by Mike Hill / 1992

Alien Workshop / Duane Pitre / by Neil Blender / 1994

Alien Workshop / Duane Pitre / by Mike Hill / 1993

Neil Blender

Alien Workshop / Bo Turner / by Neil Blender / 1995

Alien Workshop / Bo Turner / by Neil Blender / 1994

Alien Workshop / Scott Conklin / by Neil Blender / 1995

Alien Workshop / Duane Pitre / by Neil Blender / 1994

Neil Blender has an amazing sense of humor. He embraced individuality with a creative do-it-yourself ethic that influenced what skateboard culture would become. | Chris Miller

Alien Workshop / Bo Turner / by Neil Blender / 1995

Alien Workshop / Duane Pitre / by Neil Blender / 1993

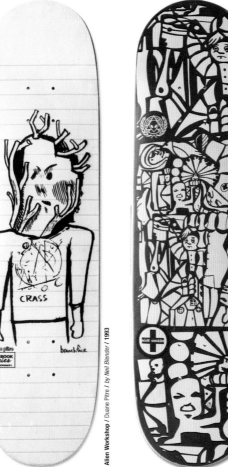

Alien Workshop / Scott Conklin / by Neil Blender / 1996

Alien Workshop / Duane Pitre / by Neil Blender / 1996

Alien Workshop / Josh Kalis / by Neil Blender / 1997

The Firm / Lance Mountain / by Neil Blender and Lance Mountain / 1993

The Firm / Ray Barbee / by Neil Blender and Lance Mountain / 1993

Consolidated / Steve Bailey / by Neil Blender / 1999

Larry Bertleman / Hand painted deck by Neil Blender / 2001

Black Label / Matt Hensley / by Neil Blender / 2002

WHO MADE ME I DON'T FEEL HUMAN, I COME OUT OF TALL BUILDINGS AND THE LIGHT ATTACKS MY EYES, WHAT AM I GODAMMIT.

ETHAN FOWLER

friendly fungus

thru the gums & over the tongue watch out oblivion here we come. *ronald whaley by Santa Cruz Skateboards

Stereo / Ethan Fowler / *by Thomas Campbell* / **1994**

Stereo / Ethan Fowler / *by Thomas Campbell* / **1996**

Santa Monica Airlines / Tim Brauch / *by Thomas Campbell* / **1995**

Santa Cruz / Ron Whaley / *by Thomas Campbell* / **1996**

Thomas Campbell

Santa Monica Airlines / Israel Forbes / by Thomas Campbell / 1995

Santa Cruz / Tim Brauch / by Thomas Campbell / 1996

Santa Cruz / Tim Brauch / by Thomas Campbell / 1996

Toy Machine / Ed Templeton / by Thomas Campbell / 1994

The free-form scribblings of Neil Blender and Tod Swank probably had the biggest impact on me, as well as their overall creative movement through life—being really creative in their skating, making 'zines, taking pictures, making music, drawing and painting. Those guys were and are the shit. John Lucero and Jim Phillips are amazing as well. Most of the graphics I have done were for friends of mine who had models. At the time I was a writer and photographer for skateboard magazines and ended up befriending a lot of different skaters. It just kinda worked out somehow, whether I offered to do them or they asked.

I really like Ethan Fowler's first model graphic I did for Stereo. It was just a scribble that came about while on a trip to Morocco, in North Africa. It was really loose and jacked. I remember the first time I saw it was when I showed up at a demo in Amsterdam, and Ethan was riding it. I picked it up and was trying to see the graphic through all the regular usage scars—I was psyched. Ethan Fowler is like a song on a skateboard ... you could watch him roll straight and be like, "Damn, that's incredible." There are not a lot of people like that. |Thomas Campbell

Hand drawn board by Tod Swank / 1988

Skull Skates / Justin Lovely / by Tod Swank / 1988

Skull Skates / Justin Lovely / by Tod Swank / 1988

Skull Skates / Tod Swank / by Tod Swank / 1989

Tod Swank

I didn't realize it until much later in life, but my parents unwittingly and subconsciously affected me more than I ever knew with their creative talents. They are highly creative people in more than just "art," but in the "art of living" with anything and everything they do, whether it's creating this abstract sculpture of cement nails—that I'm still trying to score—or mowing the fricking lawn.

I took some basic photo and art classes in high school, but it was skateboarding that really made things start exploding for me. Skateboarding was the basis for all the motivating influences that made me consciously aware of creativity. I also became immersed in the 'zine world, through which I was introduced—entirely by the U.S. Post—to a whole slew of budding young artists, some who have since gone on to become world-renowned subculture gems. To name a few: Chris Johanson, Andy Jenkins, Adam Wallacavage, Peter Talbot, Neil Blender, Jeff Scholl, Thomas Campbell, Kevin Wilkins, Garry Davis, Gabrielle Holley, and O, but there are many others.

The 'zine scene was pretty damn cool. Some of my mentors had created fictitious characters in their 'zines and I unoriginally followed suit with my own: Justin Lovely. Coupled with my tendencies to be uncomfortable being the focus of anything, I think the character was a way to take the social pressure that I—solely, most likely—placed upon myself, away from self-conscious festering, when I pressed my so-called "professional" skateboarding career with Skull Skates. The Teapot image came about when I went to Scotland to skate and hang out with this Scottish crew: Grahme Stanners, Cheese, Davie Phillip, Bob, Chimp, and such. We drank a lot of tea—like all the time—and talked about all kinds of life crap. It was just lovely, wasn't it. I spray-painted teapots all over San Diego.

I always thought I'd gotten the image of the Star and Moon from the Casbah, a bar in San Diego that is owned by Tim Maze who has thrown tons of shows, but Tim started the Casbah in 1989, the same year I started Foundation with Steve Rocco after I left Skull Skates, where I had my first Star and Moon graphic—which preceded the Casbah. So it was weird that something that grew so close to me over the years started at almost the same time and we both had the same logos.

The Star and Moon stemmed from my avid readings of science fiction, namely the great Isaac Asimov, one of the most prolific science-

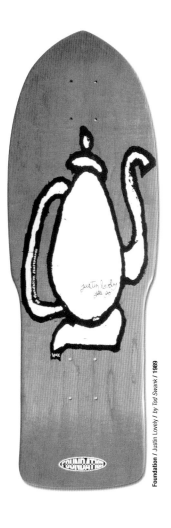

fiction writers of all time—his future perceptions of the world on scientific, social and moral basis have boggled and amazed generations with the accuracy and true insight into the future. Hence, the inspiration for the name Foundation, which comes from one of Asimov's most heralded series. The Star and Moon is a constant reminder of how ultra-rare and precious humanity is. This still stands true to me.

Recently, my friend Kevin and I were at Costco with our women. Kevin pointed out this older man wearing a Foundation OG Star and Moon T-shirt. It was only after he walked by with his family that we realized why: they were obviously Muslim, which is cool. We actually had people complaining about the logo after 9/11. Our European agent told us they could not buy anything with that logo on it. I understand why, but it doesn't matter to me. Everyone knows Foundation had the Star and Moon long before the Muslims, and we have the trademark to prove it, too.

Rocco was a surprise influence and supporter. I first met him when I was a photographer for TransWorld SKATEboarding magazine. He would always put the Swank Zine stickers on his board and was super cool to me. When I wanted to ride for World Industries in 1989, he said no, but he told me to start my own company and that he would help me out. At the time, Steve was pushing the then stagnant envelope of the skateboard industry—if not the skateboard world, as we all know now. His energy and creativity was exciting and challenging in the funniest way possible. There was no subject matter beyond reach for him to humorously jab at. Steve was no help to my early Foundation graphics except that he told me they always sucked. Reality check! | **Tod Swank**

Andy Jen

I always liked Tod Swank's art on boards. I guess the simplicity always struck me and I loved the line quality. When the first Justin Lovely Teapot board came out on Skull, I was pretty impressed by the simple graphics for how powerful they were and how far from the then current trend of detailed drawings with bright colors. I liked Ron Cameron's stuff for Blockhead, too. Other than that, I wasn't too blown away by skate graphics in general. The thing I really liked, and that really drew me, was the way certain skaters customized their boards: doing their own drawings and paintings on them, writing on them, customizing the griptape, the stickering. I still love to see certain individual skater's boards to check what they've done to them. My favorite board graphics these days are ones that have mostly been wiped away by rails, ledges and the hand of the skater—those are way more interesting than stock or shiny new graphics.

When my magazine job at *Homeboy* and Wizard Publications hit the skids in 1989, I decided to go all-out freelance. We took the articles from the last unpublished *Homeboy* and gave them to *TransWorld SKATEboarding*. Kevin Wilkins and Spike Jonze both started working for TWS and I started working part-time in their "advertising agency," which was more like just a room with a couple of toiling young freelancers in it, doing ads for Tracker, Blockhead, House of Kasai, etc. Dave Bergthold ran Blockhead, and he was way better to work with than the *TWS* ad folks, so I did more work for him on the side, including the Street Standard graphic.

Around that same time I met Perry Gladstone, a Canadian snowboarder who wanted to start his own skate company called Fishlips. When Fishlips started, Gator was on his downward slide from fame and fortune; he had parted with Vision some time earlier. I guess Perry was a bit star-

Blockhead / Team / by Andy Jenkins / 1989

Fishlips / Team / by Andy Jenkins / 1989

Fishlips / Mark "Gator" Rogowski / by Andy Jenkins / 1991

Blind / Jason Lee / by Andy Jenkins / 1989

disposable

struck and stoked with the idea of having a known pro, one-time superstar, riding for his company. Gator must have been affordable for a start-up because no one else wanted him at the time. So I met with Gator a few times, and we did the 7Eleven cup graphic and his first ad, which was to run in *TransWorld*. Then, one night, Perry calls me at home completely freaked out and tells me the story about how Gator had turned himself in for murder. He had murdered the girl during the time we were working with him. That gave me the creeps. Anyhow, the ad got pulled at the very last minute and I'm pretty sure that whole scenario took Fishlips down the drain. What a mess.

I've known Spike since he was a young kid from Rockville, Maryland and was lucky to work with him in the beginnings of his photo career at Wizard Publications. We all worked on BMX stuff, but our passions were leading us more and more toward skateboarding. Steve Rocco had the office for SMA—before he turned it into World Industries—right near us in Torrance, so we got to know the guys over there, and Spike started shooting a ton more skating, then videoing as well. He was the one to introduce me to Steve and Rodney Mullen, and since he was also working on Rubbish Heap and the Blind video, I got to meet the skaters and get to know some of them. That made it easy to slip into working on graphics.

The directions almost always came from the skaters or Rocco, like the first Dr. Seuss board I did for Jason Lee. I was a little weirded out by blatantly copying something, so I did my own drawing of a guy—supposedly it was Jason—and made him look like a Seuss-ian drawing with a Seussian styled poem to go with it. I guess that was the way I got around copying something directly, but it was inevitable that I would get sucked into the

Blind / Jason Lee / by Andy Jenkins / 1990

World Industries / Jeremy Klein / by Andy Jenkins / 1990

101 / Kris Markovich / by Andy Jenkins / 1992

101 / Gabriel Rodriguez / by Andy Jenkins / 1993

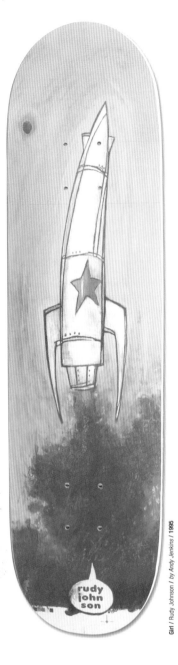

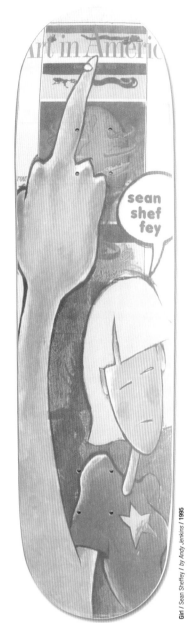

Girl / Rudy Johnson / by Andy Jenkins / 1995

Girl / Tony Ferguson / by Andy Jenkins / 1995

Girl / Sean Sheffey / by Andy Jenkins / 1995

Girl / Rick Howard / by Andy Jenkins / 1994

trend. And Rocco always paid me well. So, the next Seuss board I did for Jason had a direct drawing of the Grinch getting ready to fry up little Cindy Lou over a fire. Then there was the Mario board for Jeremy Klein. That one got a cease-and-desist letter. I always like working with Natas when he had 101, because he always wanted to do something new and original, or controversial like the Crack Pipe graphic. My favorite graphics ever, I did for 101: the Gabriel Rodriguez Grenade sculpture slick and the Evel Knievel painting for a Kris Markovich slick. Those were fun to do.

When Girl started out in 1993, they didn't have an art director. They just sort of got a few different people to interpret their ideas, and one of them was me. I think that ambivalence—driven by the lack of funds—was instrumental in creating the original Girl image, which was no image. Then about a year into Girl they hired me full-time. The only image that has held on since the early days is the bathroom-door icon—we call her the "OG" or "Original Girl"—and our sense of humor. Sure, there was a time about four years into the job where I hated the logo and tried to avoid using it. In fact, everyone here was sick of it, and we even stopped printing it on T-shirts. Big mistake. We didn't realize how popular it was until we started using it

again and it went nuts. These days it's a staple in the design process with probably 75 percent of our board graphics. And I don't hate it anymore. Now we look at it as a real challenge to try and do new things with her, and I believe it's led us down some pretty good design roads. It's good to look at required design elements as a challenge and not a disease. Otherwise you'll wind up hating what you do. I love what I do.

Collaborating with different artists just seems to be a pleasant side effect of what we do. If I see someone's work that I like, I always try to get in touch with them—and not always with the intention of working with them, but just to get a glimpse into their creative processes and lives. I guess I'm sort of looking for inspiration that way. Sometimes the artists fit with Girl, like Geoff McFetridge and J. Otto Seibold did, and sometimes they don't.

Evan Hecox was one of those people I really wanted to get in contact with because I liked the work of his that I was seeing in the ads of a snowboard clothing company called Twist. So one day I just decided to get in touch with him, and it sort of snowballed from there. It turned out he was leaving his position at Twist, and working with Chocolate was a really good

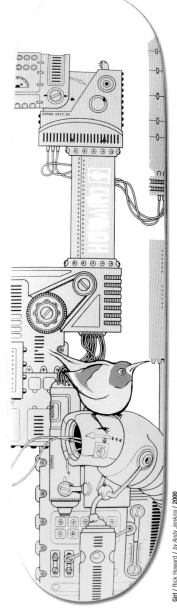

Girl / Jeron Wilson / by Andy Jenkins / 1997

Girl / Rick Howard / by Andy Jenkins / 2000

Girl / Guy Mariano / by J. Otto Seibold / 1997

Chocolate / Keenan Milton / by Geoff McFetridge / 1997

fit for him. That was just pure luck that it worked out, I think, or maybe just good timing. Every time we send Evan an idea—and it's almost always verbal and vague—he comes back with something that blows us away. He takes the ideas a step further and with his own style. He's become synonymous with the Chocolate of the late '90s and early 2000s. He's a great talent.

The concepts for Evan's first City Series were molded from our collaborative meetings here at Girl. The entire art department—or the "Art Dump" as we've dubbed it—meets at least once a week to throw ideas around. These meetings are a real benefit to what we do … even though most of the time we just goof off and come up with ideas that will never see the light of day. But we do get lucky, and some ideas bounce off one person and then another and another to morph into a solid concept for a board graphic series like the City Series or Bar Scene. I feel really fortunate that Girl—Rick Howard, Megan Baltimore, Spike Jonze and Mike Carroll—values talent in the art department. **|Andy Jenkins**

Chocolate / Street Series / by Evan Hecox / 1997

Evan Hecox

Chocolate / Bar Series / by Evan Hecox / 2000

Chocolate / Richard Mulder / by Evan Hecox / 2000

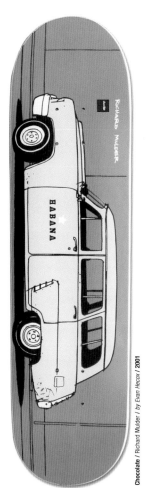

Chocolate / Richard Mulder / by Evan Hecox / 2001

GINO IANNUCCI
PROTOTYPE 4: VIDEO GAME

Chocolate / Gino Iannucci / by Evan Hecox / 1999

Chocolate / Gabriel Rodriguez / by Evan Hecox / 1998

Chocolate / Chico Brenes / by Evan Hecox / 1998

Chocolate / Keenan Milton / by Evan Hecox / 1998

Chocolate / Keenan Milton / by Evan Hecox / 1997

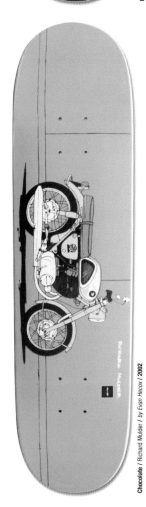

Chocolate / Richard Mulder / by Evan Hecox / 2002

DEATH DEFYING
GINO
MASTER of ESCAPE

Watch in horror as
he is lowered into
A WATERY GRAVE!

Chocolate / Gino Iannucci / by Evan Hecox / 1999

Chocolate / Keenan Milton / by Evan Hecox / 2000

Shut Skateboards

Shut / Shark / by Wylie Singer / 1989

In the beginning, Shut was a group of friends from New York, Brooklyn, and New Jersey who met through skating and were trying to make a board to better reflect the way we skated. At the time, in 1987, board designs weren't changing quickly enough, and the evolution of tricks in the streets of New York was demanding different shapes. The bulk of what was being sold was pro vert boards marketed with a California vibe and aesthetic that did not speak to us.

Rodney Smith, Alyasha Owerka Moore, and I would hand-cut, sand, and drill concave blanks on Ali's roof in Brooklyn, and give each board a custom spray paint/stencil graphic—some of those first boards were works of art, I can't believe I never saved one. We gave them to our extended crew up and down the East Coast, refining the shapes and graphics. Then shops started calling. Unknowingly, we had started a business when we were just trying to make the best boards with the hottest graphics. We never tried to be different from the established West Coast companies. It just happened that way naturally.

Aly drove our graphic direction, and Rodney and I worked on design and team. Our graphics and identity came from influences in and around New York City: hip-hop, comic book art, tattoo art, hardcore/punk music, the '80s Soho art scene, and the energy of the city. When you're skating down the street and you see a boxing poster with Warhol and Basquiat next to a full-color graffiti piece, it has an effect on you whether you know it or not. We were a product of our environment, and our scene was something we never saw in the magazines, videos, and products at the time.

We met most of our artists skating in the city. Everyone we skated with was in a band, wrote graffiti, took pictures, made art, or spun records. Someone would tell me their friend could write, and he'd come by and bring his "black book" to show what he could do. If he had skills, we would tell him that we needed a sticker or T-shirt graphic, give him some direction and see what he came back with. Often someone would bring us a drawing, lettering, or character, and we would say to apply it to a theme or adapt it to a model. A few rounds later we had a graphic. People were always stopping by, showing us what they had.

The Shark graphic was done almost entirely by Wylie Singer, who I met skating in Washington Square Park. He could be considered our in-house graphic designer. Coming from artist parents, Wylie went to music and art high school—the Fame school—and was incredibly talented and creative. He was responsible for a lot our artwork.

The first Street Posse was drawn by Hugh Gran. It was a drawing he gave us, and we made into a sticker. When we were ready to release a new shape, we'd ask him to do it as a full graphic. Hugh was very active in the NY hardcore scene, and we had mutual friends. His early illustrations definitely reflect that style.

The first Zoo York model was a way to pay respect to the crews that represented New York before us—we asked some of the older skaters, Puppet Head, Papo, Andy Kessler, and others if it would be okay to use the Zoo name—and it was a collaboration between Wylie Singer and Ducky Alex Talavera. We let them run with the Zoo and graffiti themes. Ducky focused more on the character and the cage, and Wylie on the overall graphic. Ducky introduced me to his friend Phil Frost and told me we should use him for some graphics. Phil gave me a sticker, but I never got around to calling him.

Alyasha Owerka Moore went on to play an integral role in the conception and design of several clothing lines including Phat Farm, Monkey Wrench, Mecca, Dub, Droors, Alphanumeric and Fiberops. Rodney Smith founded Zoo York and has continued representing the East. | **Bruno Musso**

Shut / Assault Vehicle / artist unknown / 1989

Shut / Street Posse / by Hugh Gran / 1989

Shut / Zoo York / by Wylie Singer and Ducky Alex Talavera / 1990

Shut / Jeremy Henderson / by Jeremy Henderson / 1990

Zoo York / Rob Gangemi / by Futura 2000 and Eli Gesner / 1996

Zoo York / Rob Gangemi / by Futura 2000 / 1997

Zoo York / Peter Bici / by Eli Gesner / 1997

Zoo York / Danny Supa / by Eli Gesner / 2001

Zoo York / 9-11 Memorial / by Horst Hamann / 2001

Andy Howell

Schmitt Stix / Andy Howell / by Andy Howell / 1989

The Ray "Bones" Rodriguez graphic was really the dawn of my emotional involvement in skating, the beginning of an era I identify with as a skateboarder. It also influenced me as an artist. I can't tell you how many times I drew lopsided skulls and crossbones trying to imitate that art. At the time, I had no idea how a board graphic was even made. It wasn't until many years later I realized there was such a thing as an art school or making a living doing art.

My first graphic was on my first board for Schmitt Stix, before we left Vision to create New Deal. It showed a few evil Stanley Kubrick A Clockwork Orange style characters with upside-down hearts chasing an innocent around a walkway that dropped off into an infinite abyss. The walkway went around a Masonic pyramid eye, which represented secret societies, money, power—all the things that were intriguing to me at the time. I did my name in sign language, because I thought it was lame to have your name on a skateboard, but then I immediately put a text version on there at the company's request—dove right in, I guess. It was a trip because so many people came up to me screaming and doing hand signs because they thought I was deaf.

When I was in art school, I started doing a lot of graffiti that I combined with the skulls and punk styles to make my own style of cartoon graphics. This combined with my history making skate/punk 'zines since junior high school, and became the style of the ads and graphics for New Deal and Element. Back then it was called the Underworld Element, which is what street skaters were basically considered by the mainstream at the time. I created the brand in the image of street and urban culture from Atlanta, where I lived, and from New York, where I stayed at Jeremy Henderson's flat in the summers.

A lot of boards and tees I did were influenced by the graffiti and music I was involved in at the time. I would be out bombing with my friends in Atlanta, and I would do the graphics I was thinking about on the walls for practice. Later they would come out as board, sticker and tee graphics, and my friends and I would crack up about it. It was a complete blast. Paul Schmitt and Steve Douglas were great to work with, although sometimes my vision fell on deaf ears when I would describe it to them.

I mean I was living in Atlanta, hanging in New York and San Francisco, while Paul had his head in the woodshop and Douglas was skating vert in San Jose. So I'm sure my ideas seemed a little wacky sometimes, like graffiti graphics on skateboards and tees; stickers of hats, pop guns, and spray cans; and gangster-style ads of our team in a police lineup with placards with their graff and city names on them. Well, I guess that's how it was back in the day, like, "Suburban-wannabe-graffiti-gangsters-create-skateboard-company-and-are-shunned-by-the-community."

So many creative minds were nurtured through the experience of riding, creating, and promoting skateboarding, and have since gone on to influence other areas of popular culture as well. Of course we were all considered outcast vandals at that time, destroying public and private property everywhere, as security guards and pedestrians often put it, "Y'all ain't never gonna amount ta nuthin', just a bunch of punk kids destroyin' our city." It was such an amazing time, and it just continues to get more and more sophisticated—a long way from the do-it-yourself-skate-company style I was so into in the early '90s.

| Andy Howell

New Deal / Andy Howell / by Andy Howell / 1990

New Deal / Andy Howell / by Andy Howell / 1991

New Deal / Danny Sargent / by Andy Howell / 1990

New Deal / Justin Girard / by Andy Howell / 1990

New Deal / Justin Girard / by Andy Howell / 1991

New Deal / Siamese / by Andy Howell and Gorm Boberg / 1990

When Chris Miller left Schmitt Stix, I knew it was over, as Vision was struggling with the downturn in the market. Steve Douglas was pushing to pull out and rallied the team together. Andy Howell, like John Lucero and Chris Miller, had done his own artwork and was a very good artist. He'd been going to the Art Institute of Atlanta and had a professional understanding about image, so Andy became the art director for New Deal. His sidekick was Gorm Boberg from Sweden. Steve, Andy, and Gorm, along with some team riders, camped out in my house in Costa Mesa for three months creating New Deal.

Andy and Gorm conceptualized and drew most of the artwork and created a look and feel for the company. Some, like Ed Templeton, did their own artwork that did not fit in. Needless to say, New Deal was rising as the established companies were falling. Everything about New Deal was opposite, from the art to the fact that the video came out before the product did. New Deal was shipped June 1, 1990, and the August issue of TransWorld SKATE Business had us as number three in the market.

|Paul Schmitt

New Deal / John Montesi / *by Andy Howell* / **1992**

New Deal / Armando Barajas / *by Andy Howell* / **1992**

New Deal / Justin Girard / *by Barry McGee* / **1992**

Underworld Element / John Montesi / *by Andy Howell* / **1994**

Underworld Element / Rick Ibaseta / *by Andy Howell* / **1992**

Underworld Element / Julien Stranger / *by Jef Whitehead* / **1992**

Underworld Element / Andy Howell / *by Dave Kinsey* / **1994**

Mad Circle / Mike Cao / *by Barry McGee* / **1993**

Mad Circle / Chris Fissel / *by Barry McGee* / **1993**

Mad Circle / Scott Johnston / *by Barry McGee* / **1995**

disposable|

Mad Circle / Scott Johnston / by Barry McGee / 1995

Moses Itkonen / Oakland, CA / 1995 / photo by Tobin Yelland

Justin Girard asked me to do a graphic for him while he was riding for New Deal, and that went okay. Then a few months went by, and he was starting a new company facade called Mad Circle and asked if I would help design stuff with him and some kid named Gorm [Boberg]. I was heavily into graffiti at that time, and so was that kid Gorm, so we just made all kinds of horrible logos with terrible concepts that the riders came up with. Barry McGee

New Deal / Ed Templeton / by Ed Templeton / 1990

New Deal / Ed Templeton / by Ed Templeton / 1990

New Deal / Ed Templeton / by Ed Templeton / 1991

New Deal / Ed Templeton / by Ed Templeton / 1991

Ed Templetor

I grew up in the shadow of Vision skateboards. They were located in Costa Mesa the next town over from Huntington Beach. I took my grandpa to Gremic Skates, the best shop in HB, to pick out a board for Christmas. Walking in was daunting because all the employees were mean, older skaters, and it was worse with my grandpa there. I remember looking around and liking all the Vision boards.

I didn't know what pros were what, so that wasn't an influence on my choice. I settled on a Grigley Old Ghosts. It had a cross on it, sprinkled with lots of smaller crosses and typical Vision squiggly hot-pink lines. It did not strike me as a religious board, just cool and scary. Vision's style was very '80s in a cut-and-paste 'zine way: really bright colors, with razzamatazz polka dots, triangles, torn paper, etc., sort of a mixture of the cheese '80s a la Patrick Nagel and the cool arty '80s of Keith Haring, Basquiat, and So Cal punk music. It had a Gary Panter feel, which was good. I was really influenced by their ads and graphics at that time.

Only once I started skating in force and hanging out in Gremic skate shop did I really get into certain graphics. The one that really stood out was Neil Blender's Interlocking Heads board. Gremic got one in from G&S that was a black-painted board with the graphics screened in black. I remember walking in and looking at the board, and when the light hit it just right you could see the graphic. I thought, "How badass!" There was something subversive about screening black onto black. It was a total not-give-a-fuck thing to do, which resonated with me.

Then Schmitt Stix came around, and its graphics really hit everyone. John Lucero's boards were so good, just well crafted and well placed for that time period, and skaters knew he did the graphics himself, making them even cooler. Chris Miller's Dog board was another one I really fanned out on. I can't explain why these graphics were good, they just were. Seeing photos of Mark Gonzales with paint pen art on his griptape was very inspiring, too. There was a photo of him doing a kickflip where he'd

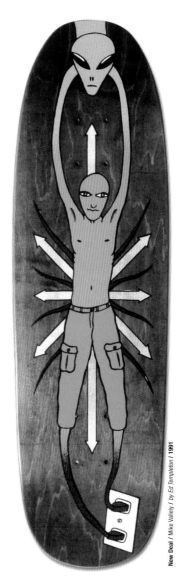

New Deal / Ed Templeton / by Ed Templeton / 1991

New Deal / Ed Templeton / by Ed Templeton / 1991

New Deal / Mike Vallely / by Ed Templeton / 1991

TV / Mike Vallely / by Ed Templeton / 1992

written, "Yes, I try to act weird," on the top of his board. I thought it was genius of him, knowing that he was going to get a photo in the mags with that showing. It was a real utilization.

Right before I turned pro for New Deal in 1990, I got into the Austrian artist Egon Schiele. His draw-ings and paintings were so wilted. I almost used one of his drawings as my first graphic, but at the last minute I changed it to a cat that I got from a Metropolitan Museum of Art catalog that my grandmother had. It was a small Egyptian-style pin they had for sale. I copied the pin shape and changed it a little bit by filling in the cat with the pattern of a woodcut I found in a book, a chaotic scene of skeletons raping and pillaging a town. There was some sexual imagery, but it wasn't immediately noticeable.

Mark Gonzales / 1987 / photo by Grant Brittain

The best part about working with Ed Templeton on graphics was that I didn't have to explain myself. I mean, most production artists would cringe if I told them I want-ed an alien with his arms wrapped around a human who is plugged into a wall outlet. They'd be like, "What the fuck?" But Ed would just say, "Cool," and then design it. I felt free to take chances, go out on a limb, and throw ideas out around Ed. We had a great relationship like that, and I think our graphics at that time were very underrat-ed and underappreciated. The coolest part about it was that we encouraged each other to be creative and expres-sive, and that's what skating and skateboard graphics are all about. |Mike Vallely

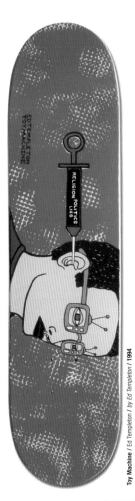

Much to New Deal's credit, I don't remember there ever being even the slightest twinge against me doing the graphic myself. The whole concept of the company was based on the premise that each pro rider had total control over their image, and we were allowed to make our own graphics and ads. I was the only one to really use that power—aside from Andy Howell, who was doing it for everyone—but I'm still surprised that New Deal didn't say something. I knew the graphic was crappy. I even made an ad that said, "Buy my board, it's the one with the crappy graphics." But it was so different from what was out there at the time and that was what I wanted to do: put out a self-made graphic regardless of how good or bad it was. The main point was to just put something out that I had created, so the kids that bought the board would know I drew my own graphic.

When I started Toy Machine Bloodsucking Skateboard Company, I continued doing my own graphics, and one of the first things I tell my team riders is that they have total control over their graphics, too. But they are very spotty. Some riders just want me to copy something off a movie poster or record cover, but it's hard for me to do that because I'm not so good at copying stuff, just creating cruddy stuff. Others will bring me ideas consistently, but sometimes I have to just make one without them knowing.

I think they still care about the graphics, but not to the level that I ever did. A lot of thinking had to go into graphics in the early '90s. The board was going to be out for six or more months, so you had to make sure it was good, that it went with the rider, and that it was going to sell. These days, all of those factors are still important, but you don't lose as much with a miss since boards are only out for three months. In the mid '90s it even got down to one graphic per month, and because of that, graphic choice is much more whimsical.

Once, while in Europe for the contests, I got a call from Tod Swank, who was freaking out about the fact that we needed another graphic for Jamie Thomas. The only thing we could think of was faxing a drawing to them in San Diego. I knew this would look like crap, but Jamie looked through my sketchbook anyway and found a drawing of a weird dinosaur/cow thing and said, "This one!" So we faxed the sketch over, and they colored it and made it into one of Jamie's boards.

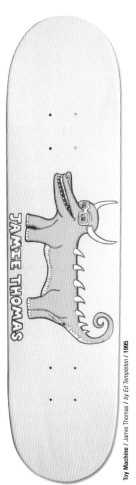

Toy Machine / Jamie Thomas / by Ed Templeton / 1995

Toy Machine / Jamie Thomas / by Cleon Peterson / 1996

Toy Machine / Jamie Thomas / by Ron Cameron / 1996

Toy Machine / Chris Senn / by Ed Templeton / 1998

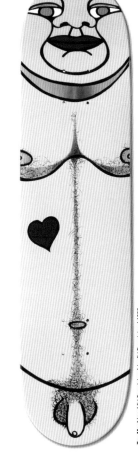

Toy Machine / Ed Templeton / by Ed Templeton / 1993

Toy Machine / Ed Templeton / by Ed Templeton / 2000

Toy Machine / Ed Templeton / by Ed Templeton / 1997

Toy Machine / Team / by Ed Templeton / 2002

Toy Machine / Ed Templeton / by Ed Templeton / 1995

Toy Machine / Ed Templeton / by Ed Templeton / 1995

It has been 14 years since I turned pro, and times have changed a lot since the early '90s. A lot of the "hand" has gone out of it. The computer is the big graphic generator these days. It has gone from doing everything by hand—cutting rubies and limiting yourself to seven colors—to being able to scan a two-inch sketch from a book, coloring it on the computer with as many colors as you want, and just emailing it down to San Diego! Logo boards seem to sell the best now.

I've been using this Transistor Sect character for a while that originally started out through my wanting to make a comic. I was trying to invent a character that would be easy to draw over and over again from different angles. That's why the Transistor Sect only has one eye and simple crab-like hands. It was a character born of laziness. I started doing boards with them on it, and it's now a recurring theme of my own graphics and Toy Machine in general. Another recurring character is Turtle Boy, who was made in the image of pro skateboarder Andrew Reynolds. Turtle Boy originated when I was on a tour with Andrew, Geoff Rowley, and photographer Atiba Jefferson. To pass the time on long drives, I would draw shitty comics with a ballpoint pen on lined paper. The comics were exclusively drawn to poke fun at the people on the tour, and I would sit mad-scientist style, drawing for 30 minutes, then we would all read it and laugh.

I started trying to draw each person as they were, but soon realized this was way too hard. So I simply changed everyone into whatever animal they looked like most, and then made their character based on that only simplified. Geoff Rowley looks like Eddie Munster, but that took too long so he became a ferret—but it looked more like a bear. Andrew looked like a turtle, so he became Turtle Boy Reynolds. I liked it so much that I told him I was going to make Turtle Boy a pro on Toy Machine. We've since made a bunch of graphics featuring Turtle Boy, and I've used the Turtle Boy comics in ads.

Aside from the comic world, I occasionally like to make a political statement with a board graphic. I feel that skaters, mostly due to their age, are not interested in the world they live in outside of skateboarding. I always wanted Toy Machine to be a place of ideas as well as skateboarding. One of my favorite boards was the Religion, Politics, Lies graphic with a drawing of a guy wearing TV-shaped glasses. He has a big syringe going into his ear with those three words in it. I wanted kids to see this and perhaps think about the stuff that gets injected into their heads from a young age. I recently came back to that theme and made a new Religion, Politics, Lies board using our newfangled four-color process style.

The last two years have been really strange. Technology has enabled us to do so much so easily that you find yourself being painted into a corner. I started three things in my life that require fulltime work for all of them to be done correctly. For the longest time I was able to juggle being a pro skater, company guy, graphic designer, and an art-fag, but as those things have grown along with emails and computing, they have intensified. Managing Toy Machine and doing the graphics is now a full-time job. Being a pro skater is now a full-time job too. You have to constantly produce new photos and video for your sponsors. And recently the amount of gallery shows I have been doing or have planned to do has become a huge time vortex.

Basically I'm fucked, and my pro skating is the one that ends up suffering the most. So over the last several years I have invited artist friends to do graphics for Toy Machine. We have had some great people do board series for us, such as, Adam Wallacavage, Margaret Kilgallen, Andrew Pommier, Jim Houser, Chris Johanson, Thomas Campbell, and many more. I really like it when my artist friends can do graphics. I get rad graphics out of the deal, and they get cash and street cred. But I still do the brunt of the graphics. | **Ed Templeton**

Toy Machine / Chris Senn / by Jim Houser / 1997

Toy Machine / Mike Maldonado / by Chris Johanson / 1998

Toy Machine / Brian Anderson / by Margaret Kilgallen / 2000

Toy Machine / Ed Templeton / by Margaret Kilgallen / 2000

Toy Machine / Elissa Steamer / by Margaret Kilgallen / 2000

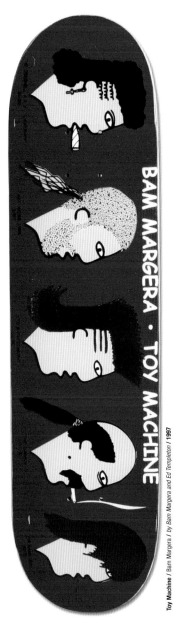

BAM MARGERA · TOY MACHINE

Toy Machine / Bam Margera / by Bam Margera and Ed Templeton / 1997

Toy Machine / Bam Margera / by Adam Wallacavage / 1997

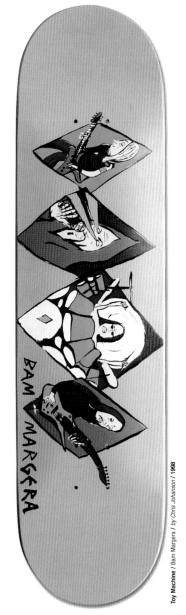

Toy Machine / Bam Margera / by Chris Johanson / 1998

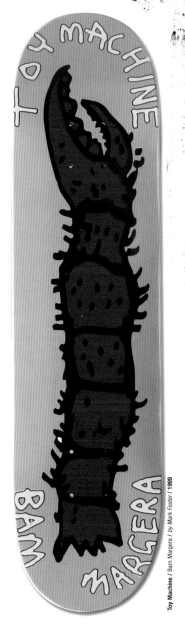

Toy Machine / Bam Margera / by Mark Foster / 1999

Bam Margera / 1997 / photo by Adam Wallacavage

We had this little haircut thing going, like the mullet, but we called it a STLB, the Short-Top-Long-Back. Then it turned into STLBSSWT, a Short-Top-Long-Back-Shaved-Sides-With-Tail. Then it just turned into STILB. So I wanted my first board graphic to just be a bunch of different STILB hairstyles, and we named them and put a percentage, like a 30/70, or a 10/90, or a 0/100, which would be like an old dude with a ponytail coming out the back. So we just made it happen, and me and Ed Templeton drew up these goofy looking faces. **Bam Margera**

Natas Kaupas

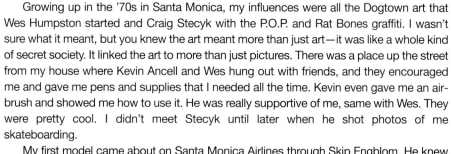

Growing up in the '70s in Santa Monica, my influences were all the Dogtown art that Wes Humpston started and Craig Stecyk with the P.O.P. and Rat Bones graffiti. I wasn't sure what it meant, but you knew the art meant more than just art—it was like a whole kind of secret society. It linked the art to more than just pictures. There was a place up the street from my house where Kevin Ancell and Wes hung out with friends, and they encouraged me and gave me pens and supplies that I needed all the time. Kevin even gave me an airbrush and showed me how to use it. He was really supportive of me, same with Wes. They were pretty cool. I didn't meet Stecyk until later when he shot photos of me skateboarding.

My first model came about on Santa Monica Airlines through Skip Engblom. He knew Ancell through the area as well, and had him draw up my graphics. I thought they were pretty good and just kinda stuck with the whole panther concept from there. Skip worked a lot by hand, and he had a lot of cool techniques using spray-paint and masking tape. The first graphic was only like two colors, but later on we felt it needed more color and thought the leaves were a good addition. Chris Buchinsky did those. I'm not sure why Ancell didn't do it … maybe he just wasn't around at the time.

Wes Humpston did the next panther design. Jim Phillips did a different rendition of it as well, but the first run was rushed through production and the word "Monica" was misspelled. Chris Buchinsky did one, but that idea didn't get fleshed out all the way, and he kinda ran with it anyway. I wasn't involved with that one enough. It was just sort of an abortion, and I think it only had one run.

In 1989, they [NHS] did a version of the Humpston graphic without letting me in on the whole thing. I only saw it when they sent me a couple finished boards that were fully silk-screened. The whole thing was done, like no sketches, nothing, and that kinda freaked me out, to not be involved in the process of having the artwork done on my own board. Maybe

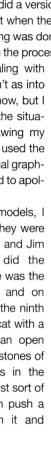

Santa Monica Airlines / Natas Kaupas / by Kevin Ancell / 1985

they were used to dealing with other people who weren't as into their graphics, I don't know, but I threw a hissy-fit about the situation and ended up drawing my own after that. They still used the panther part of the original graphic, though, and I later had to apologize for the hissy-fit.

For that last SMA models, I did the art on the one they were calling the Psycho Kitty, and Jim Phillips' son, Jimbo, did the Kitten board. Then there was the Bill the Cat knock-off, and on 101, Erik Brunetti drew the ninth version of it showing a cat with a gun to its head over an open grave. There were tombstones of all eight other graphics in the background. It was all just sort of seeing how far you can push a theme and stay within it and have fun.

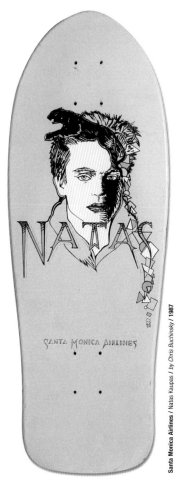

Natas Kaupas could skate like no one I had ever seen, or expected to ever see, and his first models had a panther inside a triangle. I knew I could bring that black spot in the triangle alive, and I remember telling Tim Piumarta that I could. Soon, whether from my challenge or not, I was given the job. Natas ordered up some banana leaves with a little monkey peeking out, and I made a visceral, muscular cat with killer teeth that popped out of the triangle with blue highlights, comic-book style. I upgraded the original lettering, keeping it in style, and placed some tropical flowering plants hanging around the SMA banner for effect. Some time, late at night, Santa Monica was spelled "Monca," but hardly anybody noticed. It was one of our better-selling models—however, I attribute that more to Natas' abilities on a skateboard. |Jim Phillips

Santa Monica Airlines / Natas Kaupas (Prototype) / by Justin Forbes / 1989

Santa Monica Airlines / Natas Kaupas / by Natas Kaupas and Justin Forbes / 1989

Santa Monica Airlines / Natas Kaupas / by Jimbo Phillips / 1989

For such a small company I think 101 did a pretty good job of making its mark in the graphics department. I worked with a lot of really good artists to create a lot of cool graphics. We tried to do new stuff and push some boundaries, and Rocco was really supportive of all the things we did. It's just cool to see how many 101 graphics make it into skateboard art books when we only had three pros at most. Running the company was one thing, but I really liked the graphics part the most and I learned tons. So when I began to concentrate on pretty much just graphic design, it made sense to go off and start doing freelance graphic work for other people. 101 was a great learning experience all the way around, though, and it really signified a learning experience, like "graphics life 101." It was just a good classroom. **Natas Kaupas**

Natas concept sketch / 1991 / by Natas Kaupas

Santa Monica Airlines / Natas Kaupas / by Natas Kaupas / 1990

Santa Monica Airlines / Natas Kaupas / by Erik Brunetti / 1990

101 / Natas Kaupas / by Erik Brunetti / 1991

101 / Natas Kaupas / by Marc McKee / 1991

101 / Gabriel Rodriguez / by Marc McKee / 1991

101 / Natas Kaupas / by Andy Jenkins / 1991

101 / Natas Kaupas / by "Severe" Ristagno and "Den One" Brunetti / 1992

101 / Eric Koston / by Slick / 1992

101 Skateboards Natas Kaupas Devil Worship Model

101 / Natas Kaupas / by Marc McKee / 1991

Without exerting any great deal of thought or effort, skateboarders can be generalized as a rather rebellious lot with a long history of spitting full in the face of the norm and taking taboo subject matter with a sarcastic grain of salt. Throughout the '80s this brazen defiance of the mainstream was exemplified by a proliferation of "evil" images such as skulls, blood and gore—a graphic aesthetic that fell hand-in-hand with the punk subculture—but these elements soon gave way to more clever and subversive concepts as the graphics matured to a whole new confrontational level in the early '90s.

While the World Industries Randy Colvin Censorship model certainly raised a few eyebrows in a "now you've gone too far" manner (albeit more so from uptight shop owners than skateboarders), it wasn't until the release of the 101 Natas Kaupas Devil Worship graphic in 1991 that moral psyches were unilaterally scarred, as both kiddies and adults grappled with deeply ingrained religious beliefs and superstitions. Replete with a dead Pope on a rope, a decapitated baby, an inverted pentagram, scary numerology and the Devil himself, the graphic covered virtually every Satanic base, all the way down to the detail of being printed upside-down on the deck. In one damning swoop this became the singlemost controversial graphic ever, as the stories before and after its creation became the stuff of legends—to the point that no one knew where the facts left off and the mythology took over. The great thing is, the reality of this graphic's origin is just as incredible as the rumors, or at least up until the spooky climax with Natas' broken ankle, that is.

|Sean Cliver

Mostly I recall the graphic being a jab at all the skulls from Zorlac and Powell. Marc McKee was annoyed that they weren't actually scary or hardcore and said he could do something way better. So I told him to do it. My job was then to find a rider who would want to use it. Natas was the most natural pick, but it was almost overkill with all the hype about his name. I talked with Jason Lee and at first he was all for it.

Of course, no one had actually seen the finished product yet. Then Marc unveiled it. Rodney Mullen's first reaction was pure fear. He didn't even want to be in the same room with it. I think that sort of rubbed off on Jason, and he started to back out of using it. It was at this point that I sat Jason down and wrote a 10,000 dollar check with his name on it—this was a trick that worked on Jesse Martinez every time. Jason grabbed the check, which was more money than he had ever seen, and I thought that was the end of that. Sometime in the middle of the night, Jason showed up at my house and gave back the check, saying he didn't want to burn in hell. I knew Gonz and his limited knowledge of the Catholic Church had been at work. Gonz always had a way of getting to Jason.

|Steve Rocco

The Devil Worship was originally a Jason Lee pro model for Blind. I recall Jason listening to a lot of Bauhaus at the time and wanting to come out with a board featuring a darker theme than a lot of the cartoon fare he had on some of his more recent graphics, like the Grinch and the Cat in the Hat—both unauthorized copyright infringements that got us a cease-and-desist letter from Dr. Seuss.

Mark Gonzales' cousin Ernie Mendoza, who was a contributing artist to Blind, had started on a Bela Lugosi graphic for Jason, but Rocco didn't want to produce it. So I suggested my idea and drew it up. It had the desired effect, but Jason was unsure if he wanted it, despite peer pressure from Gonz and Rocco. Finally Rocco wrote out a check for 10,000 dollars to Jason, and it looked like he was sold. That weekend we made a print run of Jason Lee shirts that contained artwork from the deck graphic. Unfortunately, Jason returned with the uncashed check, saying he'd changed his mind. I think it may have been because of the decapitated baby.

The graphic sat around for a few days despite efforts of trying to get World Industries on it instead of Jason's name, but to no avail—there was no way of putting it in there without ruining the composition. So then Natas stepped up and offered to put his name on it, seeing it as an opportunity to make a joke out of the fact he was used to getting shit from people because his name is "Satan" spelled backwards—its real derivation is a unique masculine form of the Lithuanian girl's name Natalias that his parents, who are also not devil-worshippers, came up with.

The deck sold decently and an ad we ran in Thrasher garnered many complaints, even though in Natas' own writing it said, "But seriously folks, these are jokes," which goes to show how stupid people are and that they can't read. Somewhere around this time Natas broke his ankle while skating, and a rumor emerged he was riding the Devil Worship board and it somehow jinxed him. I forget the board he was really on, but it had nothing to do with the occult. And I mean, how common are broken ankles in skateboarding?

|Marc McKee

Unreleased Jason Lee T-shirt design / 1991 / by Marc McKee

When Jason Lee backed out of the Devil Worship graphic it seemed like a perfect opportunity to thumb my nose at all the people who found a problem with my name, especially the ones who were vocal about it without doing any research. As far as an injury connection, there was no real Christian-karmic-voodoo thing, because I was riding Mike Vallely's Animal Man board at the time I broke my ankle. Maybe the vegetables were out to get me. |Natas Kaupas

Real / Max Schaaf / by Todd Francis / 1998

Stereo / Team / by Todd Francis / 1996

Todd Francis

I started working at Deluxe in 1994 as an entry-level production artist. Got hired on by Jeff Klindt, who was willing to hire anybody who could draw and be there on time. At the time, all the production work for the graphics was done traditionally—in other words "old fashioned"—as in cutting rubies [red masking film], shooting line art to film, all that crap. No scanners, no digitization of art, nothing. Still, I was happy just to be doing anything for a job that involved art in some way, and the work environment there was great. Pretty much everyone I worked with was a weirdo, which was a hell of a lot better than working in an office with a bunch of Republicans.

Soon I was able to start doing a lot of the wheel and T-shirt graphics for Spitfire and eventually got involved in board graphics for Real and Stereo. The first board graphic I ever did was for Julien Stranger, who was in jail out of state for whatever reason. It showed a judge angrily banging his gavel, and the bailiffs closing in on the accused with handcuffs. It wasn't particularly good, but it was my first. My second board

was for James Kelch, who really didn't care at all what appeared on his board graphics as long as the check arrived on time. It was this whole scene with a farmer and his daughters, running away from a tornado that is supposed to be Kelch—it's smoking a giant cigarette.

Now that I think about it, that board wasn't so bad, but over the years I've done some real stinkers. We had to churn out graphics at an alarming pace, sometimes starting and finishing a board graphic all in one day. So, sometimes the end result looked hastily done … oh well. Once you get used to the idea that the art is just going to get scraped off on a curb somewhere, it becomes a lot less about you and your artistic pride and more about deadlines and keeping people happy.

In the art room, we were expected to work closely with the pro riders on their graphics, which in some cases was great, in others was a total joke. Some guys wanted the most retarded stuff on their boards, and I couldn't just tell them that stoner crap or "Praise Jesus" themes weren't the best avenue to board sales. So sometimes I'd wind up being

Real / James Kelch / by Todd Francis / 1995

Real / Max Schaaf / by Todd Francis / 1999

Real / Max Schaaf / by Todd Francis / 1999

Real / Mark Gonzales / by Todd Francis / 1998

Real / Matt Field / by Todd Francis / 1999

THE LONG PLAYING SOUND

stereo team 93945 plume

Stereo / Team / by Chris Pastras and Judd Vetrone / 1994

JASON Lee

Stereo / Jason Lee / by Todd Francis / 1996

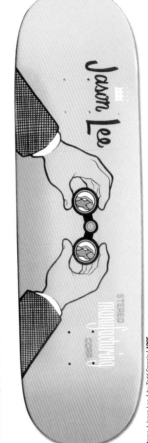

Jason Lee

STEREO manufacturing CORP.

Stereo / Jason Lee / by Todd Francis / 1996

STEREO SERIES

Stereo / Jason Lee / by Todd Francis / 1995

Stereo Presents
JASON LEE in
THE SETTING SUN
1988 - 1996

Stereo / Jason Lee / by Todd Francis / 1996

JASON LEE

STEREO

Stereo / Jason Lee / by Christian Cooper / 1995

rodriguez estereo

Stereo / Matt Rodriguez / by Jeremy Nathan / 1994

Shipman CARL

STEREO SERIES

Stereo / Carl Shipman / by Christian Cooper / 1996

stereo
carl
shipman

Stereo / Carl Shipman / by Christian Cooper / 1996

ETHAN FOWLER
STEREO THE SOUND OF REVOLUTION

Stereo / Ethan Fowler / by Tobin Yelland / 1996

stuck doing a graphic that nobody else wanted to do, and a week or two later someone would walk in holding up some horrible board, asking, "Who the hell did this?" as if it had been my idea in the first place. But lots of the guys were great with graphic ideas. Jim Thiebaud and Tommy Guerrero were, and still are, at the center of most of the decisions being made there, and they were really fun to work with. Klindt had an art background, too, so he was good at it and he was always involved.

At the time, Stereo had a real great thing going. Jason Lee and Chris Pastras were at Deluxe almost every day working on graphics and ads, and it was pretty funny to be a part of. Jason is a really easy guy to work with because he knows exactly what he wants. He'd be standing across from you, and he'd be really serious, saying, "Todd, I need this girl to be wearing this beret," or something like that, and he'd be completely insistent upon it, gesturing with his hands with this total look of seriousness on his face, and since I barely knew him I had to take him at face value. So he'd carry on for a few minutes, I'd be writing all this crazy stuff down, and then he'd lean over and say, "Todd, I'm completely fucking with you." Then he'd grin at me and start laughing, and I'd feel like an ass. Between him and Chris, they had that company's image so dialed in it was incredible. Once I figured out what they liked and disliked, it became a great company to do graphics for. Some of the graphics I did for Matt Rodriguez were the best board graphics I've ever done.

I'd never really followed Mark Gonzales all that much, but the way everyone at Deluxe treated him when he came to ride for Real, you'd think he was royalty. When he'd come into the offices, it'd get real quiet, and I'd see everyone get all nervous and itchy when he'd be sitting in the break area, doodling in his book. Guys would practically get down on their knees to shake his hand and mutter stuff about what an influence he'd been, like he was Gandhi or something. Since he wanted to get involved with the graphics for Real, I had to start working closely

with him. Don't get me wrong, I like Mark, and he's really good to work with, but since everyone else there just kissed his ass so heavily, I took it upon myself to fuck with him as often as possible. I'd leave him angry voice mails, send him threatening postcards, and it'd always get under his skin. He called me "Francis," and I'd hear him muttering my name in the halls in that nasally voice of his, then he'd come in the art room and start messing with me. One time we started wrestling, nothing serious, but for such a little guy he's real strong. I probably outweigh him by twenty pounds, and he could work me over, which is really disappointing, because I wanted to try and humiliate him as often as possible. I'm working on this really good prank that's going to piss him off to no end, hopefully by the time this book comes out I've dropped it on him.

Julien Stranger was invited to start his own company, Anti Hero, and as the months went on it became more and more my favorite company to do graphics for. Julien and I came up with the Eagle logo, which has lasted all these years, and did a whole bunch of graphics that were real funny and offensive. He was given a lot more freedom to do whatever he wanted with Anti Hero, and we had a pretty good time of it. Guys like Sean Young and Andy Roy were real good with funny ideas, Cardiel, too. Julien's the best, though. It was so fun coming up with the lousiest crap for him. There were a few times we would come up with graphics for Anti Hero that we totally loved, and for whatever reason, they'd get cut. We'd finish the board, deliver it to the printers, and then boom, we'd get a call, or Klindt would walk back into the art room carrying the artwork in his arms like it had horseshit on it.

Funny thing is, it was never tits and ass stuff. It was always political stuff that got cut. We did this one board that had a huge head of Richard Nixon on it that got somebody all riled up, and the graphic never made it to print. Who the hell is going to say we can't make fun of Richard Nixon?! I mean, that guy was just a hackey-sack for mockery, and we

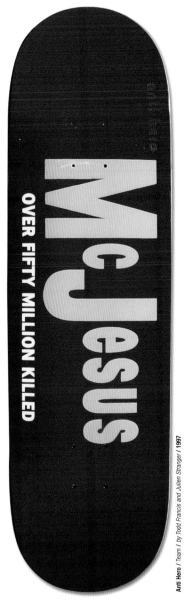

can't do a picture of him for a graphic? It wasn't like there was a swastika on his forehead or anything. We also tried to do a McDonald's board
that said something like, "Over Six Million Killed," but that
got axed real quick. You never really knew what was okay
and what wasn't.

There was one board we did called "The Texas
Chainsaw Pigfucker" that showed a redneck farmer-type
wearing a hockey mask and overalls, he's got a chainsaw
in one hand, and he's got his pants down, screwing a
hapless pig from behind. The whole thing was based on
the phrase "Texas Chainsaw Pigfucker," which was a
saying Ruben Orkin, the team manager of Spitfire and
Thunder at the time, liked to throw around in random situations, usually during a meal. Klindt heard it one day and said, "Hey, we
gotta do a board for Real of that!" It was totally senseless, and nobody
complained at all about it down the line.

The worst thing that ever happened to me at Deluxe was the time we
were instructed to do a board graphic that ripped off an old Hell's Angels
graphic from the '60s. I won't go into details, but they got really, really
angry when they found out about it. A lot of threats were made, and a

few of us were genuinely terrified for our lives months thereafter. I
thought I was going to have to jump out of the art room's second-story
windows if they arrived. A year or two later, I heard the
only thing that kept the guys from showing up and
beating our heads in once was a torrential storm that
washed out some roads. That was a really great experience. Take it from me: never ever even come close to
ripping off graphic ideas from a bunch of guys who are
really good at beating people up.

After working at Deluxe for like seven years, I was
running out of gas. I'd been in S.F. for a while and wanted to move back to L.A. to get away from the wind and
the rain—and maybe the beer. I felt like I'd done all I
could at Deluxe. I'd been art director there for five or six years, and there
wasn't any higher position I could ascend to. Plus, some of my favorite
co-workers had moved on or died. Jason had long since ceased being
a part of Stereo's operations, and the company was about to fold, so it
looked like a good time to move on. I knew I'd miss a lot of what I'd been
doing with Jim, Tommy, Chris and Julien, but in 1999 I left Deluxe and
S.F., and came back to L.A.

Anti Hero / Tony Trujillo / by Todd Francis / 1999

Real / Team / by Todd Francis / 1996

Real / Team / artist unknown / 1997

Real / Jim Thiebaud and Tommy Guerrero / by Christian Cooper / 1997

Real / Mark Gonzales / by Mark Gonzales / 1999

Stereo / Dustin Dollin / artist unknown / 1999

Krooked / Mark Gonzales / by Mark Gonzales / 2003

Element / Natas Kaupas / by Natas Kaupas and Johnny Schillereff / 1998

Element / Natas Kaupas / by Johnny Schillereff / 1998

Element / Natas Kaupas / by Natas Kaupas / 1999

New Deal / Team / by Todd Francis / 2002

New Deal / Kenny Reed / by Todd Francis and Natas Kaupas / 2001

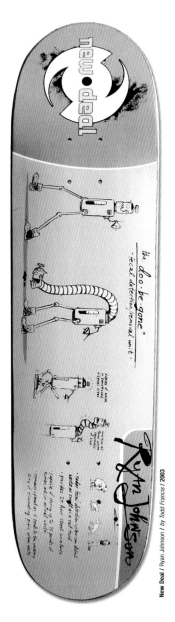

New Deal / Ryan Johnson / by Todd Francis / 2003

New Deal / Lincoln Ueda / by Todd Francis / 2002

I'd decided to give up on the skate-graphics thing, maybe try my hand at writing and drawing a graphic novel or something, but after returning to L.A., I hooked up with Natas Kaupas, and he and I started working on graphics together—it's funny that I somehow wound up back in the industry that I'd thought I'd sworn off of. I guess new faces, better pay, and a certain degree of artistic freedom will do that to you.

Of all the people I've worked with over the years, Natas is easily the best designer, graphics guy, whatever you want to call him—he's the best at it. He's just super smart, knows what he wants, a great collaborator, and really fun to work with. He introduced me to Johnny Schillereff at Little Giant, Giant's old art offices in Santa Monica, and Natas and I started doing all the graphics for New Deal.

We did that for a while, then he moved on and I kept doing them. It was funny, because New Deal was a slowly sinking ship that nobody cared about. I could have done a series of cats' asses for board graphics and it would've made it through. I wound up with total artistic freedom, could do whatever the hell I dreamed up, and as long as it looked good, then great. Some of the boards we did during that run remain some of the best I've ever done, but no one was giving two shits about New Deal, and Giant was pretty tired of keeping it afloat, so they finally put the company to rest.

Johnny and I continued to work together after that, mostly with Element. Somehow a skate company the size of Element hadn't locked in with a staff artist, and I became that for them, I guess. So it goes from making boards that nobody sees or cares about with New Deal, to making designs for boards and shirts that are everywhere. The stuff I do for Bam Margera is all over the place, and everyone knows who he is. It's nuts.

I pretty much work exclusively with Element now, and it's incredible how well things have gone. I get to work at home creating graphics, and then email the finished artwork to their offices in Irvine. The other day, after looking over some drawings I'd sent down, one of the Element designers asked around if I do a lot of drugs. I guess most of my stuff kind of comes out of left field. I should make a sign for my studio door that just says "Left Field"—I could make the letters out of corn.

|Todd Francis

Anti Hero / Team / by Chris Johanson / 2000

Anti Hero / Team / by Chris Johanson / 1999

Anti Hero / Team / by Chris Johanson / 1997

Anti Hero / John Cardiel / by Chris Johanson / 2001

Chris Johanson

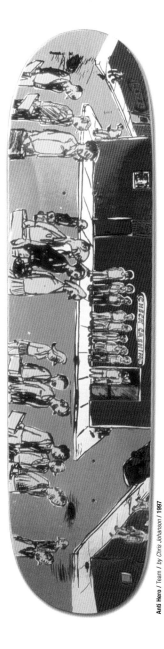

Anti Hero / Team / *by Chris Johanson* / **1997**

Anti Hero / Team / *by Chris Johanson* / **1997**

Anti Hero / Team / *by Chris Johanson* / **1997**

Anti Hero / Team / *by Chris Johanson* / **1997**

In the '80s I used to drive around to skate spots with Chris Johanson in San Jose in this big, blue piece of shit car. I don't even remember whose car it was, but he was usually on acid while the car was always on empty. He was an artist even then. His 'zine Karmaboarder was fuckin' weird, filled with odd drawings of animals skating pools, yet it was one of the most highly prized in the scene.

Eventually he moved to San Francisco and divided his time between painting and starving. His paintings at the time were almost always on found wood, an aesthetic that was most likely born out of necessity, but a detail that was essential to the bummers and the decay and the "negatrons," as he called them, that were his subjects. At the same time he formed a band called Tina Age 13. They'd wear dresses on stage and kiss each other. It was groovy. Although Chris likes to refer to it as "the damage days," it was the time that his art began to be recognized as art. The graphics he did for Anti Hero were probably one of his first successes.

Julien Stranger and I used to sit around and talk about authors like Louis-Ferdinand Celine and Samuel Beckett, so it was no surprise that we both loved Chris's paintings, which displayed a similarly dark humor. Chris has gone on to great success and is now recognized by the real "art world." His paintings were recently shown in the Whitney Biennial, one of the highest honors an American artist can achieve. |Dave Carnie

Todd Bratrud

In 1998, I was living in Minneapolis, Minnesota, and my friend Billy Kahn was getting boards from Consolidated. Once in awhile there would be one in there for me, so I'd usually send a letter saying thanks. One time I drew a picture on the envelope and soon after that I got a call from Moish Brenman, Consolidated's art director, saying they wanted to use the art for a board graphic. From the moment I stepped foot on a skateboard, all I wanted to do was skateboard graphics, so naturally I said yes. When I was younger, I'd sent ideas for graphics to almost every company and never got any response back, but I never thought to send any art to Consolidated because I knew they had their shit going pretty good.

Over the next year I did about ten graphics for Consolidated, all while living in Minnesota, mostly just random stuff. I was busy working at a consumer design firm doing art for cereal, cracker and cookie boxes, not to mention a lot of art and layout crap for Life Sucks Die magazine and Fobia skate shop. So I just did whatever whenever I had a few spare minutes and didn't put that much thought into it. I wasn't trying to get my hopes up, but I was definitely excited. I couldn't think of any company aside from Consolidated that I'd be hyped on doing art for.

My third and fourth graphics for Consolidated were these step-by-steps that made a lot of shops and people pretty mad. I was still working at the consumer design firm at the time, so I wanted to do something that was the opposite of what I was doing there, which were happy little characters. It was fun and all, but I needed to do something raw. The original idea was a series of three boards, but whoever made the final call on graphics at Consolidated didn't like the third one, which was kind of a bummer because I thought it made the whole series funny—the third board depicted a guy applying hot-pink nail polish to his fingernails. I guess it was stupid, but I liked it.

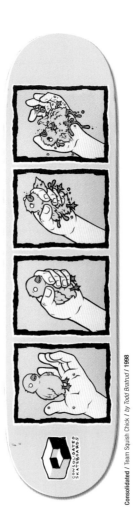

Consolidated / Scott Bourne / by Moish Brenman / 1999

Consolidated / Team Forever Shaka / by Todd Bratrud / 1998

Consolidated / Team Hand Shake / by Todd Bratrud / 1998

Consolidated / Team Squish Chick / by Todd Bratrud / 1998

Consolidated / Karma Tscheff / by Todd Bratrud / 1999

Anyway, people thought kids would somehow see these step-by-steps and try to do them in real life. One day, when I was working at Fobia, I had a mom looking at the Step-by-Step boards on the wall. She got all bent out of shape, asking how a shop could sell these boards to kids, and better yet, what kind of person would draw stuff like this. I told her I was the person who drew them. I think she thought I was just being a prick and messing with her, but I thought it was cool that someone actually paid attention to something I did.

The Skull Girls was another series I did for Consolidated before I worked there. I didn't even really know the team or what I was trying to do; I just liked the way the graphics looked. I later heard from the team that I jinxed them all with bad luck with girls though, and it was supposedly my fault because of the Skull Girl graphics. Karma Tsocheff doesn't remember telling me this, but at one point he asked me to do a graphic that would make up for the bad luck I gave him with the ladies and give him good luck with hot hippie girls. I don't know why I thought a hippie chick laying in the grass and throwing up a peace sign with hairy legs and pits would be good luck, but I did … and it wasn't.

About a year after I started freelancing for Consolidated, I got a call from Jason Jessee. He told me Moish quit and asked if I'd like his job as art director. It was a no-brainer for me; I just had to figure out how to get my wife to quit her jobs and move to Santa Cruz. But she pretty much knew this was my dream job and that was that. Two weeks later we packed up all our crap and moved to California. It was tough at first because I didn't really know what I was doing or how to do any of what I was supposed to do, like layout ads, color separations for board graphics, stickers, wheels, T-shirts, put together order forms, or edit video stuff. I just knew how to draw—and I really didn't even know how

to do that very well. I still don't really know what I'm doing, but that's kind of the way it works at Consolidated. We just do whatever we want and do it in the best way we know how.

I originally used the Giving Tree idea for Roots Skateboards, a small company from Minneapolis, and not very many were made. I don't think the boards even got out of the area. But about a year after I started working at Consolidated, the team was in Europe when I needed to get graphics done. The problem was that I couldn't get a hold of them for any ideas. I had back-ups for some of them, but not Karma. Scott Bourne had mentioned to me that Consolidated should redo the Giving Tree graphic but change the falling skateboard to the Consolidated Cube logo instead. So I made the changes to the graphic and put Karma's name on it. I didn't have time to call Todd Brown at Roots to ask if it was cool, so I decided to give them a little credit by writing "Roots" in one of the colors that got printed over by the black outlines on the boy's hair. It was hard to see even if you were told that it was there, but somehow Karma saw it and was pissed at me for it, not to mention for using the graphic in the first place on account of it being really childlike.

Unfortunately, the board sold out really quick. Leticia and Birdo wanted to run with it again, but Karma wasn't into it. So we decided to toughen it up a bit by showing the little boy crushed by the falling Cube logo. It still sold well and we needed to reorder it, but now we all felt bad about having killed the kid. So we did part three, showing the boy as an angel floating away holding the Cube logo. After the boards were all long gone, we got a call from the Shel Silverstien Foundation. The lady was yelling and screaming about a lawsuit, but Birdo talked to her for hours and by the end of the call she admitted to actually thinking the

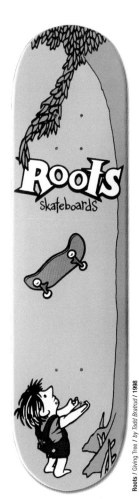

Consolidated / Karma Tsocheff / 1999

Roots / Giving Tree / by Todd Bratrud / 1998

Consolidated / Karma Tsocheff / by Todd Bratrud / 2000

Consolidated / Karma Tsocheff / by Todd Bratrud / 2001

Consolidated / Karma Tsocheff / by Todd Bratrud / 2001

graphic series was cool and that we just had to stop selling the boards. But at that point they were all gone anyway.

Consolidated never really does series graphics, but somehow I was able to persuade everyone into letting the Hurt Girls series happen. Graphics with girls never really sell that well—for Consolidated at least—but the cool thing about these was how many letters and emails we got from women's rights people. I guess we were somehow promoting the beating of women with this series. I didn't realize that by showing a girl on crutches or with a sling on her arm that it automatically meant they were beaten by men. If anything, while drawing these girls I'd imagined they were in skiing or car accidents. A handful of people also accused us of being sexist and exploiting women by showing them in bikinis. In actuality, I just thought funny-colored girls in bikinis that had been hurt in one way or another looked kind of cool. At least I drew them happy.

I've loved Anna Nicole Smith from the first Guess ads. I paid attention to all her photos that showed up in magazines, and once the tabloids started doing their thing there were a lot of good, funny photos all the time. My favorite tabloid headline was one that said huge on the cover "Anna Nicole's Boobs Explode." It didn't have a picture of her exploding like I made this graphic look, but it was still fresh. So I always had the idea to do a graphic of Anna with exploding boobs in the back of my mind.

Years later, Consolidated was doing a series of limited-edition graphics made exclusively for Nor Cal Distribution in Spain. I really didn't think the graphic was going to happen, but I submitted it anyway and for whatever reason Nor Cal was into it. I have no idea if anyone aside from me and Louise at Nor Cal actually liked this graphic, but it was cool to be able to do it.

The It's a Man graphic idea was 100 percent Birdo. The original idea, however, was "Congratulations, its Abe Lincoln!" but after a few minutes it changed to "man." There really isn't any more of a story behind this one except that it seemed funny for a second one day and we just went with it. One thing, though, is that this graphic was printed two different times. The first was kind of tame as far as colors go, because I was scared to do the graphic the way I had envisioned it—really messy with blood—and I thought Leticia wouldn't be into the idea in the first place, let alone if it were all gross-looking. So I made the afterbirth goo pink. The board ended up selling really well so we reordered it. Before it was printed though, I called Screaming Squeegees and had them change the pink color to red. I didn't tell Leticia about it. So when the boards showed up with bloody red afterbirth, I just blamed Screaming and told Leticia it must have been a printing mistake.

Some of the best Consolidated graphics of all time were done by a really good friend of mine from Windom, Minnesota—Aaron Horkey. He sends in graphics from time to time, and we've used everything he has ever sent in. All Aaron's stuff is done by hand, no computer involved at all. It also tends to be a bit on the dark side, so it really only fits Alan Petersen and Ryan Wilburn most of the time.

A lot of people were really bummed on the Rainbows graphic. I guess it comes off sort of anti-gay, but the real story behind this one is pretty far from anything at all. I walked outside of Consolidated, and Jason Jessee was working on one of his motorcycles. He was pissed and having a bad day or motorcycle problems or something. I looked up in the sky and saw a huge rainbow and pointed it out to Jason to try and cheer him up. Jason looked at the rainbow and said, "Rainbows don't mean shit." |**Todd Bratrud**

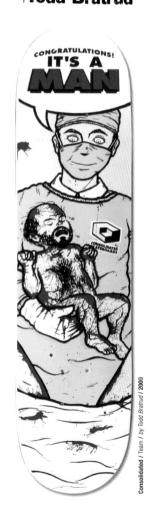

Consolidated / Team Thick / by Todd Bratrud / 2002

Consolidated / Team Medium / by Todd Bratrud / 2002

Consolidated / Team Thin / by Todd Bratrud / 2002

Consolidated / Team / by Todd Bratrud / 2000

Consolidated / Team / by Todd Bratrud / 2001

Consolidated / Amber Graves / by Todd Bratrud / 2002

CLINT PETERSON

Consolidated / Clint Peterson / by Todd Bratrud / 2001

BUTT HOLE FACE

Consolidated / Team / by Todd Bratrud / 2002

LIFE IS JOY

LIFE IS PAIN

Consolidated / Scott Bourne / by Todd Bratrud / 2000

Consolidated / Scott Bourne / by Todd Bratrud / 1999

Consolidated / Ryan Wilburn / by Aaron Horkey / 2001

CRASH & BURN

Consolidated / Alan Petersen / by Aaron Horkey / 2002

Consolidated / Jesse Paez / by Aaron Horkey / 2005

Consolidated / Alan Petersen / by Aaron Horkey / 2005

RAINBOWS DON'T MEAN SHIT

Consolidated / Team / by Todd Bratrud / 2002

Hand drawn by John Lucero / 1983

Variflex / John Lucero / by XnO / 1984

Madrid / John Lucero / by John Lucero / 1985

Madrid / Mike Smith / by John Lucero / 1985

John Lucero

I consider myself more of a designer than an artist. I hate to say that, but I've always been inspired by other skateboard art, whether it's a bold, straightforward logo-style like Santa Cruz, the VCJ stuff for Powell Peralta, or the clean artwork of Wes Humpston's early Dogtown stuff, where everything is very symmetrical. I was inspired by it all, so I might be a little more like a chameleon with my work, as I've done a few things where I've combined almost every aspect of my influences with full illustrations and very graphic backgrounds accompanied by the company logo and signature of the skaters.

In 1982, I did my first Variflex prototype with the skull, bat wings, and bone lettering. I then hand-painted it on five or six boards for trade-show samples in 1983, but the consensus was that the graphic wasn't gonna work for Variflex. It was too scary or something. I was beginning to work on some new stuff when they came back from another trade show where they had seen some graphics done by Pushead. They suggested having an artist like him do something. Since I wasn't an established artist, I felt they knew more what they were talking about than I did, so I called up

Pushead. He was already working on other graphics at the time, but he suggested I try another artist he knew, XnO from Tennessee.

I called him up, and he sent me some samples of his artwork. It was gnarly bondage stuff, and I was into it right away. I sent him a few sketches based off his artwork with a template of the board. We corresponded by phone, and the final product came out as a leather bondage bitch on top of some fucked dude tied down by his nose, lip, and earrings. Variflex sold about 200 of those boards, but a lot of them got sent back by the mom and pop stores because of the graphic nature. Today it wouldn't be much of anything, but back then that kinda stuff just wasn't out there. I still don't know how the hell it even came out, but I'm actually glad it did now because it's so fucking hot.

I quit the company shortly after that. Variflex was headed in a toy-store direction, and when a chance to skate for Santa Cruz came up I jumped at it. That was my dream team at the time. I rode for Santa Cruz for about a year, but it looked like I wasn't gonna get a pro board. I then saw Jerry Madrid at a Huntington Beach street-style contest where I got fourth

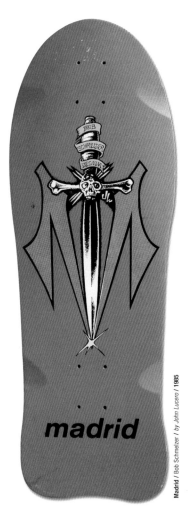

Madrid / Bob Schmelzer / by John Lucero / 1985

Madrid / Mike Smith / by John Lucero / 1986

Madrid / Bill Danforth / by Marty Jimenez / 1985

Madrid / X-Teamrider / by John Lucero / 1986

place. He offered me a spot on the Madrid team and a chance to have a pro model, but one of my conditions was that I got to draw the graphics and do whatever I wanted with the board.

My Jester board came out in 1985. This was the first graphic I ever drew by myself, and it was all my original idea. I liked the whole court jester, creepy, devious kinda thing. I wanted a hot-pink fluorescent-color board, but for whatever reason Madrid couldn't come up with the right pink. They did come up with this hot green, though, and I went with that instead. At the time there was also a race between Madrid and Paul Schmitt to produce the first stained-veneer boards, because everything done until then was all natural wood. Madrid managed to do it first, so the first ever stained-veneers were done on my Jester model in a bluish-green stain when one of the wood manufacturers finally came up with a vacuum-dyed process.

When my Madrid board first came out, 500 were produced and it sold instantly. It was the best-selling board in the history of the company. So Madrid was happy, I was happy, and every month the sales went up, which helped solidify my name in the marketplace, and it became associated with my own art and graphics. I was young and amped up and wanted to do more art, so I redesigned Mike Smith's board with the Duck graphic, did Bob Schmelzer's Dagger board, and I was working on some Bill Danforth stuff but it never came out—Marty Jimenez did Bill's Misfits graphic.

I'd gone to college and took advertising and other art-inspired class-

Jeff Grosso concept sketch / 1986 / by John Lucero

es, but a semester into it I realized that hands-on experience was the best way to go. So Madrid was a great stepping-stone for me, as it was all hands-on. They also manufactured decks for Dogtown, Suicidal Skates, and Alva, so I learned how to silkscreen boards as well.

The reason I left Madrid to hop on Schmitt Stix was simply because I was young and wanted to keep on moving on, and Paul Schmitt produced the raddest boards at the time. In Florida, he made all his boards in his mom's garage, hand pressed, and they were super strong, had really good concave, and lots of epoxy. When he made the move to the West Coast and hooked up with Vision, I approached Paul and told him I wanted to ride for Schmitt Stix. He wasn't that thrilled on the idea, but I had an ace in my pocket: I told him I had Jeff Grosso, the number-one amateur at the time who wanted to turn pro, and that we both wanted to ride for Schmitt Stix in a package deal. He jumped at the chance to have Grosso, so I got to tag along for the ride.

I already had the graphics designed for Jeff and I, and when I showed them the stuff, they were like, "Yeah, let's get it together." The first board I came out with was a little guy looking through these bars. It sold instantly, as did the Grosso with the baby blocks and the rag doll. The Grosso I drew from scratch. I just came up with this idea that Jeff was a little brat—it wasn't very publicized, but to those who knew him, Jeff's nickname was "The Brat"—and the whole thing symbolized him to a T.

Schmitt Stix / John Lucero / by John Lucero / 1986

Schmitt Stix / John Lucero / by John Lucero / 1987

Schmitt Stix / Monty Nolder / by John Lucero / 1986

Schmitt Stix / Monty Nolder / by John Lucero / 1986

My graphic, on the other hand, came from when I was a little kid, loving cereal with the prizes, and one time there was this sticker of a dungeon scene with a little guy looking through the bars. I had that thing stuck on an old chest I kept shit in before I even skated, and one day I was looking at it and thought it looked really cool. So I made my own drawing of it by fitting it on a board shape and put my name on it. I hate to admit it, but I'd say it's probably the first ripped-off graphic ever produced. During that time I also ended up getting a job in the Vision art department, and I did the Kevin Staab graphic with the mad scientist, the Monty Nolder Totem graphics for Schmitt Stix, and a lot of ads for the company. It wasn't my intent to come in there and change Schmitt Stix, but when I came to the company I brought my vibe to it, which kind of took over their vibe. This all went down in a matter of year.

When I quit Madrid they had ceased all production of my model. It wasn't until a year later, when I was on Schmitt Stix, that they reissued my Jester board as the X-Teamrider. When I first caught wind of it I was somewhat upset, but also by my nature I didn't really care. I just wanted to get a couple for myself. It also opened up the door for my second Schmitt graphic, which was kind of a payback to Madrid. The X2 turned out to be one of the best-selling boards in the history of skateboarding at the time.

John Lucero / Del Mar, CA / 1987 / *photo by Grant Brittain*

Back then I used to make a royalty of $1.50 a board as a pro skater. I didn't get a salary. So if I sold two decks I got three bucks. But since the X2 was one of the top-selling boards I got anywhere from ten- to fifteen-thousand a month—and I was only 22 years old. This eventually helped me start my own business, buy my first house—it helped me with everything. I never had to worry after that. Well, until I started my business, that is, and lost all the money and had to start over again.

During the time I had my X2 board out mini models were getting popular, but I didn't want to have a mini. I wanted to have a street board, so I made the Street Thing and that started to do well, too. The average board produced at the time was 10" x 30", and if you went outside that range people started asking questions, but I had an idea to make a bigger board, because I only rode 32-inch long decks that Chuck Hults custom-made for me. So I came up with this new graphic, the Red Cross, which was a completely different direction than my previous boards—it was real bold and simple—and I came to Paul with the idea of producing this as a larger board.

The argument started off, "The board's not gonna sell, it's too big." I go, "That's okay by me, I just want to put out something different that people might want to ride." I hate to think it was some kind of crazy argument, but what it came down to was the fact that they didn't want to produce the

board and they told me I didn't know what it took to make a skateboard company. I took offense to this and said, "Don't tell me I don't know what it takes, I've been working with you guys for a long time—this is everything to me. You guys are no better than me. I'll produce the boards myself. I'm gonna start my own company." I had no intention of quitting the team. They just caught me on the wrong day. I felt embarrassed and ridiculed, and I took it into my own hands. A couple nights later I went to dinner with Brad Dorfman and Paul to discuss it. I said, "Hey, you guys did it, so there's no reason I can't do it." I finished my steak, they handed me my last check, and I woke up the next day without a sponsor and no idea how to start a company.

I went a couple weeks without really doing anything about it. I was just cruising around and called a few places to get some prototypes made. Then I went to a contest and ran into Steve Rocco, who used to be the team manager of Sims, Vision, and Schmitt Stix. I'd gone on a tour and done a couple other things with Rocco, so I was friendly with him. He was trying to start his own company at the time, SMA Rocco Division, so we were just kicking back and laughing about it. He was all excited when he heard I'd quit to start my own thing, but I told him I didn't know jack shit about what I was doing. Rocco said, "I've got it all figured out. Come on down and I'll show you every step."

So I went down to his place—he was working out of his house—and he showed me everything he was doing. We then decided to form our own distribution company and sell both our products. The original name of the company was Prime Time Distribution. I made up the name, and he put the whole business together. We put some money into it, got a warehouse, and started producing stuff, but I wasn't really happy with the boards from

the woodshop we were using, so I was just producing stickers and T-shirts. Soon all the money I'd made as a pro skater pretty much disappeared and I started to get cold feet. Rocco's a great guy, but he just has his own way of doing things and started getting involved with some shady people.

Grosso was riding for Santa Cruz at the time, and being my best friend he let them know what I was up to and how I was off to a slow start and having second thoughts. So Santa Cruz called me up and said, "Hey, we understand you're having some problems. If you want, we'll take it over and you just go back to skating and doing artwork while we run the show." Right away I was like, "That's what I want to do." So I told Rocco, and he wasn't happy about it at all. I then sold my half of Prime Time to Rodney Mullen for a couple-thousand dollars.

When I left, Prime Time had orders for the Lucero Red Cross board, and Rocco went ahead and manufactured them anyway. It didn't mean much to me, but I did end up getting in a little fight with him. I knew the guys who owned the screen-shop that printed those bootleg Red Cross boards, so I got a couple and painted Kill Rocco on them as a joke.

Lucero Ltd. / John Lucero / by *John Lucero* / **1989**

Lucero Ltd. / John Lucero / by *John Lucero* / **1989**

Lucero Ltd. / Jeff Grosso / by *John Lucero* / **1989**

Lucero Ltd. / Riky Barnes / by *Riky Barnes and John Lucero* / **1990**

Lucero Ltd. / Riky Barnes / by *Riky Barnes and John Lucero* / **1990**

Lucero Ltd. / John Lucero / by *John Lucero* / **1990**

Lucero Ltd. / Ben Schroeder / by *John Lucero* / **1990**

Black Label / Ben Schroeder / by *John Lucero* / **1991**

John Lucero concept sketch / 1989 / by John Lucero

I started Lucero Ltd. with Santa Cruz. The first board produced was the Red Cross board. I had no idea I would get in any trouble with that one, but apparently having a red cross on a white field is a trademark infringement of the Geneva Convention—the Red Cross isn't even a company but they do own the rights to it. From there, I did the Lucero 12XU, which was an extension of the Schmitt Stix graphic with the Jester in a black and white suit with an eight ball hanging from his ankle. Then there was the Thumbhead and Riky Barnes graphic. Riky wasn't really an artist, but he used to draw these trippy little guys called Yuck Mouths, and I would blow them up on a Xerox to make them even more fucked up and then add a background design. The original version of the Grosso baby doll on the mushroom that I came up with had a sun in the background, but for whatever reason it looked too busy. Once I took the sun out I liked it better, because the graphic had a more classic look. There were about fifteen prototypes made with the sun, and Jeff actually got some photos in a magazine with it.

When we got Ben Schroeder on the team, he was just a big dude who ate shit all the time. I thought he always looked like a crash dummy, so it was a natural thing to do for a graphic. The Schroeder with the crash dummies all twisted up is one of my favorite graphics that I've ever done and probably one of my least known.

The company went through another change of hands when I ran into some people at Vision and they reminded me of the old days and how many boards I used to sell with Schmitt Stix. Lucero Ltd. wasn't going as well as I thought it could at Santa Cruz, so I felt it was time to take the company over on my own again, like I'd originally planned. So I just started the company over, changed the name, and got a fresh start. The main reason I changed the name from Lucero Ltd. to Black Label was because I didn't want my name on it anymore. I just started feeling too egocentric about having my name on the company and I wanted to get more in the background of things anyway.

I've done so many boards over the last ten years that I feel it has become more of a cut-and-paste operation than putting a lot of artwork and technique into the graphics. Three or four years ago we were able to get more run out of a graphic on Black Label and we were able to do three-to four-thousand of a board. Now there have been times we can only do one hit of a board because the market requires more new stuff, which is always the hardest thing for me to do—I never wanted to be a cookie-cutter producer of skateboards. But oftentimes I find myself in that business, so over this last year I've tried to get more excited about doing skateboard graphics.

Back in the old days, when there were much fewer pro skaters and companies, a graphic would last a couple years, so every one that came out really meant something. Now I'm trying to put that same theory back into it. The graphics mean something to the kid who's buying a board, so they should mean something to us. Graphics make a skateboard.

John Lucero

Lucero Ltd. / Jeff Grosso (Prototype) / by John Lucero / 1989

I really dug the Bukowski graphic that I got John to do for me on Black Label, because I'm a Bukowski freak. This company got a hold of Lucero, though, and they were all upset because this kid had drawn that Bukowski image, and we'd just taken it off a sticker, slapped it on the board, and cut-and-pasted a few things behind it. The board, in my opinion, was supposed to be done differently, but John had a vision of it, and anything John does is okay by me. I like it when John draws. I wish he'd draw more often.

I realize the skateboard market doesn't really want those kinda graphics anymore. Now they just cut-and-paste a logo, throw their name underneath it, and they're good to go, rather than trying to come up with their own little "flair" or whatever they call it. That's why it's such a shame now ... back when we were doing it you got a skateboard graphic and it was gonna be with you for a year, maybe a year and a half. And if it was real popular, it was gonna be your icon for the rest of your life. It was just so different then; everything was so tight-knit and small. You felt like you were part of a subculture and that there were meanings behind what people put on boards.

That's what was cool about our era—you could have somebody draw graphics that were personalized. So if somebody had a graphic of Conan with a sword, it meant something to that guy. He either was Conan, or wanted to be Conan, or something gay like that. But I see the kids now, like some of the young guys on Black Label, and John tries to approach it the way we did, he wants to get a feel for the kid, but they don't even care. They're like, "Oh, a skull and a spider web, that's cool." Plus, people don't use rails now, and the graphics are gonna be gone in two ledge-slides. So the graphics are kind of incidental. They only really matter to old fogies like us. | Jeff Grosso

BLACK LABEL

Black Label / John Lucero / by John Lucero / 1991

Black Label / Jeff Grosso / by John Lucero / 1991

Black Label / John Cardiel / by John Lucero / 1992

Black Label / Jeff Grosso / by John Lucero / 2000

Black Label / Wade Speyer / by John Lucero and Mike Miller / 2000

Black Label / Kristian Svitak / by Mike Miller / 2000

Black Label / John Cardiel / 1993

Black Label / John Cardiel / by John Lucero / 1994

Black Label / Tim Upson / by John Lucero / 1996

Black Label / Mike Vallely / by John Lucero / 1999

Black Label / Jeff Grosso / by Mike Miller / 2000

Black Label / Salman Agah / by John Lucero / 2001

Black Label / Matt Hensley / by Mike Miller / 2001

Red Cross / John Lucero / by John Lucero / 2002

Red Kross / Steve Olson / by John Lucero / 2003

Red Kross / Duane Peters / hand painted by John Lucero and Duane Peters / 2003

Cover:
Lance Mountain / Garden Grove, CA / 2004 / photo by Eric Simpson

Page 1:
Suicidal Skates / Possessed to Skate / photo by Eric Simpson

Pages 2-3:
Top Row:
Z-Flex / Jay Adams / 1977
Dogtown / Bob "Bullet" Biniak / by Wes Humpston / 1978
Powell Peralta / Beamer / 1978
Alva / Splat / by Eric Monson / 1979
Kryptonics / Steve Alba / 1979
Powell Peralta / Jay Smith / by V. Courtlandt Johnson / 1980
Seaflex / Bob Denike / by Mike Mahoney / 1983
G&S / Mark "Gator" Rogowski / artist unknown / 1983
Santa Cruz / Duane Peters / by Jim Phillips / 1984
Steve Olson Skates / Steve Olson / artist unknown / 1984
Powell Peralta / Steve Steadham / by Craig Stecyk III / 1985
Zorlac / Team / by Jeff Newton / 1986
Brand-X / Bob Schmelzer / by John Lucero / 1987
Tracker / Lester Kasai / artist unknown / 1988
Dogtown / Scott Oster / by Wes Humpston / 1988
Magnusson Designs / Tony Magnusson / artist unknown / 1988
H-Street / Art Godoy / by Art Godoy / 1988
Santa Cruz / Rob Roskopp / by Jim Phillips / 1989
Bottom Row:
H-Street / Danny Way / artist unknown / 1989
SMA Rocco / Jef Hartsel / by Jef Hartsel / 1989
Santa Monica Airlines / Julien Stranger / artist unknown / 1990
Life / Sean Sheffey / artist unknown / 1991
Blind / Jordan Richter / by Marc McKee / 1992
Swindle / Team / by Aaron Springer / 1992
TV / Ed Templeton / by Ed Templeton / 1992
Blockhead / Laban Pheidias / by Dave Bergthold / 1992
Milk / Christian Hosoi / by Mark Gonzales / 1993
Alien Workshop / John Drake / by Mike Hill / 1993
Real / Julien Stranger / artist unknown / 1994
Consolidated / Jesse Paez / by Moish Brenman / 1995
Think / Duane Peters / artist unknown / 1996
Evol / Ben Erpelding / by Niko Achtipes / 1995
The Firm / Lance Mountain / artist unknown / 1995
Flip / Geoff Rowley / artist unknown / 1997
Chocolate / Mike York / by Evan Hecox / 1998
Consolidated / Team Presto / by Todd Bratrud / 2001
Anti Hero / Team / by Julien Stranger and Mike Novak / 2002
Bulldog Skates / Sacred Heart / by Wes Humpston / 2002
Santa Monica Airlines / hand painted by Skip Engblom / 2003

Page 5:
Tony Hawk / Del Mar, CA / 1987 / photo by Grant Brittain

Page 9-10:
Powell Peralta / Mike McGill / photos by Eric Simpson

Page 12:
Mike McGill / Del Mar, CA / 1987 / photo by Grant Brittain

Page 17:
Zorlac / Craig Johnson / photo by Eric Simpson

Page 21:
Barry Smith / Toledo, OH / 2003 / photo by Steve Buddendeck

Page 24:
Powell Peralta / Ray "Bones" Rodriguez Brite Lite deck from the collection of Jimmy Anderson / photo by Jimmy Anderson
Alan Gelfand / Gainesville, FL / 1978 / photo by Jim Goodrich

Page 30:
Powell Peralta / Ripper / photo by Eric Simpson

Page 32:
Steve Rocco / 1987 / photo by Grant Brittain

Page 42:
Chet Thomas / Huntington Beach, CA / 1989 / photo by Rick Kosick

Page 45:
Lance Mountain / Huntington Beach, CA / 1989 / photo by Rick Kosick

Page 47:
Tommy Guerrero / San Francisco, CA / 1986 / photo by Grant Brittain

Page 56:
Jason Lee / Santa Cruz, CA / 1990 / photo by Tony Roberts

Page 61:
Tony Hawk / Carlsbad, CA / 1990 / photo by Grant Brittain

Page 67:
Mike McGill / Encinitas, CA / 1990 / photo by Grant Brittain

Page 72:
Shiloh Greathouse / Torrance, CA / 1992 / photo by Doug Winbury

Page 81:
Rick Kosick / Tokyo, Japan / 2002 / photo by Jeff Tremaine

Page 82:
Mike Smith / Torrance, CA / 1991 / photo by Rick Kosick

Pages 100-101:
Top Row:
Real / Mark Gonzales / by Mark Gonzales / 2000
Shorty's / Chad Muska / artist unknown / 1999
Krooked / Mark Gonzales / by Mark Gonzales / 2003
Krooked / Christian Hosoi / by Mark Gonzales / 2003
Birdhouse / Donny Barley / by Sean Cliver / 2003
Birdhouse / Vinny Vegas / by Sean Cliver / 2003
Birdhouse / Tony Hawk / by Sean Cliver / 2003
Blind / Gershon Mosley / by Marc McKee / 2001
Conscience / Team / by Jesse Geboy and Matt DeAngelis / 2004
Powell / Steve Caballero / artist unknown / 2000
Middle Row:
Santa Cruz / Stefan Attardo / by Aaron Horkey / 2002
Girl / Rick Howard / by Tony Larson / 2002
Birdhouse / Steve Berra / by Jeff Tremaine / 1998
Think / Dan Drehobl / by Dan Drehobl / 2000
Chocolate / Kenny Anderson / by Evan Hecox / 2002
Fuct / Team / by Erik Brunetti / 1999
Sideshow / Chris Pontius / by Chris Pontius / 1998
Zoo York / Team / by Futura 2000 / 2002
Supernaut / Tony Cox / by Phil Frost / 2001
Supernaut / Matt Pailes / by Matt Pailes / 1999
Bottom Row:
The Driven / Jason Jessee / by Mark Gonzales / 2002
Shorty's / Chad Muska / artist unknown / 1997
Enjoi / Louie Barletta / by Marc Johnson / 2002
Enjoi / Team / by Marc Johnson / 2002
Hessenmob / Mark Gonzales / by Mark Gonzales / 2002
Death / Scott Bourne / artist unknown / 2002
World Industries / Mike Crum / by Bret Banta / 2005
Alien Workshop / Team / by Don Pendleton / 2001
Zero / Team / by Dave Lively / 2001
Zero / Adrian Lopez / by Nilo Naghdi / 2001

Page 106:
Paul Constantineau / Skatopia, CA / 1977 / photo by Jim Goodrich

Page 108:
Eric Dressen / 1987 / photo by Grant Brittain

Page 110:
Tony Alva / 1986 / photo by Grant Brittain

Page 119:
Brand X / Weirdo deck from the collection of Dale Smith SRFSK851@aol.com / photo by Mike Carroll

Page 122:
John Grigley / 1986 / photo by Grant Brittain

Page 128:
Mark "Gator" Rogowski / Phoenix, AZ / 1984 / photo by Jim Goodrich

Pages 130:
Mark Gonzales / Gemco / 1986 / photo by Grant Brittain

Page 136:
John Gibson / 1984 / photo by Grant Brittain

Page 139:
Craig Johnson / Dallas, TX / 1986 / photo by Grant Brittain

Page 143:
Hand painted deck by Pushead / 2003 / photo by Pushead

Pages 146-147:
Skull Skates / Diehard, Hackett, and Peters deck photos from the Skull Skates collection / photos by Joel Fraser

Page 150:
Duane Peters / Upland, CA / 1980 / photo by Jim Goodrich

Page 159:
Jeff Grosso / Stone Mountain / 1987 / photo by Grant Brittain

Page 161:
Santa Cruz / Skull deck detail art courtesy of Jim Phillips

Page 176:
Chris Miller / 1988 / photo by Grant Brittain

Page 178:
Neil Blender / 1987 / photo by Grant Brittain

Pages 180-185:
Alien Workshop / Assorted icons and logos by Mike Hill

Page 190:
Skull Skates / Justin Lovely Tea Pot deck from the Skull Skates collection / photo by Joel Fraser

Page 203:
Moses Itkonen / Oakland, CA / 1995 / photo by Tobin Yelland

Page 205:
Mark Gonzales / 1987 / photo by Grant Brittain

Page 206:
Ed Templeton / Huntington Beach, CA / 1992 / photo by Spike Jonze

Page 209:
Bam Margera / 1997 / photo by Adam Wallacavage

Page 210:
Natas Kaupas / Santa Monica, CA / 1986 / photo by Grant Brittain

Page 212:
Natas Kaupas / Los Angeles, CA / 1992 / photographer unknown

Page 232:
John Lucero / Del Mar, CA / 1986 / photo by Grant Brittain

Page 239:
Garry S. Davis / Del Mar, CA / 1984 / photographer unknown (photo courtesy of Garry S. Davis)

Page 240:
Powell Peralta / Steve Caballero / by V. Courtlandt Johnson / 1986
Powell Peralta / Per Welinder / by V. Courtlandt Johnson / 1987
Schmitt Stix / Bryce Kanights / by Kevin Ancell / 1989
Santa Cruz / Jason Jessee / by Jim Phillips / 1988
Santa Cruz / Corey O'Brien / by Kevin Marburg / 1990
Zorlac / John Gibson / by Pushead / 1990
Black Label / Jeff Grosso / by John Lucero / 1992
Real / Tommy Guerrero / artist unknown / 1992
101 / Natas Kaupas / art directed by Natas Kaupas / 1993
Santa Monica Airlines / Ron Whaley / by Thomas Campbell / 1995
Alien Workshop / John Drake / by Mike Hill / 1996
Toy Machine / Ed Templeton / hand painted by Ed Templeton / 1995
The Firm / Lance Mountain / hand painted by Lance Mountain / 1996
Woodstock / Simon Woodstock / by Jimbo Phillips / 1996
World Industries / Team / by Marc McKee / 1997
Transit / Mike Valllely / by Stacy Lowery / 1998
Hessenmob / by Andy Jenkins / 2002
Hand painted by Johnny "Mojo" Munnerlyn / 2003
Skateboard Pimp / Big Pimp / by Wes Humpston / 2003
Subvert / Skull and Bones (Limited Edition) / by Grime / 2003
Conscience / by Sean Cliver / 2004
Flip / Ali Boulala / by Daniel Dunphy / 2004

Inside Back Cover:
Jason Jessee / Fallbrook, CA / 1989 / photo by Grant Brittain

Back Cover:
Schmitt Stix / John Lucero / photo by Eric Simpson

Were it not for the contributions, recollections, time, assistance, support, and generosity of several people this book of skateboard art would not be getting thumbed through on the toilets that it is today. So it is with immense gratitude I'd like to acknowledge the following individuals:

Bill Ackerman at Bill's Wheels / Salman Agah / Steve Alba / Jimmy Anderson / Joe Antonik / Artofskateboarding.com / Tom Audisio Megan Baltimore / Bret Banta / Ray Barbee / Matt Barker / Karen and Kevin Barry / Kelly Belmar / Dave Bergthold / Brian Betschart / Marco Bianco David Billick / Birdo / Eric Blais / Neil Blender / Tory Boettcher / Al Boglio / Philippe Bouyer / Aubry Boutin / Bod Boyle / Brian Brannon / Todd Bratrud Mike Brillstien / Grant Brittain / Don Brown / Neil Brown / Stephen Brown / Dana Buck / Steve Buddendeck / Tim Butler / Steve Caballero / Mike Cahill Ron Cameron / Thomas Campbell / Justin Carloni / Dave Carnie / Chris Chicarella / Chicken / Pauline Clark / James and Norma Jean Cliver Emerson Cliver / Christian Cooper / Peter Ducommun / Cris Dabica / Bill Danforth / Garry S. Davis / Eric Dressen / Dan Druff / Daniel and Liam Dunphy Rob Dyrdek / Vanessa Eisman / Brad Ellman / Dimitry Elyashkevich / Matt von Ende / Josh Etherington / David Ettinger / Mark Felt / Jim Fitzpatrick Ray Flores at The Board Gallery / Todd Francis / Joel Fraser / Michael Gatti / Tim Gavin / Jesse Geboy at Conscience Skateboards / Alan Gelfand Art and Steve Godoy / Sean Goff / Jason Goodman / Jim Goodrich / Claus Grabke / John Greeley / John Grigley / Grime / Jeff Grosso / John Guderian Tommy Guerrero / Dave Hackett / Nick Halkias / Tony Hallam / Sharon Harrison / Tony Hawk / Bill Heiden / Greg Hill / Mike Hill / Christian Hosoi Rick Howard / Andy Howell / Jason Huber / Todd Huber at The Skatelab Skatepark and Museum / Wes Humpston / Chuck Hurewitz / Chris Ilaria Andy Jenkins / Jason Jessee / Marty Jimenez / V. Courtlandt Johnson / Parker Johnson / Rudy Johnson / Scott Johnston / Spike Jonze / Stephen Joy Roy Kalin / John Kami / Bryce Kanights / Natas Kaupas / Alan Keller / Tim Kerr / Jeremy Klein / Jim Knight / Rick Kosick / Greg Lamson / Jason Lee C.J. LePage / Mark Lewman / Sean Lickert / John Lucero / Kevin Marburg / Bam Margera / Kris Markovich / Walt and Dan Marsden / Matt Majors Jim McDonnell / Barry McGee / Mike McGill / Marc McKee / Tim Medlin / Keith Meek / Chris Miller / Damon Mills / Tom Miyao / Mofo John Montessi at Westside Skateshop / Lance Mountain / Jim Muir / Rodney Mullen / Chris Mullins at Skateboard.com / Johnny "Mojo" Munnerlyn Lee Murphy / Bruno Musso / Eric Nash / Matt Newell / Chris Nieratko / Scott Obradovich / Corey O'Brien / Gavin O'Brien / Matthew Ochoa Brad Overacker / Stephen Paccione / Jamie Passama / John Pearson / Stacy Peralta / Jim Phillips / Jimbo Phillips / David Pifer / George Powell Pushead / John Ramsayer / Brad Ramsey / Don Redondo / Tony Roberts / Steve Rocco / Chris Rodgers / Aaron Rose / Rob Roskopp / Aaron Ruark Steve Saiz / Michael Schmidt / Paul Schmitt / Richard Schroeder / Josh Schwartz / Justin Sharp / Eric, Callie, Pasha and Danica Simpson Clyde Singleton / Skullandbonesskateboards.com / Terry Slywka at META Skateboards / Barry Smith / Dale Smith / Greg Smith / Jeff Snavely Kyle Sokol / Chris Solomon / Devin St. Clair / Craig Stecyk III / Tim Steenstra / Richard Stephens / Helen Stickler / Eric Stricker Jason Strubing at Skateworks / Tod Swank / Andy Takakjian / Michael Teele / Ed Templeton / Jim Thiebaud / Jamie Thomas / Muir Tinnerstet Paul Tippin / Tracy Topping / Bernie Tostenson / Jeff Tremaine / Mike Vallely / Francisco José Burgos Villarrubia / Adam Wallacavage / Mark Waters Blair Watson / John Weaver / Mikey "Rat" Whaley / Kevin Wilkins / Doug Winbury / Simon Woodstock / Tobin Yelland

There is, however, one person who ultimately made this book possible and that is my wife, Shari. To her I owe the biggest thanks of all, because not only did she put up with staring at the back of my head for two years as I carried on a love affair with a computer, but she believed in the book from start to finish, suggested the designer and copy editor, provided invaluable editorial critiques throughout all stages of the manuscript, and knowingly sacrificed her time with me so I could pursue the most self-indulgent thing I've ever done in my life. So yeah, this book is dedicated to her—with love.

I'd also like to extend a special thanks to Michael Brooke and Per Welinder for enabling this book to be entirely created, designed and produced by skateboarders for skateboarders.